STRANGERS
AT OUR GATES

STRANGERS AT OUR GATES

Canadian Immigration and Immigration Policy, 1540–2015

Fourth Edition

VALERIE KNOWLES

DUNDURN
TORONTO

Fourth Edition Editor: Cheryl Hawley
Design: Jennifer Gallinger, Courtney Horner
Cover Design: Laura Boyle
Cover Image: William Kurelek, *The Ukrainian Pioneer, No. 2*. National Gallery of Canada and the Isaacs/ Innuit Gallery on behalf of the William Kurelek Estate.
Printer: Webcom

Library and Archives Canada Cataloguing in Publication

Knowles, Valerie, author
        Strangers at our gates : Canadian immigration and
immigration policy, 1540-2015 / Valerie Knowles. -- Fourth
edition.

Includes bibliographical references and index.
Issued in print and electronic formats.
ISBN 978-1-4597-3285-8 (paperback).--ISBN 978-1-4597-3287-2
(epub).--ISBN 978-1-4597-3286-5 (pdf)

        1. Canada--Emigration and immigration--Government policy--
History. 2. Canada--Emigration and immigration--History.
3. Immigrants--Canada--History. I. Title.

JV7220.K56 2016   325.7109   C2015-906828-2
                                                        C2015-906829-0

1   2   3   4   5   20   19   18   17   16

  Canada

Conseil des Arts du Canada   Canada Council for the Arts

ONTARIO ARTS COUNCIL
CONSEIL DES ARTS DE L'ONTARIO
an Ontario government agency
un organisme du gouvernement de l'Ontario

We acknowledge the support of the **Canada Council for the Arts** and the **Ontario Arts Council** for our publishing program. We also acknowledge the financial support of the **Government of Canada** through the **Canada Book Fund** and **Livres Canada Books**, and the **Government of Ontario** through the **Ontario Book Publishing Tax Credit** and the **Ontario Media Development Corporation**.

VISIT US AT
Dundurn.com | @dundurnpress | Facebook.com/dundurnpress | Pinterest.com/dundurnpress

Dundurn
3 Church Street, Suite 500
Toronto, Ontario, Canada
M5E 1M2

— CONTENTS —

Preface   7

Introduction   9

1. The Beginnings   11

2. Canada's First Large Influx of Refugees   33

3. British Immigration Transforms the Colonies   48

4. Immigration in the Macdonald Era   68

5. The Sifton Years   84

6. Forging a New Immigration Policy   105

7. Immigration Doldrums   127

8. Immigration's Post-War Boom (1947–1957)   155

9. Major New Initiatives   179

10. A New Era in Immigration   199

11. The Turbulent 1980s and Beyond   221

12. Immigration Grabs Attention, 1996–2006   247

13. Developments 2006–2015: Pruning the Queue   264

14. Issues in the Twenty-First Century   283

Appendix: Tables and Figures   293

Notes   301

Select Bibliography   319

Index   327

— PREFACE —

THE IDEA FOR THIS BOOK originated with Kirk Howard, Dundurn Press's publisher, who asked me in 1988 if I would undertake a two hundred-page survey of the history of Canadian immigration and immigration policy. When I agreed to take on the assignment, I little dreamt that in 2015 I would be toiling away on a fourth edition of the book. At times, I have been overwhelmed by the magnitude of the task, and by the challenge of compressing a wealth of material into a short history that touches on most of the key topics that should be raised in an introductory work of this nature.

Fortunately, I have had a lot of assistance along the way, most of which has been acknowledged in earlier editions. Nevertheless, I still owe a debt of gratitude to several people who played a role in the evolution of this fourth edition. I am most grateful to Joe Bissett, who answered questions during an interview and who provided a valuable print summary of immigration developments in recent years. I also owe a vote of thanks to Gerry Maffre and Mike Molloy, who read chapter 13 and made suggestions for its improvement. Anne Arnott made a huge contribution to this chapter as she checked all the facts, even rising to the occasion when she was on holiday overseas! For editorial expertise, I enlisted the help of my amazing Toronto editor, Kate Merriman, who edited chapters 13 and 14. Cheryl Hawley of Dundurn Press did a final copy edit and piloted all the chapters through their final stages. And finally I would like to express my gratitude to my husband, David Knowles, who was frequently called upon to solve computer problems and print chapters.

— INTRODUCTION —

THE SIGNIFICANCE OF THE ROLE played by immigrants in Canada's history is underscored by an observation made by William Scott. In or around 1913, the superintendent of immigration from 1903 to 1924 observed: "More important than the drilling of armies, more important than the construction of navies, more important than the fiscal policy of this country is the question of who shall come to Canada and become part and parcel of the Canadian people" (William Scott, "Immigration and Population," *Canada and Its Provinces*, edited by Adam Shortt and Arthur Doughty [Toronto: The Publishers' Association of Canada, 1913], vol. 7, 589).

Closer to the present day, Richard Tait, chairman of the Canadian Immigration and Population Study, which issued the Green Paper of 1975, echoed these sentiments when he said, "A hundred years from now, I don't suppose people will care all that much whether we legalized marijuana or not. But decisions about who you let into Canada will decide the kind of country we have 100 years from now."

The people who have come to Canada have, by their efforts and talents, fashioned this country's institutions, political and economic character, and cultural diversity. In short, they have made Canada what it is today. The purpose of this book is not to re-tell the important story of what these people endured and accomplished but rather to describe *briefly* the different kinds of immigrants who have settled in this country over the centuries and the immigration policies that have helped to define the character of immigration in various periods. Special attention is paid to some of the key policy-makers and moulders of public opinion. And, because racism frequently plays a role in the Canadian immigration story, it is also discussed, as is the effectiveness of various policies in achieving Canada's immigration goals. The last part of the book touches on the realities of the 1990s and the early years of the present century that influence the framing of immigration policy, and tries to make some sense of the current debate about this country's immigration and multiculturalism policies.

— CHAPTER 1 —

The Beginnings

The Beginnings

THE PREHISTORIC ANCESTORS OF CANADA'S present-day Indians and Inuit became this country's first immigrants when they journeyed to America by way of the Bering Strait, at a time when a land bridge, now vanished, still connected Asia and America. Centuries later, according to an unconfirmed hypothesis, Irish monks visited Newfoundland. Then, starting around the year 1000, Vikings made occasional stops, overwintering at points on Baffin Island, Labrador, and the northeastern tip of Newfoundland (L'Anse aux Meadows). Still later, in 1497, the Italian mariner John Cabot, sailing in the service of England, glimpsed the shores of Newfoundland while searching for the country of the Great Khan (Asia). After viewing the Grand Banks, he sailed back to Bristol with amazing tales of an ocean dense with schools of codfish. The European fishery, if not in existence in these waters before Cabot's sighting, certainly came into being shortly after. And, as it developed, knowledge of the resources and configuration of the northeastern coast of North America spread throughout the fishing ports of western Europe.

Among the beneficiaries of this knowledge was a group of Portuguese who established a colony on Cape Breton Island between 1520 and 1524. Their exploits were eclipsed, however, by those of a remarkable Italian-born explorer who sailed in the service of France: Giovanni da Verrazano. In 1524, Verrazano struck out on a new route to North America, hoping that it would lead him eventually to the "blessed shores of Cathay" and the fabled riches of Asia. Although he failed in his mission, the Italian succeeded for the first time in history in charting the Atlantic seaboard of the

North American continent from Florida to Cape Breton. On this spectacular voyage the explorer also conceived the name "Nova Gallia", envisaging a New France that would encompass all of North America from Spanish Florida to the far north.

But it was Jacques Cartier, a Frenchman carrying on the exploration started by Verrazano, who paved the way for permanent European settlement in Canada. On July 24, 1534, Cartier clambered up the Gaspé shore of the Baie de Chaleur, erected a thirty-foot cross and claimed the newly discovered territory for His Most Christian Majesty, Francis I. On his second voyage, made the following year, the French explorer journeyed up the St. Lawrence River and visited Stadacona (Quebec). Then he went on to Hochelaga (Montreal) before wintering on the Sainte-Croix River near Stadacona. When he returned to France in 1536, having lost a fourth of his crew to scurvy, the hard-bitten St. Malo seaman had discovered the St. Lawrence River, explored the continent's interior as far as Montreal, and proven that Anticosti and Newfoundland were both islands.

Five years elapsed before Jacques Cartier returned to the New World, and when he did, he was on a major expedition designed to found a settlement "in the aforementioned countries of Canada and Hochelaga". To give the undertaking adequate stature, it was placed under the direction of Jean-François de La Rocque, Sieur de Roberval, a court favourite. Cartier was appointed chief pilot. That spring the master mariner and five ships sailed for Canada, expecting the expedition's leader to follow. Roberval, however, delayed his departure until the spring of 1542, by which time a discouraged Cartier was on his way back to France, having abandoned the settlement of Charlesbourg-Royal that he had founded at Cap Rouge above Quebec. Roberval re-established the colony at Cap Rouge, but after a disastrous winter there he and his colonists followed Cartier's example and returned to France.

The failure of the Charlesbourg-Royal colony and renewed war with Spain diverted French thinking from colonizing ventures to developments in Europe. Then came bitter conflict between Huguenots and Catholics, which was to distract France for almost another forty years. New France, meanwhile, was left to the fishermen and the fur traders, who returned each year to exploit its bounties. In the half-century that followed Cartier's last venture, French fishermen journeyed westward from Brittany, the Bay of Biscay, and the Channel ports to Newfoundland, seeking to corner the seemingly inexhaustible supply of cod at the expense of their Spanish, Portuguese, and English competitors. Further west, fur traders, following in the wake of Cartier, sailed up the St. Lawrence River to the interior to obtain furs, the most prized being beaver, which was felted and made into fashionable hats. Not until the close of the sixteenth century, when order had been restored to their country by Henry IV, did the French once again turn to colonizing their overseas possessions such as New France. There, they would pursue their goals in Newfoundland; in Acadia, an area that lay within the present day boundaries of Nova Scotia, New Brunswick, and Prince Edward Island (known as Île Saint-Jean until it was ceded to Great Britain in 1763, at which time it was called the Island of Saint John); and in Canada, the St. Lawrence River settlement that centred on Quebec and Montreal.

In order to establish settlements in the New World, Henry IV had recourse to that venerable European institution, the trade monopoly. By means of this widely accepted device, wealthy merchants or nobles, singly or in groups, were granted exclusive rights of trade and control of parts of overseas empires in exchange for a commitment to develop the possessions and found settlements. It was a method whereby France, using the privileges of the Crown, hoped to extend her dominions in the New World without becoming actively involved in overseas colonization. The first French monopolists failed in their attempts to establish sustaining colonies on the Magdalen Islands in the Gulf of St. Lawrence; on that desolate pile of sand off Nova Scotia known as Sable Island; and at Tadoussac at the mouth of the Saguenay River. But when these risk-takers did at last succeed, credit was due not to the noblemen or merchants in France but to their agent in Canada, Samuel de Champlain, a navigator, visionary, soldier, geographer, and ardent Catholic, to name but a few of the descriptions that apply to this remarkable pioneer.

THE FRENCH BEACHHEAD IN NORTH AMERICA

With one Atlantic voyage to the West Indies and Central America already behind him, Champlain journeyed up the St. Lawrence River in 1603 as a member of a group of fur-trading associates. He embarked on his first colonizing mission the following year when he sailed for North America on an expedition headed by the Protestant, Pierre Du Gua de Monts. Their choice of site was St. Croix Island in the Bay of Fundy, but after scurvy killed thirty-six of the eighty-odd settlers, the colony was moved across the bay to Port Royal, which Champlain had discovered earlier. Here, in present-day Nova Scotia, Champlain and De Monts maintained a base for three years, abandoning the tiny settlement only after their fur-trading privileges had been revoked. Not until 1610 did French colonists return to Acadia and then it was to face repeated intrusions from the English, who also contested the territory.

Having helped to establish a French foothold in North America, Champlain returned to the New World in 1608, again in the employ of De Monts's company, but this time in command of a ship. After sailing up the St. Lawrence, the explorer ordered the construction of a huge, barn-like habitation on a site thirty miles above Cap-Tourmente, overlooking the mighty river and the way into the heart of the continent. For twenty-six years Quebec would be the only French settlement on the St. Lawrence, a tiny but vital fur-trading post dependent on France for virtually all its supplies.

Although it was important, the fur trade was not the sole reason for the settlement's existence. In the eyes of Champlain and other devout Frenchmen, it was also an invaluable commercial tool to be used in the pursuit of a higher goal: the conversion of the Indians to Catholicism. In exchange for their furs the Hurons and Algonquins received not only European goods but Récollet brothers (friars of the third order of Franciscans) fired with missionary zeal. Commerce was therefore desirable because it could lead to conversion. But Champlain also realized that colonization was essential to both conversion and commerce. European settlers were required to demonstrate the Christian way of life to the Indian converts and to make the settlement self-sufficient. In 1618, therefore, when he was living in France, Champlain presented a memorial to Louis XIII and another to the Chambre du Commerce of Paris in which he made a strong pitch for emigration to New France. Notwithstanding the force of his arguments, the explorer's efforts were of little avail. The court was indifferent to his plans for overseas expansion. And, despite the impressive net profits that they were raking in from their fur-trading operations, the merchants balked at providing more than minimal support to the Récollets, who had arrived in Canada in 1615, and the first Jesuit missionaries, who had sailed to Quebec in 1635.

Large-scale colonization was destined to remain a dream as long as settlement was tied to the fur trade, for bands of Indians supplied all the labour necessary for its operations and there was no other economic activity in New France to attract immigrants from overseas. The impetus for colonization had to be provided by a change in thinking, and this occurred with the rise of seventeenth-century mercantilism, the theory that called for a state to increase its monetary wealth by severely restricting imports of manufactured goods and obtaining as many of its raw materials from abroad as possible. Colonies were an indispensable ingredient in the equation, they could supply the necessary raw materials for the mother country's manufacturing industry and theoretically they could also furnish a market for some of its exports.

In the first quarter of the seventeenth century, when mercantilism began to figure prominently in European economic thinking, France had no colonial economy, only the seasonal fishing industry and fur trade of New France. But there were influential Frenchmen who believed that North America offered tremendous possibilities should France decide to base her power on a colonial economy. One of these was, of course, the determined lobbyist, Champlain. When Cardinal Richelieu first became a member of Louis XIII's royal council, Champlain seized the opportunity to plead New France's cause once again. He appealed in vain. Not until Richelieu was appointed for a second time to the council and became "chef du conseil" did the cardinal become fully convinced of France's need to embark on an aggressive colonization policy.

THE COMPANY OF NEW FRANCE

To launch France on this daring new course, Richelieu, in 1627, spearheaded the establishment of a powerful commercial company designed to establish agricultural settlements, encourage missionary activity in New France and exploit its resources. Officially known as Compagnie de la

Nouvelle France, it was composed of more than a hundred associates (hence the frequent reference to the Company of One Hundred Associates), who provided working capital of 300,000 livres. In return for title to all the lands claimed by France in North America and a monopoly on all commerce except fishing, the company undertook to settle 4,000 French Catholics in its domains between 1627 and December 1643. Like its predecessors, it had the intimidating task of securing French claims in Acadia, France's hotly contested seaboard possessions in North America, and "Canada", the tiny, feeble fur-trading post on the St. Lawrence River. Unlike previous enterprises of this kind, however, the Company of One Hundred Associates was the most ambitious colonizing vehicle ever launched by France — and it had the Crown's full backing.

Unfortunately for the cause of colonization and its shareholders' pocketbooks, the Company of New France was plagued by tribulations that were of the same magnitude as its pretensions. Its greatest misfortune was to be launched at a time when England and France were at war and safety at sea was a forlorn hope. In 1628, the luckless company's first expedition was wiped out by the buccaneering Kirke brothers, three brothers who had been born and raised in France, but who now sailed under the English flag. In 1629, the efficient brothers followed up their conquest by helping the Scot, Sir William Alexander, Jr., establish a settlement near the earlier French settlement of Port Royal in Acadia. Lewis and Thomas Kirke then sailed up the St. Lawrence and captured Quebec, thereby temporarily smashing French power in North America.

In 1629, the Company of New France dispatched another expedition to the New World, and once again the commercial organization suffered a total loss. This, and the closing of the St. Lawrence to the French for three years, depleted the monopolists' funds still further. Not until 1634, two years after England had agreed to evacuate all the places that she occupied in Acadia and Canada, did the company succeed in supplying the St. Lawrence colony with any sizeable group of settlers. With the arrival of this first influx since 1617, the advance of population was pushed upriver from Quebec and Canada began the transition from a mere fur-trading post to a true colony. In the next decade, settlement would concentrate not only around Quebec but also around two new regional centres of population: Trois-Rivières and Montreal.

THE FIRST WAVE OF IMMIGRANTS

Among these early waves of immigrants were merchants, professional men, and some landless nobles, for whom the alluring prospect of a seigneury in Canada more than compensated for the anticipated rigors of a long, rough voyage across the Atlantic. There were also skilled workers such as blacksmiths, coopers, joiners, and carpenters, some of whom may have succumbed to the powerful propaganda of the Jesuits, who attempted to recruit settlers for the colony by advertising its attractions in their *Relations* (a series of annual reports compiled by Jesuit missionaries in New France and sent, between 1632 and 1672, to their Paris office). In his role as a propagandist, the noted Jesuit, Father Paul Le Jeune, observed in 1635: "There are a great number of craftsmen in France who, for lack of work, or for lack of owning a little land, spend their life in pitiful poverty and want... Now, as New France is of such great size, such a large number of settlers can be sent there that those who remain in Old France will be able to employ their skill honourably."[1]

Because Canada's manpower needs were so pressing, the system of indenturing was often invoked, a period of three years being the usual length of time selected. One Frenchman recruited for the colony by this method was Jacques Ragot, who signed a contract on April 9, 1643 with the chief clerk of the Company of New France agreeing to enter the service of Sieur Guillaume Couillard.[2] The immigrants' ranks also included the inevitable soldiers and members of religious orders. On August 1, 1639, for instance, two groups of nuns disembarked at Quebec, one comprising Hospitalières from Dieppe, the other Ursulines led by Mother Marie de l'Incarnation. When six Jesuits also got off the ship, Father Le Jeune was able to hail the arrival of a vessel bearing "a college of Jesuits, a house of Hospitalières, and a Convent of Ursulines".[3]

Irrespective of occupation, the overwhelming majority of those who disembarked at Quebec in these years were Roman Catholics because Richelieu had effectively barred Huguenots and naturalized foreigners from settling permanently in the colony. New France, like France, was expected to be a completely homogeneous community — one religion, one language, and loyalty to one monarch. In any event, the French Protestants were no longer interested in colonizing ventures. After being actively involved in three such undertakings in the Americas in the six-teenth century, including Roberval's colony, they had concluded that they could get a better return on their money in other types of ventures.

As part of its program for recruiting colonists, the Company of One Hundred Associates continued the practice, begun earlier, of granting large tracts of land to organizations or private individuals who agreed to estab-lish settlers on them (the seigneural system). Robert Giffard, surgeon and apothecary from Perche, that little "pays" so famous for its draught horses, was one entrepreneur who took up the challenge. In 1634, he secured the seigneury of Beauport near Quebec, signed a commercial partnership agreement with another gentleman from Perche, and then set sail with his family and a sizeable number of other colonists for Canada.[4] The follow-ing year he recruited other families for his seigneury, including the pro-genitors of some of French Canada's most prominent families. One, the Sieur des Chatelets, later obtained his own seigneury at Cap Rouge above Quebec. In less than thirty years, seventy such seigneuries would be grant-ed along the banks of the St. Lawrence between Quebec and Montreal.[5]

La Societé de Notre-Dame de Montréal pour la conversion des Sauvages de la Nouvelle France, an offshoot of the semi-secret, pietistic Compagnie du Saint-Sacrement, founded Ville Marie (Montreal) and in 1642 initiated settlement of the Island of Montreal. To launch its evan-gelistic activities, the Societé dispatched a band of pious colonists to Quebec, led by an experienced soldier and earnest Christian, Paul Chomedy de Maisonneuve, and Jeanne Mance, who would later found the Hotel-Dieu hospital of Montreal. In 1653, they were joined by a con-tingent of settlers, numbering over a hundred men.

Although the Company of One Hundred Associates was the first group of monopolists to recruit settlers in significant numbers for the St. Lawrence colony, it did not meet with outstanding success in pro-moting settlement there. In 1641, one year before Maisonneuve and Jeanne Mance founded Ville Marie, and nine years after French reoccu-pation of the St. Lawrence, the settlement's population numbered only about two hundred. This was certainly far short of the goal of 4000 set-tlers stipulated in the company's contract.

Most of these permanent settlers, as opposed to the numerous *hiver-nants*, who came only as sojourners, had been brought out by the

Company of New France, a few wealthy noble speculators, and religious communities that had funds to invest in the clearing of land and the recruitment of labourers. Only a few had arrived in Canada courtesy of ships' captains because royal orders that commercial vessels bring out colonists in proportion to their tonnage were largely ignored. Even Champlain had failed lamentably in his attempt to promote population growth with the declaration to assembled native chieftains that "our sons shall marry your daughters and together we shall form but one people." [6]

Burdened by an enormous debt, the Company of New France decided, in 1645, to relinquish its fur trade monopoly to the St. Lawrence colony, while retaining its rights of ownership over all of New France. In accepting the monopoly, La Communauté des Habitants — in reality a small group of businessmen — assumed the obligations of the Company of One Hundred Associates, including the responsibility for bringing out settlers. Conditions in the colony were such, however, that the Communauté's affairs deteriorated rapidly. Battered by Iroquois attacks and religious strife and plagued by administrative instability, shortages of supplies, and military and commercial insecurity, the struggling settlement issued repeated appeals to the mother country for help. What was clearly needed was a complete reorganization of its affairs, and in 1663 Louis XIV responded by taking New France out of the hands of the Company of One Hundred Associates altogether and making it a royal province to be governed directly by the Crown. According to the royal plan, France would henceforth assume full responsibility for administration, security, justice, economic development, and finance in all her possessions in North America.

THE ADVENT OF ROYAL GOVERNMENT

As soon as the Company of One Hundred Associates resigned, the French monarch appointed a new governor, a *conseil souverain* (sovereign council) and an intendant of justice, public order, and finances. But no sooner were these institutions in place in New France (before the arrival of an intendant) than Louis and his *intendant de finance*, Jean-Baptiste Colbert, shifted gears and established the Compagnie des Indes occidentales (the French West Indies Company), to which they entrusted a role in the ownership and administration of New France. In still another replay of history, they granted the new organization a monopoly of the colony's fur trade and commerce for forty years. Once again, monopolists were to have a role in New France's development.

With the introduction of royal government, the St. Lawrence settlement crossed the threshold of a new era. For a few brief years, before the mother country became distracted by the later wars of the mature Louis XIV, the colony would emerge from the economic stagnation that had been its lot for decades and begin to fulfil some of the promise expected of it back in 1627.

The royal official placed in charge of New France's destinies in May 1663 was a methodical minister of driving ambition, forty-four-year-old Jean-Baptiste Colbert. Called "Monsieur Nord" by Louis's courtiers, he was a cold, intimidating functionary who craved power and found his only pleasure in hard work. At this critical juncture in the colony's history he held only the post of intendant of finance, but he would soon become a minister, a member of the great council of state and, under Louis XIV, the most powerful man in France. Practically everything in the kingdom that did not come under the jurisdiction of the ministers of war and foreign affairs was to come under his direction: industry, commerce, finance, arts and letters, science, royal buildings, the navy, and, of course, colonies.

Although Colbert frequently resorted to expediency in his master plan for France's growth and development, he did make a genuine effort to put into practice the principles of mercantilism, which linked together industrial growth in the mother country, colonial expansion, and state power. France, in his view, had to be made economically self-sufficient, which meant utilizing to the full the kingdom's resources, including her overseas possessions. In this scheme of things, Acadia and Canada would have an important role to play — especially Canada, which now numbered some 2,500 people.

To begin the remaking of New France, Colbert chose the skilled and ambitious administrator Jean Talon. Jesuit-trained, he had served as an intendant with the French army and then as intendant of Hainaut. When the newly-appointed intendant of New France embarked for the wilds of North America, and the colony on which he was to have such an impact, he was about forty years old, an imaginative and energetic man whose drive, initiative, and vision would have served him in good stead as a captain of industry in a later century.

Jean Talon was determined to make Canada self-supporting. Furs, especially beaver pelts used in the manufacture of high-crowned, wide-brimmed fur-felt hats, had been the colony's only export in the past. But given the vagaries of this luxury trade, Talon decided that the colony had to develop other, more stable, sources of revenue, such as lumbering, mining, fishing, manufacturing, and trade with the West Indies. In order for these sectors to be developed, however, it was imperative that the settlement have capital, men with managerial talent, and skilled labour, all three of which were in short supply in Canada. Once again immigration became a top priority, but this time it was to be well-ordered, and subsidized by the government. Nevertheless, before settlement could get under way in earnest, the Iroquois had to be quelled; to accomplish this, 1,000 officers and men of the Carignan-Salières regiment were sent to the colony in 1665.

Jean Talon.
Coloured Engraving by
Theophile Hamel.

National Archives of Canada, C7100

While serving as New France's most important official, Talon worked tirelessly to encourage agriculture, crafts, and industry in the St. Lawrence colony, to provide it with a system of swift and impartial justice, and to stimulate trade with France and the French islands in the West Indies. Along with Colbert, the great intendant also mounted a major assault on the problem of a glaring shortage of men with entrepreneurial talents and skilled workers such as shipwrights.

No sooner had he arrived at Quebec than Jean Talon began to attack the population question. First the intendant completed a nominal census of the settlement. Then, despite all the misgivings that he had about the Company of the West Indies, he concluded an agreement with it to bring a number of settlers to New France. This agreement and the advent of royal government set the stage for a dramatic rise in immigration to the St. Lawrence colony. Indeed, the decade 1663–73 represents the one period in the history of pre-1760 Canada when immigration figured prominently in its development. Some 2,000 settlers were sent out from France in these years. They came from all the French provinces, although three-quarters originated in districts west of a line between Soissons and Bordeaux. The principal sources of these immigrants were Normandy and Île-de-France, followed by Poitou, Aunis, Brittany, and Saintonge.[7] Not all the new arrivals were French or Catholic. In 1668, for example, one ship brought Dutch, Portuguese, and German colonists, for although official policy required settlers to be French Roman Catholics, some 350 settlers, from many countries, came to New France before 1760.

Although the newcomers who came to Canada during Talon's time included families, most of them were unmarried men. Some were indentured workers (*engagés*), who had signed three-year contracts to work in Canada, where their service was regarded as a kind of apprenticeship. Others were clerks, and impressive numbers were soldiers, who were later given liberal discharge grants as an inducement to remain in the colony. When the Carignan-Salières regiment, for example, was recalled to France in 1668, more than 400 of its men decided to take advantage of the generous concessions and stay on in the settlement. Additional soldiers came in 1669, including six army captains, who arrived with six fifty-man companies and a total of twenty-four junior officers, all of whom were encouraged to settle on the land.[8] Among the officers who accepted grants of seigneuries from Talon and whose names still live on in the place-names of Quebec were St. Ours, Chambly, Verchères, Contrecoeur, Berthier, La Valtrie, and Saurel.

Because the overwhelming majority of immigrants were single males, some thought had to be given to redressing the numerical disparity between the sexes. Accordingly, the authorities persuaded a substantial number of unmarried young women to emigrate to the colony, offering husbands as the prize at the other end. In the summer of 1666, ninety of these so-called *filles du roi* were shipped out at the king's charge; by mid-November of that year eighty-four of them were married. A second group arrived the next summer, and once again, an impressive number (102) of the women who got off the ship found husbands by mid-November.[9]

Drawn for the most part from the houses of charity in French cities, these women were largely orphans and foundlings. Their ranks also included, however, young women incarcerated for vagrancy, prostitution, and illicit Protestantism. In the words of a contemporary observer, they were "a mixed cargo", part of the forced immigration that helped to populate numerous colonies at that time. Talon had requested that only "strong country girls" be sent out, but as luck would have it the only viable source of recruitment of young women was the charitable institutions, such as the Hôpital générale.[10]

Among the *filles du roi* there were also some young ladies of higher social standing who were sent out to become wives of military officers. In the seventeenth century women made up a third of all immigrants, but after 1673 their number dropped to an average of three per year, a level that persisted until the end of the French regime.[11]

The young women received accommodation in special hostels, but the idea was to get them married as quickly as possible; to hasten that outcome, bachelors in the colony were forbidden to go hunting or fishing or to participate in the fur trade from the time the ships docked until all the young women had been led to the altar. Such aggressive measures to promote settlement were necessary because Canada, with its harsh winters and hot summers, Iroquois attacks, and great distance from France, was an unattractive destination compared to the Antilles. Moreover, the king had warned Talon that war with Holland left France little money to spare for Canada and that henceforth Canada and Acadia would have to stand on their own feet. From 1672 on, this would become all too evident, for beginning that year organized immigration came to a virtual halt.

To impede the return of established settlers to France, visas issued by the governor and intendant were required, and rarely granted. But these and other immigration-related measures were not enough to populate the colony, and steps were taken to encourage natural increase. Fathers, as heads of families, were rewarded with a family allowance bonus if they had at least ten children "living and not in holy orders", and were fined if their sons and daughters were not married at an early age. And, since not all young men were attracted by the idea of early marriage, Talon in 1671 issued an ordinance forbidding them "the enjoyment of the right to hunt and fish and trade with the Indians and even to go into the Woods."[12] But such decrees failed to produce the desired results and, in 1683, most of them were repealed.

By 1700, Canada's population had climbed to approximately 15,000, with most "Canadiens" concentrated in and around the towns of Quebec and Montreal. During the seventeenth century some 6,000 immigrants had come to and remained in Canada compared to about 20,000 who had gone to the Antilles and some 8,000 French Huguenots who had emigrated to the various Anglo–American colonies.[13]

Acadia, the Neglected Outpost

Acadia, France's second area of settlement in New France, witnessed even less activity than the St. Lawrence settlement in these years. As late as 1686, only "885 âmes", according to a census, lived in this part of France's North American domain, chiefly at the head of the Bay of Fundy and in the Annapolis Valley.[14] Acadia, in stark contrast to Canada during the St. Lawrence settlement's prosperous years, received minimal assistance from the Crown and, as a consequence, little immigration. France's neglect of this part of her North American possessions was so great, in fact, that in 1686 Intendant Jacques de Meulles could report to Louis XIV, "Acadia is at present of so little importance, since it is supported in no way and receives no help from France, that most of the settlers, because of their frequent contacts with the English and the trade that they carry on continually with them, have abandoned these shores to go live around Boston." [14] The north south exodus, which would later become a pattern of population movement in Canada, was already under way. There had been a time, however, when the tidewater colony had loomed large in French colonial thinking, when its prospects had even appeared more promising than those of the St. Lawrence settlement. This was back in 1632, after Acadia had been returned to France by the Treaty of St.-Germain-en-Laye. In phase one of a projected settlement program, Governor Isaac de Razilly arrived that year with "300 gentlemen of quality" and moved the capital from Port Royal to La Heve, located on the south shore of present-day Nova Scotia. By concentrating France's colonizing efforts on the Atlantic seaboard, the governor and Richelieu hoped to transform Acadia into a defensive bulwark against dynamic New England, which had been growing by leaps and bounds since 1630.

Unfortunately, these plans collapsed when de Razilly died in 1635, leaving two rival seigneurs, Charles de Menou d'Aulnay and Charles de La Tour, to quarrel over his succession. With d'Aulnay's sudden death in 1650, the bitter jurisdictional disputes between the two foes came to an end, but not other territorial disputes, which continued to rage during the period when Acadia was in English hands (1654–67) and into the eighteenth century.

As a result of all this instability the colony saw little new settlement in these years. What little French colonization there was took place chiefly in the 1630s, 1640s, and 1670s, with most of the immigrants coming from south of the Loire in France, chiefly Poitou. These would form the backbone of the highly self-reliant Acadian population, which farmed, raised livestock, fished, hunted, and even pursued commercial ties with the English colonists in America, often against the wishes of the French authorities.

Left completely to her own devices, Acadia soldiered on without the benefit of any sizeable influx of immigrants. When France ceded her eastern seaboard possessions (minus Île Royale, Île Saint-Jean, and the region north of the isthmus of Chignecto) to Great Britain in 1713, the population numbered only about 1,500 to 2,000 Acadians in the drained marshlands area of the Bay of Fundy and scarcely a hundred white inhabitants in continental Acadia.[15]

IMMIGRATION IN THE EIGHTEENTH CENTURY

In the eighteenth century, the state dispatched soldiers, artisans, and brides to the St. Lawrence colony in about the same numbers as during the previous century. As a result, total immigration from France during the entire *ancien régime* numbered no more than 12,000 permanent settlers. There

Esther Brandeau: Among the more colourful of the first arrivals in New France was a sailor who disembarked at Quebec in 1738 from the schooner Saint Michel. Something about his person aroused the suspicions of colonial authorities, who questioned him and discovered that Jacques La Farge was in reality a nineteen-year-old French Jewess, Esther Brandeau. The young woman would have been allowed to remain in the colony had she been prepared to convert to Catholicism, but she had other ideas. Despite months of cajoling, persuasion, and threats on the part of church authorities, Brandeau would not capitulate, and so, in 1739, she was shipped back to France at the expense of the French government. (Irving Abella, A Coat of Many Colours: Two Centuries of Jewish Life in Canada [Toronto: Lester & Orpen Dennys, 1990], 1-2.)

was virtually no individual, church-sponsored, or seigneurial-sponsored, immigration. The immigrants' ranks were boosted, however, by the presence of state-exiled poachers, counterfeiters, and salt-smugglers, who found little opportunity to continue their illegal activities in the colony, but who undoubtedly elicited the admiration of the independent-minded habitants. In 1739, for example, a dispatch from Jean-Frédéric Phélypeaux de Maurepas, minister of marine and colonies, reported that eighty-one salt smugglers were being sent to Canada and that they were to be incorporated into the troops or assigned to individuals and communities offering good work contracts.[16] Available records indicate that almost a thousand were sent out in a ten-year period.

Indian and black slaves also formed a significant addition to the colonial population. Over a period of 150 years some 2,700 Amerindian and 1,400 black slaves were recorded in Canada, most of them kept as domestic servants by the religious communities, military officers, and merchants, but some of whom were employed as agricultural workers. Large numbers of the Amerindian slaves were members of the Pawnee tribe from what is now the state of Nebraska, and since their name in French was Panis, this word became synonymous with Indian slave. Fifty percent of all the slaves, including the blacks, most of whom came from the Antilles, were to be found in the Montreal region, with the remainder concentrated in the towns of Quebec, Detroit, and Trois-Rivières.

In 1706, European merchants and their agents were granted permission to set up shop in the colony. Soon a score of importers in

Montreal and Quebec were making a comfortable living doing business with about a hundred *negociants* — traders, outfitters, shopkeepers — in Montreal, who were perpetually in debt to them. By 1765, the population had climbed to 69,810,[17] largely through natural increase, and the colony was able to support a variety of small industries and commercial enterprises, such as sawmills, grist mills, family craft shops, the royal shipyards outside Quebec (subsidized and controlled by the state), and the St. Maurice ironworks near Trois Rivières. Both the shipyards and the ironworks stimulated the importation of skilled workers from the *metropole* (mother country).

The outbreak of the War of the Austrian Succession (1744–48), in which France and Great Britain again declared war on one another, saw contingents of regular troops dispatched from France to defend the colony. Even greater numbers were sent out after 1755, during the Seven Years' War. Since there were no barracks, the soldiers were billeted with habitants. Relationships developed between the colonials and the newcomers, marriages took place, and by the end of the war some 800 military men elected to remain in the colony as settlers. These soldiers probably represented the largest single influx of immigrants that the colony had ever received. Their numbers helped to swell the population to more than 70,000 people by the time the Capitulations of Montreal transferred Canada to Britain in September 1760. It is an impressive number when one realizes that just under 9,000 settlers had made their way to the St. Lawrence colony during the 150 years of the French regime. With immigration from France cut off by the British conquest, however, Canada's francophone population would grow only through natural increase.

Colonization was not restricted to the St. Lawrence Valley. In 1701, the picaresque adventurer Lamothe Cadillac founded the post and agricultural settlement of Detroit. On the heels of the fur traders in the Illinois country came soldiers and settlers. In 1720, upon the completion of Fort de Chartres, near Kaskaskia in the Illinois country, a convoy of 120 colonists arrived from the Montreal area. Soon the settlement boasted forty-four soldiers and 108 families engaged in farming.[18] Meanwhile, along the shores of Lake Superior, the offspring of Canadian traders and native women began to form their own distinctive villages.

DEVELOPMENTS IN EIGHTEENTH-CENTURY ACADIA

Although the peninsula of Nova Scotia had been ceded to Great Britain in 1713, Île Royale and Île St. Jean remained French. With the surrender of mainland Nova Scotia to Britain, France shifted her attention to the wild, almost empty Île Royale (Cape Breton). Here, several hundred civilian refugees from Placenta and other French settlements in Newfoundland, who had been largely engaged in the fishing trade, settled. For their part, some sixty Acadian families decided to settle in the interior of the island, away from the fortress of Louisbourg, which was then being built to protect the fishery and provide an Atlantic naval base. With the growth of the fisheries and the construction of Louisbourg, the largest fortress of its kind in North America, Île Royale became a major entrepôt. Soon the town of Louisbourg itself, the centre of population, numbered several thousand people — soldiers, fishermen, merchants, and artisans. While most of the women had been born in the New World and the majority of the men had come from western France, there were town dwellers representing all the French provinces as well as other parts of Europe.[19] After capturing Louisbourg in 1758, the British blew up the fortifications and abandoned the town. Île Royale, renamed Cape Breton, saw most of its French inhabitants return to France. By 1785 only about a thousand Acadians remained and they were in the south of the island. From now on this part of the world would see British, American, and German immigration, but not French.

THE FOUNDING OF HALIFAX

Between 1760 and 1800, immigration to British North America was largely haphazard as Britain had no stated policy for populating its North American colonies. Indeed, the English Parliament by and large opposed the outward movement of British citizens, convinced that emigration would sap the nation's vitality.[20]

One striking example of a departure from this thinking involved the founding of Halifax, Nova Scotia's capital and Atlantic Canada's largest city. Its establishment resulted from a deliberate attempt to make Nova

Scotia an instrument for thwarting French attacks against New England. To achieve this goal, British authorities decided to erect extensive fortifications in and to people the province with subjects loyal to the Crown.

The principal architect of this plan was the First Commissioner for Trade and Plantations, Lord Halifax, who thought that the Acadians posed the greatest danger to British interests. Accordingly, the settlement scheme proposed that English and Protestant settlers be mingled with French-speaking subjects so that they would lose their identity as a separate people and become obedient to royal authority. This plan also had additional goals in mind, however, goals that were equally important: exploiting the rich cod fishery, procuring masts for the British navy, and restraining French fishermen from using British waters.[21]

After Louisbourg was returned to France in the peace treaty of 1749, Halifax proposed that some three thousand individuals, mostly discharged soldiers and sailors, form the nucleus of new settlements in Nova Scotia, and in May of that year Colonel Edward Cornwallis set sail for the province, followed by ships bearing settlers and supplies. The future governor intended to superintend the settlement of Nova Scotia from Annapolis, but when the wind did not favour the Bay of Fundy, he made the pivotal decision to stop at Chebucto instead and to keep all the settlers there until the following summer.[22] As a result, the projected settlement of the province occurred on the Chebucto peninsula and the new town of Halifax, not Annapolis, became the home of the three thousand newcomers.

These townspeople were soon joined by merchants and fishermen from New England and by immigrants from other seaboard colonies. The population gradually declined, however, when residents moved to the Nova Scotia townships or to New England. Halifax would only revive when, on the evacuation of Boston in 1776, it became a naval and military base and a home for Loyalists fleeing the American Revolution.[23]

THE NEW ENGLAND PLANTERS

England's expulsion of the Acadians in 1756 precipitated an influx of New England Planters, the largest of several immigrant groups to put down roots in Nova Scotia in the last half of the eighteenth century. The arrival of the Planters (an Elizabethan name for colonists) was heralded by Nova Scotia Governor Charles Lawrence's proclamation of October 12, 1758, which invited loyal subjects from New England to locate on the fertile Nova Scotia farmland vacated by the expelled Acadians. In response to this invitation, agents, representing potential settlers, started to arrive in the colony the following year. Immigration began in earnest in 1760 and within eight years approximately eight thousand New Englanders had established themselves in the colony.

Although they were a heterogeneous group, most of these settlers were either farmers or fishermen, driven to emigrate by economic and social pressures in their hometowns. Indeed, poverty was a stark reality in colonial New England, where many early eighteenth-century towns also faced land shortages that would force subsequent generations to seek new opportunities elsewhere. Chatham, Massachusetts was a typical eighteenth-century New England town in that it experienced land shortages by the 1720s and boasted a noticeably large poor population by the 1750s. As a result, many of its residents went in search of opportunities elsewhere, including approximately two hundred people, many of them young and poor, who left for Nova Scotia's south shore between 1760 and 1763.[24]

The farmers, who hailed primarily from Rhode Island, Massachusetts, and Connecticut, were offered a maximum 1,000-acre parcel of land that came rent-free for the first ten years. These terms were also extended to the fishermen, most of whom came from Massachusetts and had been visiting Nova Scotia's shores for decades, attracted by its abundant fishery. Both groups succeeded in permanently transforming Nova Scotia.

EARLY IMMIGRATION TO NEWFOUNDLAND

Europeans were first attracted to Newfoundland by the rich supplies of cod that John Cabot observed off its Grand Banks in 1497. French and Portuguese fishermen, soon joined by Basques, conducted the earliest trans-Atlantic migratory fishery. English fishermen, all of whom came from a specific part of England — the West Country — arrived relatively late on the scene. However, although they did not come in significant numbers until the 1570s, they controlled most of Newfoundland's eastern Avalon Peninsula by 1600.[25] In 1583, Sir Humphrey Gilbert formally claimed possession of the island, but his colonization schemes in Newfoundland came to nothing, Sir Gilbert drowning on his return trip to England.

European settlement in Newfoundland began with the establishment of a resident fishery, carried out by fishermen resident on the island. This began to occur in the seventeenth century, when caretakers remained in some harbours over the winter and family residences were built. French settlement was confined to the South Shore (notably at Placentia) while English overwinterers were scattered among thirty harbours and coves.[26] In 1610, the first English colony was established at Cupids in Conception Bay by colonists sent out by a group of merchants from London and Bristol. By now, other ports in England, Wales and even Ireland had become interested in the lucrative cod industry. With the founding of this settlement as a resident fishery the way was paved for Newfoundland to become an English colony.

Visiting English fishermen, who undertook the long voyage from England each summer, bitterly opposed this colony as well as all succeeding moves to establish permanent settlements on the island. They resented the fact that resident fishermen enjoyed a longer fishing season and lower costs. Of even greater concern to these visiting fishermen, however, was the fear that residents would occupy the best beaches for drying their fish. The merchants from southwest England, often referred to as the West Coast Merchants or the Merchant Adventurers, fought the establishment of permanent settlements, periodically enlisting the support of monarchs and parliaments in their struggle. Nevertheless, Sir David Kirke, (Quebec's captor) managed to establish a successful colony and resident fishery by 1637. From then on, although confronted by countless difficulties, including French hostility, English settlement on the island slowly grew.

Between 1660 and 1690, the English government wrestled with the concept of permanent settlement in Newfoundland. At one point it went so far as to attempt to remove residents from the island. In 1699, however, an act was passed that formally recognized the presence of inhabitants.[27]

In the eighteenth century, southeastern Ireland, notably the area within a 30-mile radius of Waterford City, provided Newfoundland with a steady source of new settlers. In fact, some 30,000 Irish settled in the offshore colony from the 1770s to the 1830s. The Atlantic fisheries, in other words, supplied the first significant Irish settlement in what would eventually become Canada. Many of these migrants would subsequently move from Newfoundland to the British North American mainland and New England.[28]

CHAPTER 2

Canada's First Large Influx of Refugees

IMMIGRATION BEFORE THE REFUGEES' ARRIVAL

AFTER THE SIGNING OF THE papers of capitulation in September 1760, the surviving French troops in Canada boarded ships and sailed back to France. So did most of the colony's leaders and merchants. For although New France had been a century and a half in the making, France now wanted nothing more to do with her. In the eyes of French officialdom, the colony had swallowed huge sums of money, but had yielded little in the way of returns. With the crushing of the French empire in North America, therefore, came a brutal severing of New France's ties with the mother country. From now on France would show little interest in her former subjects and there would be virtually no French immigration to the country that the sharp-tongued Voltaire had contemptuously dismissed as "1500 leagues [of] glacial deserts."

French immigration ceased abruptly, to be replaced by the first wave of Scottish settlers in Canada: soldiers from disbanded Scottish regiments that had served in the Seven Years' War. Among the ten Highland regiments raised for the war were the Montgomery Highlanders, the Fraser Highlanders, and the Black Watch, which were dispatched to Canada. The Fraser Highlanders, in fact, played a pivotal role in the British capture of Quebec.[1]

At the end of hostilities the British government was confronted with the problem of what to do with the Highland regiments raised for service in the conflict and the equally perplexing question of how to solidify control over the newly conquered French population. Eager to reward the soldiers for their service but reluctant to reintroduce large numbers of them into the Highlands, then convulsed by rapid social and economic change, the government decided to give the men free land in North America. Settled in the Thirteen Colonies, they would be available for military service should the discontent so evident in that British possession erupt into open rebellion. Established in the territories newly acquired from France, they would provide the skilled manpower necessary to deal with a possible French-Canadian insurrection, or protect Nova Scotia and Quebec from possible invasion from the Thirteen Colonies. At the war's end, therefore, men from the Fraser Highlanders and the Black Watch settled in Quebec and Nova Scotia, principally around Murray Bay and Mount Murray on the north shore of the St. Lawrence River.[2]

THE PROCLAMATION OF 1763

Great Britain had high hopes that the end of the Seven Years' War and the issuing of the Proclamation of 1763 would herald the arrival of a large influx of English-speaking settlers into Quebec and Nova Scotia. The Proclamation had even been framed with a view to attracting immigration. Not only did it define the boundaries of the newly created province of Quebec, it prohibited settlement west of the Appalachian Mountains, thereby effectively closing off the Ohio Valley to pioneers venturing west of the Thirteen Colonies and encouraging the belief that colonists would be directed north to Nova Scotia and Quebec. In anticipation of a large influx of English-speaking settlers, the ordinance promised that British institutions, including representative government, would soon be introduced into Quebec, now reduced to a narrow parallelogram that comprised only the settlements along the St. Lawrence River. But contrary to the government's expectations and designs, Canada saw little immigration in the years immediately following the Treaty of Paris and the issuing of the controversial Proclamation.

It turned out that the Proclamation was based on false hopes. The ordinance undoubtedly encouraged some settlement in Nova Scotia, where the New England Planters had settled in increasing numbers after the expulsion of the French Acadians in 1755. Between 1763 and 1767,

Nova Scotia's population climbed from above 8,000 to approximately 13,500.[3] This figure also included, however, Protestant Germans, who had settled in the province between 1749, when Halifax was founded, and 1752; English settlers in and around Halifax; and remnants of the Acadians, particularly on Cape Breton Island or in areas of what would become the provinces of New Brunswick and Prince Edward Island.

The Proclamation of 1763, in other words, had only limited success in luring settlers from the Thirteen Colonies north to Nova Scotia. It had even less success in promoting Anglo–American immigration to the province of Quebec, where it was hoped a tide of English-speaking newcomers would submerge the French-speaking population. With its foreign culture and harsh climate, Quebec had little appeal for New Englanders, New Yorkers, and others. Not even the Proclamation's promise of the early establishment of an elective assembly and British patterns of law and land ownership was enough to direct more than a trickle of English-speaking settlers to the colony from the Thirteen Colonies and Britain.

The few who did venture into Quebec after the British victory were, for the most part, merchants, often contractors and suppliers for the British occupying forces. These newcomers settled in Montreal and Quebec and, thanks to their British and American business connections, became the dominant force in the province's economic life, especially its rich fur trade. Although relatively small in numbers, this rising Anglo–American business class would spar frequently with British administrators, military men, and governors, who came to regard them as grasping, self-seeking demagogues, bent on controlling the province's political institutions to serve the promotion of commerce.

The Quebec Act

Since few English-speaking settlers expressed an interest in the colony, successive British governors concluded that Britain's policy of anglicizing Quebec was unrealistic. Furthermore, many British officials came to sympathize with, and admire, the French Canadians. The first British governor, General James Murray, refused to introduce the elective assembly promised by the Proclamation and his successor, Sir Guy Carleton, soon came round to the view that "barring a catastrophe shocking to think of this country must, to the end of time, be peopled by the Canadian race."[4] Convinced that Canada would always boast a French-speaking majority, Carleton contended that Britain should replace the Proclamation with a new set of governing principles that respected the French Canadians' institutions, laws, and traditions of government. He also urged that steps be taken to ensure the allegiance of French Canada's leaders, the seigneurs and the clergy. They must be welded to the British Crown and their loyalty ensured in the event of any future crisis, such as the one that he saw brewing in the Thirteen Colonies.

As a result of the aristocratic governor's recommendations, the British government introduced the provocative Quebec Act of 1774. It retained French civil law insofar as it applied to seigneurial dues, landholding, and marriage rites, guaranteed the position of the colony's Roman Catholic Church, and crushed the merchants' hopes for an elected assembly. The colony, it seemed, was going to be allowed to languish as a tranquil backwater in the outer reaches of the Empire.

THE COMING OF THE LOYALISTS

This would not be its fate for long, though, for Quebec and Nova Scotia would soon find themselves forced to accept thousands of English-speaking, largely Protestant settlers who had been uprooted by the American Revolution. Known as the United Empire Loyalists, these were largely political refugees who headed north to British North America either because they did not wish to become citizens of the new United States of America or because they feared further beatings, imprisonment, or other forms of harassment for their support of the British during the War of Independence.

Although the Maritimes had a population of about 20,000 and Newfoundland could claim about 8,000 permanent settlers in 1783, the wave of Loyalist migration that got under way that year furnished British North America with its first large influx of English-speaking settlers. All told, a total of some 40,000 to 50,000 Loyalists flocked to British North America between 1775, when hostilities broke out, and 1784, the year after the peace treaty. Of these, approximately 35,000 went to the Maritimes and 9,500 to the Province of Quebec.[5] In both the Maritimes and Quebec hard-pressed officials, with only primitive administrative structures and limited funds, suddenly found themselves swamped with new and daunting responsibilities: supplying this flash flood of humanity with food, clothing, tools, seed, temporary accommodation, and, later, land on which to erect permanent dwellings; deciding who settled where; and settling numerous land grant squabbles. The tasks were so overwhelming that many observers and participants wondered if the challenge could be met, but, to the great credit of the authorities, it was.

ORIGINS OF THE LOYALISTS

The Tory newcomers came from every part of the Thirteen Colonies, from the slave-worked plantations of Georgia to the frontier farms of New York, from well-off urban households to struggling rural home-steads. In most colonies, however, they had been concentrated in urban and seaboard areas. Only in New York and New Jersey did farmers con-stitute the majority of those who submitted claims for losses incurred in the Revolution, although in the Carolinas and Georgia they were the largest single category.[6] Irrespective of place of origin, occupation, or class, though, all held political or social convictions that could survive in America only with Britain's help or protection.

Some were uncompromising Tories like Jonathan Sewell, attorney general of Massachusetts when the Revolution broke out and later judge of the vice-admiralty court of Nova Scotia and New Brunswick. Sewell was flabbergasted that citizens privileged to live in one of the richest and freest countries on earth should "rush to arms with the ferocity of savages and with the fiery Zeal of Crusaders!"[7] Like other Tories observing the fruits of the Revolution, he was impressed by nothing so much as the rise of the lowborn and the toppling of the great. "Everything I see", he wrote, "is laughable, cursable, and damnable; my pew in the church is converted into a pork tub; my house into a den of rebels, thieves & lice."[8] In contrast to Sewell, other Loyalists resembled the socially prominent Philadelphia lawyer James Allen, who died before being able to flee Pennsylvania for

Europe. He initially subscribed to the aims of the protesters, but then broke with them when he concluded that America's liberty and prosperity could be preserved best within the British Empire. Then there were those Loyalists who were essentially apolitical, but who ended up backing the British cause after being harassed for refusing to support the Revolution.[9]

FREDERICK HALDIMAND

The man most responsible for making decisions regarding the fate of the exiles in Quebec was Frederick Haldimand, who had been governor of the province since 1777. It fell to this Swiss-born career soldier to settle a sizeable influx of embittered Loyalists, who had been congregating in Montreal and Quebec since 1775 to wage war against the American Revolution's western and northern frontier. By the end of hostilities this Loyalist population numbered nearly 10,000, mostly soldiers and their families, who had hoped to make Canada a temporary base from which to reconquer, and return to, their homes south of the border. Still more Loyalists would arrive in 1784 after the Treaty of Paris.

When their regiments were disbanded after the war, some of these Loyalist soldiers settled on the south shore of the St. Lawrence River around the garrison towns of Sorel, Fort St.-Jean, and Chambly on the Richelieu River. Others established themselves around Lake Missisquoi near the United States border, in territory that would later be officially recognized as the Eastern Townships. The choice of the townships' sites was not made with Haldimand's approval, however. Instead, the governor condemned this location, fearing that the Loyalists' proximity to the United States would lead to either conflict or smuggling, and he wanted neither. Far more to his liking was the decision of some 300 Loyalists to settle in the remote Gaspé Peninsula, where they founded towns at Gaspé and Chaleur Bay. In total, the Loyalists in these three locations probably numbered less than 2,000. That left over 7,500 exiles for whom Haldimand still had to find permanent homes. The governor realized that this would be a formidable task. To introduce a large alien population into the settled parts of French Canada, with its tightly knit society and different language, religion, and institutions, would inevitably foment tensions. Haldimand felt that, as in his native Switzerland, each language group should have its own cantons. At first he bandied about the idea of settling his charges on near-empty Cape Breton, which had just been declared a colony in recognition of the role that it could play in Loyalist resettlement. He decided, however, that the majority of the refugees would not adapt well to life on the seacoast.[10] The area south of Montreal was considered next, but dismissed in favour of locating the Loyalists in the wilderness northwest of the junction of the St. Lawrence and Ottawa rivers, on land purchased from the Indians. Settled in large blocks in the province's western reaches, these newcomers would form a potential buffer against the Americans.

In May 1784, then, at the town of Lachine, just west of Montreal, the first of countless flotillas of river boats began departing for Cataraqui (Kingston) with their crews of experienced boatmen, Loyalist passengers, and provisions. Before the westward movement was completed, approximately 7,500 Loyalists had relocated along the north shore of the St. Lawrence and Lake Ontario in territory then known as "the upper country" of Canada, but which in 1791 would become the colony of Upper Canada.

UPPER CANADA COMES INTO BEING

The Loyalists who dispersed throughout the upper country of Canada in 1784, some as far west as the Thames River and the area around present-day Detroit, were a heterogeneous group. Most of them, including Highland Scots, Germans, and native-born Americans, had earlier settled in the western frontier regions of New England, New York, and Pennsylvania. After the outbreak of hostilities they had made their way to safety at Montreal, Niagara, and Detroit. The men, serving in such Loyalist regiments as the King's Royal Regiment of New York, Butler's Rangers, and the Loyal Rangers, scattered along the frontier from Lake Huron to Lake Champlain while their families congregated in refugee encampments along the St. Lawrence, between Quebec and Montreal.

Some of these Loyalists were British and Hessian soldiers who had joined Loyalist corps during the war, but the overwhelming majority were frontier farmers, men well suited to carving out homes in the wilderness and accustomed to living on the fringes of society. Conspicuous among the newcomers to what would later become Ontario, however, were members of those Indian tribes bordering the Thirteen Colonies who had supported the British cause, believing that an alliance offered the best hope for preserving their independence and protecting their territories from land-hungry colonists. None had fought more vigorously for the king than those Iroquois, or members of the Six Nations Confederacy, led by young Thayendanegea or Joseph Brant, an ambitious and well-educated Mohawk. During the winter of 1783–84, this celebrated leader visited Quebec City, where he arranged for some of his Mohawk people to settle on the north shore of the Bay of Quinte, and for others of the Six Nations to occupy land north of Lake Erie, in the vicinity of the Grand River and the present-day city of Brantford, Ontario.

Loyalist Migrations to the Maritimes

Compared to the Loyalist migrations to Quebec, those to the Maritimes contained a much higher concentration of civilians. Most of these settlers came from the Middle Colonies (New York and New Jersey providing by far the largest share), were overwhelmingly American-born, and were from the lower and middle ranks of the societies they had fled. Popular illusion to the contrary, only a few had patrician origins like those of young, articulate Edward Winslow, a Harvard graduate who was raised in a Plymouth, Massachusetts mansion with expectations of continuing the family tradition of public service and social prominence.[11] Winslow would first go to Halifax as a Loyalist agent and then become one of the leaders of the large contingent of settlers who landed on the St. John River.

Nearly all the Loyalists destined for Nova Scotia were evacuated in 1783 by boat from the port of New York, which, along with Long Island, Staten Island, and the adjacent shores of New Jersey still remained in British hands. Some of the wealthiest Loyalists set out for England, where they pressed claims on the British government for compensation for their losses. Those unable to support themselves, however, were shipped at public expense to the closest British territory, Nova Scotia, where free grants of land and provisions awaited them.

National Archives of Canada, C96362

Loyalists Drawing Plots for their Land. Artist C.W. Jefferys.

Because he was afraid that the new arrivals would be strongly resented by resident Nova Scotians, John Parr, Nova Scotia's governor, decided that his refugee charges should be located on the mainland side of the Bay of Fundy, along the St. John River Valley, where there were only a few existing settlers and a handful of squatters. About 19,000 Loyalists had different ideas, though, and remained in peninsular Nova Scotia. There, on rocky soil, at the southwest end of the peninsula, some of them established the instant town of Shelburne. The phenomenal growth of this south-shore community, which became almost overnight the largest city in British North America, was one of the wonders of its day. Within three years, however, it was a ghost town, its inhabitants having scattered to other parts of the province or returned home to the United States.

Sydney County, located at the far east end of peninsular Nova Scotia, attracted the next largest number of grantees, followed by Annapolis County, situated across the peninsula from Shelburne.[12] Here many Loyalists settled in the town of Annapolis Royal and in the valley behind it while others put down roots at the opposite end of the basin from Annapolis Royal, founding the town that became Digby. In 1784, when Loyalists settled at Sydney and Baddeck, Cape Breton was declared a separate colony, but in 1820 it was reunited with Nova Scotia.

THE FREE BLACKS

Among those Loyalists attracted to the Shelburne area in 1783 were some 3,000 free blacks, who left in the mass evacuation from New York to become part of the first large influx of freed and fugitive slaves to Nova Scotia. Some of the free blacks settled in the future town of Shelburne, but at least half of them — nearly 1,500 — selected Birchtown, a site across the broad harbour. Together these two locations would boast the highest concentration of free blacks in Nova Scotia.[13]

Among the free blacks who settled in Nova Scotia were men and women who had heeded a British proclamation issued early in the war, offering freedom to any slave who deserted his American master during the Revolution and volunteered to serve with the king's forces. Most of the new arrivals, however, had responded to an offer of freedom made late in the conflict when it was apparent that fewer slaves than antici-pated had accepted the earlier call. Issued by Sir Guy Carleton, then commander-in-chief of British troops in North America, it guaranteed that all slaves who made formal claim to protection behind British lines would receive their freedom.[13]

The free blacks expected that they would be dealt with on the same terms as white Loyalists in their new home. Only rarely, though, were land grants and provisions distributed to them in the same manner as they were to other Loyalists. Besides the scourge of racism, the blacks also faced a host of other obstacles. Accustomed to toiling as field work-ers on the fertile land around Chesapeake Bay or back of the Hudson River, they had little knowledge about farming thin soil in a harsh cli-mate or about how best to help themselves. Bitterly disappointed in their hopes of finding equality and a good life in Nova Scotia, nearly 1,200 of them sailed in 1792 for Sierra Leone to start afresh on the west coast of Africa. Meanwhile, other free blacks as well as slaves brought to Nova Scotia by their white masters would continue to contribute their skills to the building of communities throughout the province and the newly created province of New Brunswick.

THE CREATION OF NEW BRUNSWICK

The approximately 14,000 civilian and military Loyalists who went to the St. John River Valley in 1783 also faced many difficulties in their attempts to carve out new homes in a seemingly unending wilderness of dense green. Many, for example, had to spend their first winter in tents on hastily selected house sites because of confusion, shortages, delays, and competition. This convinced Edward Winslow that the new St. John River communities should not rely on distant Halifax for assistance but instead should have their own government to attack the urgent and complex problems associated with settlement. He therefore took the lead in proposing and promoting the separation of these settlements from the colony of Nova Scotia.[14]

In 1784, Winslow's wish was granted and the Loyalists in the St. John River Valley settlements became the founding population of the province of New Brunswick. Edward Winslow, whose ancestors had sailed on the *Mayflower*, hoped that the new province would be "the most Gentleman-like one on earth", and in time the "envy of the American states."[15] A believer in paternal leadership and a highly ordered society, he envisaged New Brunswick being headed by an elite who would own large estates and provide the community with the leadership and social structure that he believed the infant province required. This vision of the promised land was shared by fifty-five other Loyalists who had been prominent in the Thirteen Colonies, and who, in 1783, had the effrontery to petition General Guy Carleton for large grants of land. But their aristocratic pretensions were not admired by the colony's ex-soldiers and working people, who refused to become tenants on the estates of the self-appointed gentry and denounced their ambitions. New Brunswick thus evolved as a society of small, independent proprietors rather than as an ordered hierarchical society of massive landed estates with large tenant populations.

LOYALIST SETTLEMENT IN PRINCE EDWARD ISLAND

Some 600 Loyalists journeyed to Prince Edward Island (P.E.I.), then known as the Island of St. John, in response to a sales pitch made by agents who had been dispatched to Shelburne by the island's governor, Walter Patterson. But in contrast to the treatment accorded the refugees in Quebec and Nova Scotia by British officials, the Loyalists who found their way to P.E.I. fell victim to duplicity and extortion. Many, as it turned out, would not be able to obtain clear title to their lands because of conditions peculiar to the island.

These conditions dated back to 1767, when the British government had granted sixty-seven townships of 20,000 acres each, by lottery, to military officers and others to whom it owed favours. To fulfil the terms of their grants, the proprietors were required to place settlers on their lands. Few, however, made any attempt to discharge their obligations and those who released their property for settlement charged steep rents or purchase fees. To make matters worse, those owners who offered their land for sale did so on ambiguous terms that allowed them to withhold legal title to the land from Loyalist purchasers for years. Discouraged by such chicanery, many Loyalists left the island for other parts of British North America.

IMPACT OF THE LOYALISTS

Although overwhelmed in numbers by later immigrants, the Loyalists and their descendants exerted a profound and lasting influence on the development of British North America. In fact, the very arrival of these refugees determined that Canada would retain its colonial ties with Great Britain. As a result, Canadians continued to maintain an interest in the culture and political development of Britain and adopted the British model for political institutions rather than the American one.

In the short term, the Loyalists not only transformed Nova Scotia and brought into existence New Brunswick, they also precipitated the division of Quebec into Lower Canada and Upper Canada (Ontario). It was thanks to a vigorous lobbying campaign mounted by the Loyalists, in which they had the support of the British merchants and other like-minded settlers in Quebec, that the new political arrangements for the province were introduced. The Constitutional Act of 1791, which was passed by the British government, divided Quebec into the province of Upper Canada in the west and the province of Lower Canada in the east. In Upper Canada, the act established British laws and institutions, which the Loyalists had been seeking, while in Lower Canada it retained French civil law and seigneurial tenure, as well as the rights accorded the Roman Catholic Church in 1774. To both provinces it granted an elective assembly.

IMMIGRATION INTO UPPER CANADA

While the Loyalists were changing the face of the Maritimes, those in Upper Canada were initiating a process of growth that would see a million new immigrants arrive in Upper Canada in less than seventy five years. John Graves Simcoe, the province's first lieutenant-governor, who arrived in 1792, was a British officer who had enjoyed a brilliant career commanding Loyalist troops in the Revolutionary War. Although not a Loyalist himself, Simcoe was as determined as the Loyalist settlers to build a superior society working from British models. Indeed, Simcoe believed that the colony should be successful enough to attract former enemies from south of the border, who, through the influence of British institutions, would become ideal subjects. And so he devoted a good deal of his famous energy and bubbling enthusiasm trying to make the colony not only a fit home for Loyalist heroes, but also an attractive location for former rebels, who were boldly invited to emigrate to Upper Canada in return for generous grants of excellent free land.

In response to Simcoe's proclamation of February 7, 1792, thousands of land-hungry settlers from the old Thirteen Colonies journeyed across New York State, Lake Ontario, and the Niagara River to Upper Canada, where the lieutenant-governor was busily initiating the construction of roads and the building of settlements. Among the newcomers were adherents of the Society of Friends, since Simcoe, hoping to encourage a movement already under way, had issued a special appeal to the Quakers, promising them exemption from military service.[16] The ranks of these early American immigrants also included members of other pacifist religious communities, such as the Mennonites and the Dunkards, who, like the Quakers, came principally from Pennsylvania and New York. These groups, who settled in Prince Edward, York, and Waterloo counties, imparted a distinct flavour to an otherwise ordinary movement of American frontier farmers.

The Talbot Settlement

The Proclamation of February 7, 1792, failed to encourage significant British immigration or settlement. That was left to individual colonizers or groups of associates operating under a variety of terms and conditions. The two most outstanding examples in this period were Colonel Thomas Talbot and Thomas Douglas, Earl of Selkirk, but of the two it is Talbot who has been acclaimed as the greatest colonizer of his era.

A member of the Anglo-Irish aristocracy, Thomas Talbot gained his knowledge of the New World during trips to the Miami River and Detroit and while serving as an aide to Governor Simcoe in 1793 and 1794. In 1803, he obtained a grant of 5,000 acres of land, noting in his application to the under-secretary of state that the settlers streaming into Upper Canada were producing a "growing tendency to insubordination and revolt," which could best be curbed by promoting British immigration.[17] The former military man took his 5,000 acres in the township of Dunwich, located halfway between the two ends of Lake Erie, and then proceeded to spend the next thirty years of his life in opening and peopling the western part of Upper Canada. Talbot was an eccentric log-cabin dictator, who summarily dispossessed any settler of his land if he failed to obey the colonel's regulations. Nevertheless, by his dedication and hard work, Talbot succeeded in settling twenty-seven townships before he was required to wind up his agency.

The success of the new communities in Upper Canada attracted waves of new immigrants, including discouraged Loyalists from Nova Scotia and New Brunswick. By and large, however, before the War of 1812, Upper Canada was peopled by Americans. Although Simcoe left the province in 1786, his policy of welcoming American settlers was continued, albeit with somewhat less enthusiasm by his successors, who did not share his conviction that virtually all American immigrants would make loyal British subjects. Still, the province required more settlers, the Americans had the necessary skills to develop a pioneer area, and there was little hope of obtaining colonists from Great Britain while the Napoleonic Wars were in progress.

The first wave of these American immigrants has often been described as "late Loyalists", a somewhat misleading term, as most of them did not emigrate for political reasons. Nevertheless, some of them were relatives of the original Loyalists, drawn to the colony by their relatives' reports of its attractions. Some were disillusioned by developments in the new republic while still others, having been lured by the advertisements of land companies to upstate New York, decided, once they had arrived there, that they would fare better in Upper Canada.[18] After the War of 1812, which was fought mainly in Upper Canada, Simcoe's welcome to American settlers was retracted. Not until late in the nineteenth century would they again be solicited as desirable immigrants, this time for Western Canada. Instead of American immigration, Canadian officials now sought British settlers because the war had focused attention on Upper Canada's need to acquire more people, particularly settlers with British sympathies. For the next century and a half British newcomers would head the list of sought-after immigrants for British America, later the young Dominion of Canada.

— CHAPTER 3 —

British Immigration
Transforms the Colonies

W HEN THE LOYALISTS POURED INTO Quebec and Nova Scotia in 1783–84, they provided British North America with not only its first large influx of refugees but also its first sizeable wave of American settlers. Americans, in fact, would make up the largest number of colonists to people British North America between 1785 and 1815. Although British immigration was considered eminently desirable, it was almost choked off by Britain's wars during this period, initially by the epochal struggle with Revolutionary and Napoleonic France, which did not end until 1815, and then by the War of 1812–14, which was but a later development in that protracted conflict.

The comparatively small number of Britons who did arrive on British North American shores during the war years were, by and large, Scottish Highlanders and were part of a steady stream of Highlanders who set sail for the New World in the final decades of the eighteenth century and the opening years of the nineteenth. The first Highlanders, in what became a mass movement of Highland Scots to the Atlantic provinces, arrived on Prince Edward Island in 1772. These were 300 tenants from the estate of Captain John Macdonald of Glenaladale. The following year the rotting old brig *Hector* discharged almost 200 destitute Highlanders at Pictou, Nova Scotia, the advance guard of a flood of Highland immigration that would make Cape Breton and Nova Scotia's eastern mainland distinctly Scottish. The ruggedness of Nova Scotia's terrain, the enveloping ocean, and, of course, the presence of other Scots all helped to make the province a favourite destination for Scottish immigrants.

Only occasionally did the St. Lawrence port of Quebec succeed in tapping into the Scottish immigrant trade during these years, as in 1790, when the ship *British Queen* arrived with ninety-six Highlanders.[1] Like so many other Highland emigrants in this period, they were dispossessed crofters escaping from recurrent famines and an impoverished society that had been convulsed by rapid and profound change since the crushing of the Stuart uprising in 1745.

The end of the Napoleonic Wars in 1815 heralded the beginning of a vast outpouring of humanity from Great Britain. This great British migration was part of what has been described as the Western world's "greatest folk movement of modern times".[2] It was a movement that saw thousands, then tens of thousands, and eventually hundreds of thousands of people leave Europe to find new homes in South America, Australasia, South Africa, and North America. By the closing years of the nineteenth century the annual exodus would number well over a million individuals.

Most of these exiles went to the United States, but many also journeyed to British North America, particularly to Upper Canada, or Canada West as it was known after the Act of Union came into effect in 1841. The newcomers who made their way to the northern attic of the American continent represented many countries in Europe, but by far the largest number came from the British Isles.

In the 1820s, British immigration reached such proportions that it began to transform the face of British North America. Throughout its vast territory newcomers from England, Scotland, and Ireland filled in the settled areas, pushed back the frontiers, and introduced welcome funds into cash-starved economies. With their skills and capital the expatriate British built new Canadian businesses and institutions. But more importantly, they reinforced British customs and values.

Thanks principally to the immigrant tide from Britain, the population of the northern provinces grew from less than 500,000 people in 1812 to approximately 2.4 million in 1850. By 1867, the year of Confederation, two-thirds of British North America's population was British in origin.

FACTORS UNDERLYING BRITISH EMIGRATION

Many factors combined to encourage emigration from the British Isles in the post-Napoleonic period, not least of which was the extensive dislocation and suffering caused by far-reaching changes in agricultural land use in England and Scotland, which had begun even before the war years. The eradication of run-rig agriculture (the practice of cultivating intermixed strips in open fields), the consolidation of the dispersed, shifting strips into compact plots, and the consolidation of farms figured prominently in these changes. For sheer drama, however, none could eclipse the Scottish Highlands chiefs' and lairds' uprooting of their tenants to provide pasturage for sheep, whose mutton and wool brought higher returns than rents. Evicted from their holdings in the notorious "Clearances," many crofters sought to eke out a living on scanty, inferior land allotted to them on the coast. Others drifted to Lowland cities. But many emigrated to the New World.

Overpopulation, another factor, figured prominently in both England and Scotland, but in the Scottish Highlands the repeated failure of the potato crop, which provided the peasantry with its staple food, added another dimension to the problem. Sweeping changes in the manufacturing sector in both countries also predisposed many people to emigrate. The shift from handicraft to machine methods in the British textile industry, for example, spelt disaster for desperate hand-loom weavers unable or unwilling to adjust to the new conditions, while the later decline of the cotton industry and extensive changes in the metal industries sealed the fate of countless other workers.

Added to these long-term factors were conditions peculiar to the immediate post-war period. In the wake of peace came the demobilization of fighting men, the slowing down of industries that had supported the war effort, and soaring unemployment. Wages slid steadily downward and poor rates became increasingly burdensome.

In largely agricultural, backward Ireland, falling prices for farm produce, absentee landlordism, and overpopulation had resulted in widespread and abject poverty. Such was the magnitude of the island's overpopulation that in 1815 some 6 million Irish struggled to survive on approximately 13 million acres of land, farmed by the most unproductive methods.[3] In fact, it was from one of the most densely populated areas of Ireland and western Europe — Ulster and the adjoining provinces of Connaught and Leinster — that the vast majority of Irish immigrants to Canada originated. For the most part they were small farmers-cum-weavers seeking to better their prospects overseas, after facing a depressed market for agricultural products and a structural reorganization of the Irish linen industry.[4] And in mainland Canada the chief attraction for these immigrants was land, available in rural areas.

GOVERNMENT-ASSISTED EMIGRATION

Paradoxically, it was an overseas war, the War of 1812–14, which revived Britain's interest in promoting emigration to her North American colonies. The necessity of defending these distant outposts of the empire focused attention on their weaknesses and led the British government to conclude that they must be strengthened by a new infusion of loyal and trustworthy subjects. If immigration provided British North America with a much larger population, reasoned British officialdom, the colonies would be in less danger of being absorbed by their overpowering neighbour to the south.

Well before the end of hostilities, political and military leaders in Upper Canada had voiced their concern about the number of residents who were fast transforming the province into "a compleat American colony".[5] They feared that if Americans continued to pour into the colony after the return of peace, Upper Canada would become even more vulnerable to American peacetime encroachment or invasion. The secretary of state for war and the colonies, Lord Bathurst, shared this worry, for he was convinced that the War of 1812 had demonstrated all too forcefully the need to increase the province's British component. In 1813, therefore, he proposed that his government assist Scottish Highlanders to settle in the province, where they would provide good recruits for the militia and help to aid the growth of a loyal population along the northern shores of Lakes Ontario and Erie.

From this evolved a post-war settlement policy that called for demobilized British regulars and selected immigrants to be offered free land

and provisions to settle in the province. To discourage further American immigration into British North America, Bathurst also announced a brand new policy with far-reaching consequences: he ordered that no land be granted "to Subjects of the United States" and that every effort be made to prevent their settling in either Upper or Lower Canada.[6]

MILITARY SETTLEMENTS

When peace returned, the British government began implementing plans to establish an interior line of communication between Montreal and Upper Canada to safeguard Britain's tenuous hold on the province and the area to the west. Central to this scheme was the Rideau Lakes system, where the government spearheaded the establishment of settlements at Perth (1816), Richmond (1818), and Lanark (1821).[7] Composed of demobilized military regulars and loyal citizens with military potential, these strategically placed towns were designed to serve as a "second line of defence" in support of the Loyalist settlements along the upper St. Lawrence River. In Lower Canada, similar considerations led to the founding of Drummondville, east of Montreal.

Perth

The best-known of these so-called military settlements was Perth, located on the River Tay in what is now eastern Ontario. Its early settlers were mostly Highland Scots, many of whom were undoubtedly small farmers whose position had become increasingly precarious as a result of the widespread agrarian changes then transforming the remote rural Highlands.

Those who set sail from Glasgow in the summer of 1815 were attracted by the British government's promise of free passage, 100 acres of land, and supplies for the first six months. Unfortunately, when they arrived in Canada the Scots discovered that the surveys of their lands had not been completed and that their allotments were not ready for occupancy. It was not until late in 1816 that they could take possession of their properties, located by the newly named River Tay, where the depot of Perth had been established. A shortage of money and food, constant bickering between the different layers of the joint civil-military administration, and unfamiliarity with pioneering techniques plagued the early days of the settlement and drove many disaffected settlers south of the border to join friends and kinsmen. Many, however, braved the hardships and stayed on to make Perth one of the most prosperous and un-military-like settlements in British North America.

The Richmond and Pinhey's Point Settlements

Officers and men of regiments discharged from service in the 1812 war formed the basis of settlement at Richmond and at nearby Pinhey's Point in the Township of March. One of the most colourful founders of the celebrated March Colony of "officers and gentlemen" on the Ottawa River was not a soldier but a wealthy and cultured adventurer, Hon. Hamnett Kirkes Pinhey. Formerly a London ship and insurance broker, who had served as "king's messenger" behind Napoleon's iron curtain, Pinhey set out from cosmopolitan Georgian London in 1820 for the Canadian wilderness. Here, overlooking the scenic Ottawa River, he built an impressive estate on 2,000 acres, entertained lavishly, and became a leading public figure.[8]

Quite different in origin were settlements established by unemployed textile workers from the Paisley and Glasgow areas, who took up land in 1821 northwest of Perth in Lanark and Dalhousie townships. For this purpose they were provided with government assistance in the form of free land and personal, repayable cash loans. This type of assistance was also provided in 1823 and 1825 to Irish settlers brought out by Peter Robinson, the first commissioner of Crown lands in Upper Canada.

PETER ROBINSON AND IRISH SETTLEMENT

The condition of the poor was bad enough in England and Scotland, but it was even worse in Ireland, where endemic tumult in several counties threatened to erupt into a serious political uprising. In the hope of quieting Ireland and providing a new start in life for some of its poor, the British government conceived the idea of offering free passage to Upper Canada and assistance in getting established on the land to selected Irish from troubled districts. To Robinson was entrusted the task of superintending such a settlement scheme and in 1823 he visited Ireland, where he selected nearly 600 candidates, all but ten of whom were Roman Catholics.[9] These were sent to Upper Canada, where they took up lands in Ramsay, Pakenham, and other townships to the east and north of Perth. In 1825, Robinson brought out a still larger contingent of Irish settlers, some 2,000 in all. Most of these were placed north of Rice Lake, where around the village of Peterborough, named after him, they launched a thriving community.

Although these two Irish settlement ventures were eminently successful, especially the second one, the British Parliament, after an extensive review of the subject in 1826 and 1827, voted not to allocate any more funds for such undertakings. It decided that such schemes were just too expensive to be repeated. In any event, the publicity surrounding the assisted emigrants spurred independent emigrants to follow, and follow they did in large numbers during the great emigration fever that gripped Britain in the 1830s and 1840s.

When they sailed for the New World, over 90 percent of all these emigrants occupied steerage, where they endured the most horrendous of conditions during their six-week voyage. They travelled not in passenger ships but in cargo vessels that carried wood from Quebec and Saint John to Britain each summer. As human ballast, crammed into windowless, dark holds, they solved the difficult problem of finding cargo for the return trip to North America and earned higher returns for ship owners than the transport of timber and other goods.

CHARITY-ASSISTED EMIGRATION

Many British immigrants to Canada in the years after 1815 were poor and destitute individuals, who received assistance not from official government sources but from individuals and organizations with a social conscience. Some were enabled to emigrate by English parishes, which obtained contributions from private benefactors to send deserving poor to the colonies. Other newcomers were members of machinists', weavers', and other comparable societies, which taxed their members to raise the necessary funds to remove impoverished colleagues to the New World. Still others came under the auspices of such groups as the Children's Friendly Society, the Female Emigration Society, and the Poor Law Ragged Schools.[10] Large numbers, however, were sent out by philanthropic and not-so-philanthropic English, Scottish, and Irish landlords.

LORD SELKIRK'S COLONIZING SCHEMES

Foremost among those landlords who promoted settlement in British North America was Thomas Douglas, Earl of Selkirk, a deeply committed philanthropist, who sold land cheaply, often on credit, furnished supplies, and provided sorely needed guidance to his colonists. Pursuing his dream of creating new havens for dispossessed Scots, the Scottish landlord dispatched some 800 Highlanders to Prince Edward Island in 1803. Originally destined for St. Mary's in Upper Canada, they arrived at Point Prim during a period of heavy Highland Scots emigration to Prince Edward Island (1801–1803).[11] Selkirk's P.E.I. colonists adjusted so well to their surroundings that the landlord sent in fresh contingents over the next few years to join them. If this initial colonizing effort was a dramatic success, however, a second settlement that he started the following year at Baldoon near Lake St. Clair in Upper Canada was a disaster. Nevertheless, despite this failure Selkirk went on to launch his most notable colonizing venture, the first farming settlement in northwest British North America, the Red River Colony.

This small, isolated community of Scots and Irish, from which present-day Manitoba would arise, was located below the confluence of the Red and Assiniboine rivers on land that the earl had acquired in 1811 from the Hudson's Bay Company. Its location, deep in the heart of the continent, far removed from civilization, almost proved its undoing. For the Selkirk settlement not only sat astride the North West Company's vital trade route to the North West, it also occupied land that yielded the fur company's essential pemmican supplies. These were obtained largely through the Metis, who in turn saw their very existence as proud buffalo hunters threatened by the advance of settlement.

The Nor'Westers succeeded in dispersing the colony for a time, but eventually it was re-established with the aid of a Hudson's Bay counterforce. But then, in 1816, Robert Semple, the colony's governor, and a party of settlers were killed by the Metis in a skirmish at Seven Oaks. Selkirk's response was to attack Fort William, the North West Company's inland headquarters, using hired veterans of the 1812–14 war, German, Swiss, French, and Polish mercenaries, who later settled on the Red River. William McGillivray, the company's chief leader, was arrested and a new settlement founded at Kildonan, but at a heavy price. The Seven Oaks skirmish and the seizure of Fort William spawned a series of costly suits and countersuits in the courts of Upper Canada that broke Selkirk's spirit, ruined him financially, and led to his untimely death in 1820. Without the earl's active interest and promotion, immigration to this part of the world dropped off markedly. Nevertheless, after the amalgamation of the Hudson's Bay Company and the North West Company in 1821, many company servants obtained land in the area, thereby vindicating Selkirk's belief in the viability of a permanent settlement on the Red River.

LAND COMPANIES

Land companies also contributed to the settlement of British immigrants in nineteenth-century Canada. In terms of measurable success, top marks must undoubtedly go to the Canada Company, one of only three colonizing undertakings to reach full maturity, the other two being the British American Land Company and the New Brunswick and Nova Scotia Land Company. The creation of British investors, the Canada Company acquired over 2 million acres of land in Upper Canada, for which it agreed to make annual payments to the provincial government between 1827 and 1843. As part of an aggressive marketing campaign, the company placed agents in key British ports as well as in centres throughout the Canadas and distributed a barrage of publicity material to every city, town, village, and hamlet in the United Kingdom. As a result, Upper Canada became known as a destination fit not only for the poor but also for men "of capital…of education and intelligence".[12]

The agency's chief promoter was John Galt, the well-known, high-spirited Scottish novelist. In his capacity as secretary and, later, superintendent of the company, Galt lived in Upper Canada from 1826 until 1829, during which time he plodded through the woods with his Scottish literary friend, William "Tiger" Dunlop, planning improvements. In 1827, he founded the town of Guelph, located approximately fifty miles west of York (now Toronto).

The company injected new vigour into land settlement before it ceased active operations with the expiry of its contract in 1843. It not only made available impressive sums of capital for the building of roads and other improvements, it also attracted large numbers of settlers to the province who might otherwise have headed for the United States.[13] Its shortcomings notwithstanding, the agency earned the distinction of being the corporate equivalent of Thomas Talbot, the individual colonizer.

Establishment of a Canadian Immigration Service

The Canadian immigration service also traces its embryonic beginnings to the 1820s. The first moves in this direction were taken in 1828 after the British government introduced still another Passenger Act in a long succession of such acts, alternately lax and stringent, to regulate conditions on board the "floating coffins" that carried emigrants to the New World. In that year, the Colonial Office, under its vigorous new secretary, William Huskisson, appointed a chief emigration agent, Alexander Carlisle Buchanan, Sr. Although stationed at Quebec, where the vast majority of immigrants to British North America landed, Buchanan acted on behalf of both Lower and Upper Canada.

Before he retired, exhausted by repeated exposure to typhus and other diseases, Buchanan carried out a wide range of official duties. These required him to receive immigrants on landing, distribute landing money, if available, clothe and feed the indigent, hear complaints, launch proceedings against shipmasters violating passenger vessel laws, direct newcomers to places of employment, help new arrivals to locate their friends, and trans-ship newly arrived immigrants to their destination.[14]

In due course, the chief agent at Quebec had a network of agents in other centres reporting to and receiving instructions from him. Depending on the needs of the day, these agents might be located in such places as Montreal, Ottawa, Kingston, Toronto, and Hamilton. Initially the entire cost of this operation was borne by the British government, but after the withdrawal of an imperial grant in 1854 the cost was assumed by the government of the Province of Canada.[15]

Immigration in the 1830s

The year 1830 marked both the start of a new decade and a surge in the overall volume of British immigration to British North America. Between 1829 and 1830, the numbers of Britons giving British North America as their destination jumped from 13,307 to 30,574,[16] while the number of recorded arrivals at Quebec went from 15,945 to 28,000.[17] Which of the two sets of figures is more reliable is, of course, a moot point since figures from this era can't be accepted at face value. What is significant is the impressive jump in numbers, which, as it turned out, was not an isolated case. In fact, annual increases of comparable magnitude were experienced between 1833 and 1834, and 1835 and 1836.

This dramatic increase in immigration occurred at a time when the colonization views of the British social reformer, Edward Gibbon Wakefield, were gaining in popularity. These views were inspired by Wakefield's three-year sojourn in Newgate Prison, following his abduction of a young heiress. Shocked by what he learned in Newgate of the penal system at home and transportation overseas, the budding reformer decided that systematic colonization was the best preventative measure for much of the poverty and crime resulting from Britain's steep rise in population. Land in the colonies, he argued, should be sold at reasonable prices, not given away in large tracts, and the funds so raised used to transport deserving individuals to a new life abroad.

Before Wakefield began urging the removal of selected emigrants to the colonies by a plan that would finance itself, people had looked upon life in the colonies as demeaning and having a lot in common with penal transportation. With the spread of his teachings they began to regard emigration to Canada and other imperial outposts as a means of both improving their prospects and strengthening the Empire.[18]

Interest in, and support for, emigration had also been whipped up by extensive parliamentary debate on the subject during the 1820s and by the findings of select committees of the British House of Commons. One of these, the Select Committee of 1826, concluded that the grossly

Josiah Henson: Although blacks have lived in Canada since the French regime, by far the largest number arrived in this country in the mid-years of the nineteenth century. These were American blacks who escaped north of the border using a network of secret routes known collectively as the "Underground Railroad." It is estimated that some 30,000 slaves made their way to Canada before the outbreak of the American Civil War.

One of these slaves was the celebrated Josiah Henson, who was the prototype of Uncle Tom in Harriet Beecher Stowe's famous novel, Uncle Tom's Cabin. Unlike the cringing figure portrayed by Stowe, however, Josiah Henson was an energetic, resourceful man of action. Born a slave in Maryland, he became the overseer of a plantation in Kentucky. On learning in 1830 that his family was to be broken up, he escaped from Kentucky with his wife and four small children to Canada.

Risking recapture and the cruel punishment doled out to runaways, he returned, at least three times, to the United States to bring out 118 other slaves. Although he had no schooling when he arrived in Canada, Henson became the leading spirit in the founding of Dawn, a cooperative settlement of fugitive slaves near Dresden, Ontario.

He also became a self-appointed spokesman for his race and an internationally known celebrity who was feted by London society. (Margaret K Zieman, "The Story Behind the Real Uncle Tom," Maclean's Magazine, June 1, 1954, 20-21, 42-44.)

National Archives of Canada, C14124

Edward Gibbon Wakefield.
Engraving by B. Holl from a drawing by
A. Wivell.

under-populated colonies could provide gainful employment for Britain's excess workers. Of even greater significance was the work of a wide-ranging 1830 House of Commons inquiry into the state of the Irish poor. As a result of its findings, it recommended large-scale emigration as a remedial measure for Ireland's many social ills.

Recommendations such as these only reinforced the British government's interest in promoting emigration to British North America, especially that of the poverty-stricken Irish, who, it was feared, might one day swarm into Britain in unprecedented numbers. To encourage emigration to British North America, the government routinely made the passage to that part of the world cheaper than to American ports and, in addition, provided free transportation in barges up the St. Lawrence River to poor emigrants who declared their intention of settling in Canada.[19]

It has been estimated that about two-thirds of those who staggered onto the docks at Quebec in these years were from Ireland; two-thirds of the remainder were from England, while approximately one-tenth of all the new arrivals hailed from Scotland.[20] No matter what their origins, however, most of them were destined for Upper Canada.

In this phase of immigration to the colonies, the Maritimes would be largely bypassed. Immigration to Nova Scotia, for example, would begin to decline after 1838, because by that time most of its last frontiers had become pretty well occupied. More than half of the approximately 40,000 newcomers to the province between 1815 and 1838 were Scots, who came to make up the third-largest group after the Loyalists and the pre-Loyalist New Englanders.[21] Scots had also emigrated to Prince Edward Island in impressive numbers, but that province, like Newfoundland, which was chiefly populated by Irish and English from the west of England, did not share in the large British immigration of the 1830s. Only New Brunswick received significant numbers of immigrants in these years and most of these were Irish.

THE CHOLERA EPIDEMIC OF 1832

By far the heaviest influx of immigrants in this decade occurred in 1832, when almost 52,000 immigrants arrived at the port of Quebec.[22] It was not the immigration totals that made 1832 so memorable, however, but rather the large number of people struck down by cholera. A regular visitor to the Canadas in these years, it arrived early in June on one of the overladen immigrant ships that docked at Quebec. Before the epidemic had run its course in October, it had killed approximately one-twelfth of the newly arrived immigrants and thousands of residents of Lower and Upper Canada. So devastating was the epidemic's impact, that it goaded authorities into introducing the first Canadian public health legislation and regulation. The epidemic also unleashed turmoil among French Canadians, who were already suspicious and fearful of immigration. Thinking that the disease represented a deliberate attempt to exterminate their people, crowds of French Canadians lined the shores of Lake Champlain that July, weapons at the ready, threatening to fire on any steamers that did not turn back.[23]

FRENCH CANADA AND IMMIGRATION

The crowds' hysterical behaviour stemmed from the French Canadians' long-standing equation of immigration with disaster. Just as today many Québécois harbour deep fears for their survival and integrity as a cultural community so did many of their ancestors as far back as the first decades of the nineteenth century. Although numerically superior in these years, they saw themselves under constant threat from Lower Canada's English-speaking minority whose members ran the economy and the executive branch of the government and controlled the Legislative Council.

For French Canadians this threat was personified by the so-called British Party, which controlled the levers of power. Its members were strange bedfellows, representing all social classes, but they were united in fighting for the progress of commerce and immigration and in attacking French Canada and everything that it represented. In the eyes of these anglophiles, French Canadians were a backward, inert, and ignorant people, whose fitting destiny was assimilation by the English-speaking population. This, it was thought, could be accomplished by a variety of means, some of which were spelled out in a memorandum written in 1810 by Jonathan Sewell, son of the United Empire Loyalist of the same name and chief justice of Lower Canada.

Writing to Sir James Craig, then governor of both Canadas and an energetic foe of French Canadians, Sewell stated that French Canadians were "still French; their habits, religion and laws are still those of Frenchmen and absolutely opposed to the habits of our people."[24] The chief justice then went on to recommend that French Canadians be assimilated by means of large immigration, the union of both Canadas so as to place French Canadians in a minority position in the Assembly, and the implementation of close control over education and the Roman Catholic clergy.

The views of Sewell and other members of the British Party were repeatedly challenged by the Canadian Party, in which the rising tide of French-Canadian nationalism found its most vocal expression. Through its official mouthpiece, *Le Canadien*, the party attempted to refute accusations levelled against French Canadians by such foes as the *Quebec Mercury*, the British Party's newspaper, which proclaimed that it was necessary to "unfrenchify" the colony. In its counter-attacks *Le Canadien* assailed the goal of assimilation, invoking an argument that has a conspicuously modern ring to it. The assimilation of French Canadians, particularly by American immigration, predicted the newspaper, would eventually lead to the Americanization of the province, but retention of French Canada's distinct society would prevent such a catastrophe.

French-Canadian fears of assimilation were further reinforced by a union bill that was introduced in the House of Commons in 1822. It was eventually defeated by the violent opposition of French Canada and the Speaker of Lower Canada's assembly, Louis-Joseph Papineau, who journeyed to London to lobby against it. The idea of union would continue to be a pet project of Lower Canada's English-speaking population, however, and would later surface in the famous Durham Report, which also had a good deal to say about immigration.

The Durham Report and Immigration

When the Melbourne ministry in Britain asked John George Lambton, scion of one of the oldest and wealthiest families in the north of England, to take on the government of the British North American colonies, it had every hope that he would prescribe a solution for a particular political problem: what form of government to install in the Canadas, where open rebellion had erupted in 1837 after a prolonged period of increasingly bitter conflict between the appointed executive government in each province on the one hand, and the elected legislative assembly on the other.

Since it was the crisis in Lower Canada that was chiefly responsible for bringing Lord Durham to British North America, the radical Whig politician devoted most of his five-month sojourn on this side of the Atlantic to studying the situation in that province. His trenchant analysis of the rebellion's root causes led him to conclude that the perennial feud between French and English could only be ended by impressing an English character on Lower Canada, and that could be achieved, declared Durham, by submerging the French Canadians in an intercolonial union and by following this up with a "judicious system of colonization". Immigration, in other words, should be used as "an effective barrier against the recurrence of many of the existing evils",[25] in short, as one of several tools for assimilating a people whom Durham considered decidedly inferior to the English-speaking minority.

Durham's provocative assessment of the problem in Lower Canada and his two key recommendations for the Canadas — union and qualified responsible government — have often deflected attention from two other themes that are raised throughout this well-known state document: immigration and land policy. In fact, two sections of the report are devoted entirely to immigration or "emigration", as it is labelled, and the disposal of public lands. Thought to reflect the views of the ubiquitous Edward Gibbon Wakefield, who served as one of Durham's principal, if unofficial, aides on his Canadian mission, they contain some interesting observations on land policy and immigration in the 1830s.

The method of disposing of public lands in British North America comes in for withering criticism. Its numerous shortcomings, claims the report, not only hinder settlement and discourage immigration, they also promote emigration to the United States, which boasts a highly efficient land-granting policy. Referring to the loss of immigrants to the U.S., the report observes that "the number of people who have emigrated from Upper Canada to the United States since 1829, must be equal to more than half the number who have entered the Province during the eight years."[26] Another estimate places the number of people who crossed into the United States between 1816 and 1828 at three-quarters of the more than 120,000 United Kingdom immigrants who arrived at Quebec during this period.[27]

Upper Canada could probably claim, with some justification, that it attracted four-fifths of the immigration destined for British North America in this period. But it appears that once immigrants arrived in the province most of them kept right on going until they reached Canada's southern neighbour. This diversion or loss of immigration to the United States would be a recurring theme in nineteenth-century Canadian history. From the 1860s to the closing years of the century, in fact, more people would leave the country than enter it.

The 1840s: A Decade of Contrast

Immigration to British North America plummeted in 1838 because of the rebellions in the Canadas. But it soon gathered momentum, with fairly equal numbers of English, Irish, and Scots reaching the colonies in the first half of the next decade.[28] Because they provide a fascinating study in cause and effect, two years in particular stand out in the first half of the decade: 1842 and 1843.

In February 1842, Sir Charles Bagot, governor general of British North America, advised the colonial secretary, Lord Stanley, that there would be plenty of work for unskilled labourers in the Province of Canada the following summer. The Colonial Office, therefore, promoted emigration and over 44,000 people sailed to Canada in 1842, many expecting to find employment in canal building. Unfortunately, Bagot's predictions were ill-founded. Much of the work that he had promised failed to materialize and as a result hordes of newly arrived immigrants became destitute. Many, despairing of finding jobs in Canada, made their way to New York, hoping to find employment there, but to no avail. Disillusioned and discouraged, some 9,500 Britons returned to their homeland from New York in the autumn and winter of 1842–43. This would be the only "backwater movement" of the decade and one of only a handful in the years to come.[29]

The following year's immigration saw the customary number of small farmers and merchants, but a sharply reduced number of labourers. Immigration, in fact, was down, with less than half the new arrivals being Irish. Nevertheless, the immigration of this year was long remembered in New Brunswick and the Province of Canada as one that was a real asset to the colonies. Quite different, however, would be the memories of the "famine" immigration that transformed the character of immigration in the second half of the decade and triggered a renewed groundswell of opposition in the colonies to the dumping of paupers in their midst.

BLACK '47

In this decade of heavy immigration one year stands out above all the others as being one of the most dramatic chapters in the entire history of British immigration to North America: 1847, the year when a mammoth tide of penniless and starving immigrants arrived on Canada's shores, many afflicted with typhus and dysentery.

This was the summer that saw forty sailing vessels stretch for three kilometres down the St. Lawrence River below Quebec, their filthy holds crowded with sick and dying passengers waiting to be processed at the government quarantine station at Grosse-Île. Over 5,000 people died that summer on the island, described by one official as "the great charnel-house of victimized humanity."[30] But it did not end there. After healthy immigrants passed inspection at Grosse-Île and landed at Quebec, they continued to fall ill, carrying typhus further upriver to Montreal and then on to Kingston and Toronto. All told, more than 30,000 people succumbed to disease in this epidemic, the overwhelming majority of them Irish. Writing in the French-Canadian paper *La Minerve*, Ludger Duvernay reported, "L'année 1847 sera nommée dans notre histoire l'année de l'émigration. Près de cent mille malheureux ont quitté l'Irlande pour venir chercher du pain sur le rivage du Saint-Laurent; pour comble de malheur la fièvre les a décimés."[31]

THE IRISH

Of the approximately 105,000 emigrants who left British and Irish ports for British North America in 1847, nearly all were destitute Irish fleeing the ravages of the horrific 1845–46 famine, caused in part by the failure of the potato crop. The potato crop also failed throughout the rest of northwestern Europe in 1845–46, but because it was the basic food staple in Ireland its failure represented a calamity of unequalled magnitude in that country. There was food aplenty in Ireland during the famine years, but the people could not afford it. What little money they had was used to pay their rents and since money for rent came from the sale of grain and oats, the peasantry faced starvation when potatoes were nonexistent. Confronted by this dire prospect, many chose to emigrate or were consigned by their landlords to emigration.

During the peak immigration years, 1846 to 1854, over 400,000 people set sail from Britain for British North America, most of them Irish. So many Irish were attracted to Ontario in these and the pre-famine years that two-thirds of the people living in the province at the time of the first Dominion census (1871) classified themselves as Irish.[32] Two-thirds of these, contrary to popular perception, were Protestant and over three-quarters of those who classified themselves as Irish lived in rural areas.[33] Sheer numbers alone, however, account for the shift in political power that occurred as a result of the Irish influx in the late forties and early fifties. In 1848, Upper Canada boasted 57,604 persons of Irish birth, while in 1851–52 the census reported an equivalent statistic of 179,963.[34] This increase of 118,358 in the number of Irish-born was just enough to shift the population balance and therefore the balance of political power between Canada West and Canada East.

British immigration to British North America dropped dramatically in 1855 because of the revival of trade in the United Kingdom and the demand for men to serve in the Crimean War. Not until after Confederation would it resume on the same scale and then it would be of a very different character from the "famine" emigration.

IMMIGRATION PROMOTION

The decrease in British immigration, the continuing loss of large numbers of immigrants to the United States, and the exodus of increasing numbers of French Canadians to that country led the Province of Canada to embark on an immigration promotion program in the 1850s. While in the 1840s the colony's principal concern was its lack of control over the quality of immigrants pouring into it, now its main preoccupation was overseas recruitment of immigrants, particularly suitable British ones. To this end, the province earmarked a small sum of money in 1854 to advertising its attractions in England and on the Continent.[35] This first appropriation was used largely to finance the publication of pamphlets, which were distributed abroad by agents of the Department of Agriculture, which had responsibility for immigration.

A landmark step in the active recruitment of immigrants was taken in 1859, when A.B. Hawke was dispatched to England to open an office in Liverpool and begin promotion work in the United Kingdom. The following year William Wagner was sent to Germany by the Crown Lands Department. He was armed with literature on the province and instructions to discourage the "promiscuous" emigration of mechanics, clerks, and house servants, for whom there was then no demand in Canada. Instead, he was urged to promote the emigration of small farmers and agricultural labourers.[36]

The work done by these immigration salesmen foreshadowed the activities carried out by the network of immigration agents established after the Dominion of Canada came into being. Like their predecessors these later agents targeted Britons, especially British agriculturalists. British immigration had done much to stamp the character of Canada between 1760 and 1867 and would continue to play a notable role in Canadian society in the years immediately after Confederation.

— CHAPTER 4 —

Immigration in the Macdonald Era

FOR THE FIRST THREE DECADES after Confederation, large-scale immigration was a dream rather than a reality. But this was not because Sir John A. Macdonald and the Conservatives, who were in office for most of the period, did not attach a high priority to luring new settlers to this country. They did, especially Sir John, the nation-builder, who had long dreamt of a vibrant Canada extending from the Atlantic to the Pacific.

When the new federal union came into official existence on July 1, 1867, Macdonald and the other Fathers of Confederation could congratulate themselves on having achieved a great deal. In a very real sense, however, the largest part of their program remained unrealized. In the East, Prince Edward Island and Newfoundland still hung on the sidelines, while in the West the future of the North-West Territories, Rupert's Land, and British Columbia remained undecided.

Of all these considerations, by far the most important was the future of the West because failure to include it in the new union would have dealt a severe blow to the expansionist urge which had figured so prominently in the Confederation movement. As far as Macdonald and the Conservatives were concerned, it was essential that the West be brought into Confederation — and as quickly as possible in view of the threat posed to it by the imperialist ambitions of Canada's neighbour to the south. The race to incorporate British Columbia and the domains of the Hudson's Bay Company into Canada therefore became the most urgent task facing Macdonald and his government. And closely allied with this was the need to promote large-scale immigration into that sparsely settled plain that stretched from the Lakehead to the Rockies. As never before, immigration would receive top billing, yet, despite its enhanced stature, it would not rate a department of its own. Between 1867 and March 1892, immigration would come under the Department of Agriculture and from then until October 1917, under the Department of the Interior.

Establishing the Immigration Framework

No sooner had the fledgling dominion come into being than measures were taken to establish a network of emigration agents to advertise this country's attractions to prospective immigrants. Until the advent of the First World War, these immigration salesmen would target farmers with capital, agricultural labourers, and female domestics, preferably from Great Britain, the United States, and northern Europe, in that order. In the picturesque words of one assistant superintendent of immigration, those sought were "men of good muscle who are willing to hustle".[1] Not so welcome were individuals with professions, clerks, or other prospective immigrants of sedentary occupation. They were actually discouraged from emigrating to Canada, while artisans, mechanics, and tradesmen, if not discouraged from doing so, were certainly not courted.

Sir John himself did not hesitate to let it be known whom he would target in any immigrant recruitment program. When detailing recent appointments to the ranks of government immigration agents, he informed the House of Commons that a Scotch agent would also be appointed, "Scotch emigration being as a rule, of the very best class".[2] On the other hand, Macdonald was quick to discourage the immigration of those he considered undesirable. In this category fell certain "loose" women who had taken advantage of a program of assisted female emigration to Canada to come to this country. The scheme had been designed to attract suitable wives for prairie settlers, but had succeeded only in demonstrating that it worked better in theory than in practice. Upon learning of its shortcomings, Sir John, as minister of the interior, had it abolished.[3]

Before the first agents could be appointed, the federal and provincial governments had to decide how to share the joint responsibility for immigration conferred on them by section 95 of the British North America Act, now known as the Constitution Act, 1867. The section of the act that recognizes immigration as a concurrent power reads:

> In each Province the Legislature may make Laws in rela-
> tion to Agriculture in the Province, and to Immigration
> in the Province; and it is hereby declared that the
> Parliament of Canada may from Time to Time make laws
> in relation to Agriculture in all or any of the Provinces,
> and to Immigration into all or any of the Provinces; and
> any Law of the Legislature of a Province relative to
> Agriculture or to Immigration shall have effect in and for
> the Province as long and as far only as it is not repugnant
> to any Act of the Parliament of Canada.

With a view to arriving at some decisions regarding this shared
responsibility, a federal-provincial conference convened in 1868 to define
respective spheres of action in the field of immigration promotion. As a
result of the delegates' deliberations, it was decided that Ottawa would
open an emigration office in London and one on the Continent, followed
by other agencies when the need arose. The provincial governments were
to be free to appoint their own agents as they saw fit. Almost immediately a "Dominion Agency of Immigration" was established in London
under the direction of William Dixon, who had earlier organized the
Province of Canada's aggressive immigration promotion campaign in
Great Britain. With his two small rooms in London's Adam Street and a
staff comprising two clerks and a messenger, Dixon can probably be
described as the Dominion of Canada's first resident immigration agent
abroad.[4] His appointment was soon followed by the installation of an
emigration agent on the Continent and by the appointment of other permanent agents, located in Glasgow, Belfast, and Dublin.

It was not long, however, before the carefully formulated plans for
immigration promotion began to unravel. An immigration conference
that convened in 1874, for example, quickly concluded that separate and
independent action by the provinces in promoting immigration had led to
waste and inefficiency and, in some cases, to actual conflict with the federal government. Accordingly, the participants decided that, in the future,
the federal minister of agriculture would assume full control of all immigration promotion in the United Kingdom and Europe and that "independent agencies for any of the provinces [would be] discontinued".[5]

THE FIRST IMMIGRATION ACT

In 1869, one year after the London office opened, Parliament passed Canada's first act dealing with immigration matters. Reflecting as it does the prevailing laissez-faire philosophy of the time, it says nothing about which classes of immigrants should be admitted and which categories should be proscribed. Not until 1872 was the act amended to prohibit the entry of criminals and other "vicious classes" into this country and not until 1879 was an order-in-council passed excluding paupers and destitute immigrants. With the introduction of these amendments, the pattern was set for future Canadian immigration policy: it would be evolutionary and implemented largely by amendments to the current immigration act, thereby avoiding the difficult and time-consuming job of introducing new acts, and enabling the government to put new policies into effect quickly — usually in response to pressure from the general public and vested interests. Authorization for such amendments is provided by the Immigration Act, which delegates power to the cabinet to make rules and regulations in the form of orders-in-council, designed to adapt the act's broad provisions to changing circumstances.

CHINESE IMMIGRATION

The laissez-faire policy reflected in Canada's first immigration act remained virtually intact during the Macdonald era, with one notable exception. This was an act passed in 1885 "to restrict and regulate Chinese immigration" (the head-tax act). It was introduced in response to pressure from British Columbia, which was concerned about the large numbers of single Chinese males who had entered the province to work on the Canadian Pacific Railway (CPR). In a related move, the Canadian parliament also passed an act depriving the Chinese in Canada of the vote.

When introducing the head-tax bill, Secretary of State Joseph-Adolphe Chapleau conceded that placing racial limits on immigration abolished a long tradition of whereby "British soil was open to any member of the human family". He lauded the contributions that Chinese immigrants had made to Canada and refuted the claim that they introduced disease or caused trouble. Indeed, opposition to them, he said, could be attributed solely to "the competition of cheap labour with labourers who want to exact a higher price". Having said this, Chapleau went on to observe that "it is a natural and well-founded desire of the white population of the Dominion ... that their country should be spoken of abroad as being inhabited by a vigorous energetic white race of people."[6]

Chinese immigrants first arrived in Canada from California in 1858, at the beginning of the Fraser River gold rush in British Columbia. Then, starting in 1859, more came directly from Hong Kong on chartered ships. By far the largest numbers, however, began arriving in the 1880s, after Andrew Onderdonk, an American contractor, was awarded the contract for building the section of the CPR that runs from the Rockies to the Pacific. Between 1881 and 1884, an estimated 15,701 Chinese males entered British Columbia, most to participate in the construction of that historic stretch of railway, which winds through dangerous passes, canyons and mountains.[7] Without these Chinese labourers, many of whom lost their lives to disease and injury, the construction and completion of the CPR would have been postponed indefinitely.

Nevertheless, while white British Columbians opposed the Chinese because they were traditional sojourners and "cheap labour," the federal government and the railway welcomed them for just these reasons. Once the last spike had been driven on the CPR, however, Ottawa was prepared to repatriate the Chinese. The federal government, like Victoria, wanted only white British, American, and Northern European settlers.

The views of Sir John A. Macdonald typified the views of those Canadians opposed to Chinese immigration. In 1883, for instance, the prime minister informed Parliament that he was "sufficient of a physiologist to believe that the two races cannot combine and that no great middle race can arise from the mixture of the Mongolian and the Arian." For Sir John a Chinese was "a sojourner in a strange land ... and he has no common interest with us ... gives us his labor and is paid for it, and is valuable, the same as a threshing machine or any other agricultural implement which we may borrow from the United States or hire and return to its owner."[8]

Although the act did not ban Chinese immigration outright, it levied such a stiff head-tax ($50) as to deny entry to the province to a significant number of Chinese. Still, this was not enough to satisfy British Columbia and so the tax was raised to $100 and then to $500 in 1903. At that level, as Sir Joseph Pope, who had been Macdonald's private secretary, noted, it "so effectually restricted the inflow from China that it ceased to be a cause for alarm."[9] The foundations had been laid for a restrictive (later exclusionist) immigration policy that would shape a unique, long-surviving bachelor community with its own distinctive cultural and organizational features.[10]

The Hudson's Bay Company's sale of Rupert's Land and the North-West Territories to Canada in 1869; the creation of the "Postage Stamp Province" of Manitoba the following year; and British Columbia's entry into Confederation in 1871 with the promise of a transcontinental railway threw the whole question of immigration into sharp focus, for now there were vast new areas to be settled. Indeed, only a populous West under the plough would ensure the economic viability of the projected transcontinental railway and safeguard the forty-ninth parallel against encroachment from Canada's rapacious neighbour, where at least one state legislature (Minnesota) had cast covetous eyes on the Red River district.

Officials had estimated total Canadian immigration between 1861 and 1871 at 179,000 and natural increase at 550,698. Although this represented a rate of increase of only 14.2 percent as against 32.6 percent for the previous decade, it was nevertheless a good rate of growth in what had been essentially a prosperous decade. Still, it was patently obvious that immigration must be promoted as never before if the Dominion's new lands were to be filled with people and its resources sufficiently exploited to justify such a daring undertaking as a transcontinental railway.

Against this backdrop the government staged the first of a series of conferences on immigration in Ottawa in 1871. Then, to encourage settlement on the recently acquired prairies, the Conservatives introduced the Dominion Lands Act (1872). This act, which was modelled on the United States Homestead Act of 1862, set in motion a vast, twelve-year land survey, never since equalled. Subsequently amended, although not altered in principle, the Dominion Lands Act granted 160 acres of free land to any settler twenty-one years of age or older who paid a ten-dollar registration fee, lived on his quarter section for three years, cultivated thirty acres, and built a permanent dwelling. By anyone's standards, including the

Americans', this was a most generous offer. But not many newcomers from outside Canada were tempted by it in the 1870s and 1880s, when prairie settlements were few, tiny, and separated by oceans of waving prairie grass.

In fact, homestead entries averaged under 3,000 between 1874 and 1896, and in many years new entries barely exceeded cancellations.[11]

Only in Canada itself were the prairies a magnet for significant numbers of people. So many Ontarians migrated to Manitoba in the 1870s that the province acquired the nickname "Ontario West". Maritimers and English-speaking Quebeckers also journeyed to the West as did French Canadians. But the French Canadians came in significantly smaller numbers. The picture of a poverty-stricken West painted by French Canadian missionaries as well as the climate of opinion surrounding the events of 1869-70 in the Red River discouraged emigration from Quebec to the prairies. For French Canadians the major attraction was New England, located right on the province's doorstep and a ready source of factory and labouring jobs.

With the colonization of the West only limping along, the Mackenzie government (1873–78) decided that another approach was necessary to attract settlers to the prairies. Despite the demonstrated failure of colonization companies in the past, it decided, in 1874, that the newly implemented Dominion Lands Act should be amended to provide that if any party (or parties) undertook "to settle any Dominion lands free of expense to Government, in proportion of not less than sixty-four families in any township" under the act's homestead provisions, the township(s) in question would be withdrawn from the market and sold, in whole or in part, to the colonization company(ies) at reduced prices.[12]

Unfortunately, numerous colonization schemes and companies launched under the new regulations met with resounding failure, including the Canada West Land and Agency Company, headed by Sir Hugh Allan, founder of the Allan Steamship line and railway promoter. Thoroughly disillusioned, the government decided, in 1877, to discontinue the practice of surrendering large tracts of land to colonization companies. Four years later, however, the Macdonald government decided to allow the establishment of colonization companies composed primarily of the friends and supporters of government willing to invest capital in public improvements designed to attract settlers to the

West. However, of the more than twenty companies that signed an agreement under these provisions, some of which boasted British peers as their leading sponsors, only one fulfilled its promises punctually; the remainder defaulted and were liquidated.[13] Once again the federal government failed to settle the Northwest by entrusting the job to colonization companies. As a result, this approach was abandoned, not to be revived until the Laurier regime.

THE MENNONITES

Among the small number of immigrants from outside Canada who did enter the West in the 1870s and 1880s was a group of Mennonites, an Anabaptist sect that spoke a Low German dialect and embraced a simple lifestyle and pacifism. Their search for a new home was precipitated by the introduction of a policy of Russification in the schools of the Ukraine, where they lived, and by the implementation of universal conscription, which went against their pacifist beliefs. In a precedent-setting concession, the Canadian government offered them freedom from military service and from swearing the oath of allegiance. In response to these offers, as well as the promise of the "fullest privilege of exercising their religious principles", government travel assistance of $30 per adult to "Mennonite families of good character", and bloc settlement, some 7,500 Mennonites left the Ukraine for Manitoba in the 1870s. There they settled on two reserves, one southwest and the other southeast of Winnipeg. As the former reserve was located on open prairie, the Mennonites had the distinction of being the first post-Confederation European immigrants to farm prairie land.

John Lowe, in his capacity as secretary to the Department of Agriculture, visited the oldest of the Mennonite colonies, the Rat River settlement, in 1877. There, on the east side of the Red River, in a colony containing about thirty-eight villages and 700 families, he found such "thrift and manifest prosperity" as to move him to make the following heart-warming observations to the House of Commons' Select Standing Committee on Immigration and Colonization:

These people were put down on the naked prairie in the middle of summer, barely three years ago, about 14 miles distant from any wood, and at a still greater distance and out of sight of any human habitation. They had to dig wells for water for their daily use on their arrival, and sleep, with their women and children, under the shelter of their wagons. They broke a little sod for the beginning of a crop the first year, and built temporary huts or houses ... the first winter. They subsequently built the substantial houses and out-buildings of the villages we saw... besides carrying on the large farming operations... and besides furnishing the Winnipeg market with eggs, poultry and other farm produce.... The secret of this result I found to be that every man, woman, and child in the settlement is a producer. We saw women ploughing in the fields as we drove into the settlement. We next saw a woman thatching the roof of a building... a girl plastering the outside of a house.... We saw very young children take out and bring in the cattle...we saw men, women, and children going out into the fields to work before the morning was grey.[14]

The Icelanders

This period also saw some 2,000 Icelanders leave for Canada after volcanic eruptions in 1873 deposited pumice over a wide area of farmland in their impoverished country. One group established themselves at Rosseau, in the Muskoka region of Ontario, but this settlement was short-lived. Another party tried their luck at Kinmount, in Victoria County, Ontario. From here, eighty left for Markland, Nova Scotia, where they put down roots for several years. Neither settlement lived up to expectations, however. As a result, the Icelanders decided to look elsewhere and in 1875, they founded the community of Gimli (meaning paradise) on the southwest shore of Lake Winnipeg.

From the beginning they were beset by hardships, including floods, wet weather, brutal cold, a smallpox epidemic, grasshopper plagues, and a scarcity of food, which drove them to the brink of starvation; by 1881, more than half the settlers had left for North Dakota. As devastating as these setbacks were, though, the original settlement soldiered on with the aid of an $80,000 loan from the Mackenzie government and even managed to prosper in the 1880s.

Despite a concerted effort by Canadian officials to persuade Scandinavians to settle in Canada during these years, few responded to the government's overtures, although thousands were pouring in through the Canadian corridor to destinations in Iowa, Michigan, Wisconsin, and Minnesota. Not until 1886 was a Scandinavian colony of any size established in the West. That year a party of Norwegian skilled workers journeyed from Eau Claire, Wisconsin, to Calgary, where they set up the Eau Claire Lumber Mill, which became one of the city's major industries.

JEWISH SETTLERS

Individual Jews and Jewish families from Britain and Europe started to trickle into the West as far back as the 1850s as farmers, fur traders, merchants, and gold miners, but it was not until the 1880s that they began to arrive in appreciable numbers. Jews began fleeing Russia in hordes after the assassination of Czar Alexander II unleashed pogroms in Kiev, Odessa, and other towns and villages. Homeless, hungry, and penniless, they poured into Austria, not knowing where they would end up.

Slow at first to acknowledge the plight of these unfortunates, the West finally responded in a frenzy. Mass meetings were called, the most important for Canadian Jewry being one that was held at the Mansion House, the official residence of the lord mayor of London. Among those who left the meeting determined to aid the refugees was Alexander Galt, Canada's first high commissioner to Great Britain. Eager to find some suitable immigrants for Canada and to interest the banker, Lord Rothschild, and his friends in investing in Canada, Galt raised the issue of Jewish immigration with Sir John A. Macdonald. Jews, he informed the prime minister, were a superior people who had the necessary funds to get established in Canada and he wanted to see his country play a part in the refugee movement.

For his part, the prime minister approved of the idea of bringing some Jews to Canada and instructed government officials to make land available. Alluding to the stereotypical image of the Jew as an old clothes pedlar, he predicted that a sprinkling of Jews would be good for the Northwest as they would involve themselves in peddling and politicking.[15] Accepting Galt's assurances that Canada's empty prairie lands would make a good home for the refugees, the Mansion House Committee decided that a party of Jewish refugees should settle in Manitoba as farmers.

In April 1882, therefore, 240 refugees left for the Canadian northwest, the first of several such parties sponsored by the Mansion House Committee or by relief committees in Berlin, Paris, and New York. The most celebrated of the agricultural settlements founded by the Russian Jews was New Jerusalem, which was established in 1884 on an inhospitable tract of land near Moosomin in present-day southeastern Saskatchewan. Although this experiment failed, several Jewish colonies would later succeed at Hirsch, Qu'Appelle, Wapella, and Oxbow, in what would later become Saskatchewan.

Hungarian Settlement

This period also saw the beginning of Hungarian settlement on the prairies. The first Hungarian colony in the West, indeed in Canada, was established in Manitoba through the efforts of a colourful adventurer, Count Paul d'Esterhazy. In 1885, this immigration agent brought a group of Magyar and Slovak families from the United States to a location near the town of Minnedosa, Manitoba. The following year he established another group of settlers near the site of present-day Esterhazy, Saskatchewan.

It was clearly evident, however, that the Dominion Lands Act of 1872, the reliance on colonization companies to introduce settlers, and the establishment of the North-West Mounted Police in 1874 to secure law and order were not enough to produce a tidal wave of new settlers. These developments had to be complemented by favourable economic conditions, advances in agricultural technology, and a transcontinental railway that provided the West with a lifeline to Eastern Canada and honoured the pledge made to British Columbia when it became a province. Without a "trail of iron", east-west trade and extensive western settlement were impossible.

In the 1870s, settlers wishing to journey from Toronto to Manitoba via British territory had to face the most daunting of trips on the so-called Dawson route, an all-Canadian route that ran from present day Thunder Bay to the Red River district. On the first leg of this arduous journey they went by steamer across the Great Lakes. Then, from Port Arthur's Landing, on Lake Superior, they bumped along a fifty-mile wagon road to Lake Shebandowan. The next stage found them travelling by steamboat over eastern Manitoba's rivers and lakes until they reached the newly completed Dawson Road, a mere trail that wound its way from the northwest corner of the Lake of the Woods to Fort Garry (Winnipeg). Over the whole Dawson route to Fort Garry, travellers had to contend with some seventy loadings and unloadings and often leaking boats. Their only other option was to detour through the United States, usually by Duluth, Minnesota, where not too scrupulous land agents subjected immigrants to a plethora of temptations and falsehoods in an effort to induce them to make the U.S. their final destination instead of Manitoba.

BUILDING A RAILWAY

A transcontinental railway had long figured in Sir John A. Macdonald's plans for Canada. Indeed, even before 1867 he had worked out the three pillars of his grand design for this country's economic growth: the development of industry in the East, construction of an all-Canadian transcontinental railway, and settlement of the very thinly populated West. All presented major challenges and none more so than building the railway and populating the West.

On November 5, 1873, the Macdonald government resigned because of the notorious Pacific Scandal, which arose over Sir John's and other prominent Conservatives' solicitation of election funds from a railway-building syndicate headed by Sir Hugh Allan. Alexander Mackenzie, the self-made fellow Scot who succeeded Macdonald as prime minister, also had plans for railway construction and western settlement. But his plans were blunted by declining government revenues, resulting largely from a fall in imports and import duties. Unable to persuade private capitalists to undertake extensive railway construction, Mackenzie and the Liberals proceeded cautiously with railway building and met with little success in encouraging western settlement. By the time that they were defeated in the 1878 election, they had only succeeded in pushing the main line of the Pacific Railway westward from the head of Lake Superior and eastward from the Red River. Between the two railheads of Keewatin (later Kenora) and English River remained a gap of 181 miles, which had to be bridged if the Red River community was to gain access to the East through Canadian territory and immigration into the West was to receive a badly needed shot in the arm.

WESTERN SETTLEMENT

After being returned to office in 1878, Macdonald and the Conservatives assigned top priority to three interrelated national policies: protective tariffs (dignified by the title "National Policy", but commonly referred to as the "N.P."), transcontinental railways, and western settlement. It was western settlement, however, that became Macdonald's main concern. As an indication of the importance he attached to this undertaking, Sir John himself took on the post of minister of the interior. A relatively new portfolio, it had been created in 1873 to manage all the important aspects of expansion in the West. Its principal task was promoting western settlement, and in the autumn of 1878, when Macdonald took control, the department was ready to attack its job effectively.

The preliminary work in western settlement had already been completed with the extinguishing of the aboriginal title to the land (in the 1870s a series of patiently negotiated treaties formally ceded Indian title to western lands to the federal government); the displacement and settling of most of the native peoples on reserves; the enactment of the Dominion Lands Act; and the swift establishment of an effective system of law and order. Now it was essential that the construction of the CPR be hurried forward if Sir John's economic strategy was to be realized and

British Columbia prevented from leaving Confederation. To this task Macdonald applied dogged determination, devoting weeks in the eventful summer of 1880 to negotiating the famous contract that granted $25,000,000 and 25 million acres to a Montreal-based syndicate and paved the way for the completion of the Canadian Pacific Railway.

The CPR — constructed chiefly, it should be recalled, with Chinese immigrant labour in the Rockies — opened up the West for settlement by providing a transportation lifeline to Eastern Canada. But since the CPR believed that occupied land would help to generate traffic for the railway, it also participated directly in the settlement of the prairie West by selling its lands to individual colonists and farmers. As early as 1881, the company appointed a land agent in London, England and started stoking an advertising campaign for its lands. That same year it also established a land department in Winnipeg and in 1882 it instituted provisions permitting the sale of large blocks of land in a forty-eight-mile belt to individuals and companies.[16]

The government policy of allowing land companies to purchase land remote from the CPR for colonization purposes also helped to further the cause of settlement, albeit in a minor way. But despite initiatives such as this and the railway, settlers did not arrive in the hoped-for numbers. Large-scale immigration might be essential for the success of the railway and the triumph of Macdonald's own plans, but it would not become a reality in the old chieftain's lifetime. At Sir John's death in 1891, the population of the Prairies stood at only 250,000. Even more discouraging, the previous decade had witnessed an unprecedented exodus to the United States; between 1880 and 1891 over a million Canadians and immigrants — equivalent to one-fifth of Canada's total population — had headed south of the border in a search for greater opportunities. And this phenomenon would be repeated in the ensuing decade.

Several factors contributed to the West's slow growth, chief of which were worldwide adverse economic conditions, known as the "Great Depression" (1873–96). Grain prices were relatively low from 1874 to the mid-1890s and in the West, with its short growing season and low rainfall, farming became more risky and experimental, especially outside Manitoba's Red River district. High freight rates to ship grain to the Lakehead were another drawback. Many settlers therefore preferred the

American West, which, besides offering better farming conditions, also boasted a more complete transportation system, even after the CPR's completion in 1885.

Canada's immigration prospects only began to look up in the 1890s. By then there was a general economic recovery in both North America and Europe and an increased demand for Canadian foodstuffs. Europe was also in the midst of a population explosion, a phenomenon not

The Parting Hour, published in 1832.

unfamiliar to the British, who for years had packed off their surplus population overseas. By the turn of the century, however, the problem in southern and eastern Europe had become both relatively new and more severe. A wide variety of conditions, ranging from high taxes and debt burdens to land clearances and ethnic tensions, would lead many in this part of the world to try their luck overseas — in Canada.

Thanks to such breakthrough developments in Canadian agricultural technology as the development of better strains of wheat (notably the earlier maturing Marquis) and the chilled steel plough; the adoption of dry farming techniques that permitted the successful exploitation of semi-arid prairie lands; the widespread belief after 1890 that the United States was finally running out of good free land; and higher returns for farm products, Canada would at last become a preferred destination for immigrants. And poised to take full advantage of these new developments was the Liberal government under Prime Minister Wilfrid Laurier, which had swept to power in 1896. In the years preceding the First World War vigorous expansion would be the order of the day — expansion in numbers, wealth, and enterprise that would prompt Sir Wilfrid's celebrated prediction in 1904: "As the nineteenth century was that of the United States, so I think the twentieth century shall be filled by Canada."

— CHAPTER 5 —

The Sifton Years

CLIFFORD SIFTON AND HIS POLICIES

I F THERE IS ONE MAN who, more than all others, symbolizes the aggressive expansion of the Laurier years, it is Clifford Sifton, who was appointed minister of the interior in 1896 at the age of thirty-five. In this powerful portfolio, he would exploit his relentless drive and celebrated energy to the full and become the most important member of the cabinet next to the prime minister himself.

Born and educated in Ontario, Sifton had joined thousands of other Ontarians in migrating to the West in the 1880s. Once arrived in Manitoba, the six-foot lawyer established a law practice in Brandon with his brother Arthur. Using this as a springboard, he embarked on a twenty-three-year political career, first in the provincial arena, where he served for five years as an influential member of the Greenway Liberal government, and then at the federal level as a member of Laurier's cabinet (1896–1905). His entire federal career was spent in the Department of the Interior portfolio, from which he resigned in 1905 after a bitter quarrel over the issue of separate schools in the new provinces of Saskatchewan and Alberta.

A born organizer, Clifford Sifton was determined to revamp the lacklustre immigration service that he had inherited, and fill the empty prairies with suitable farmers as rapidly as possible. Like the good provincial booster that he was, he had unbounded confidence in the West. At the same time the new minister was firmly convinced that massive agricultural immigration was the key to general Canadian prosperity; if primary resources were developed, then industry and commerce would follow naturally. They did not need to be stoked by immigration. This close-mouthed man stated his immigration goals nowhere more explicitly than in a memorandum that he wrote to Laurier in 1901. Said Sifton:

> Our desire is to promote the immigration of farmers and farm labourers. We have not been disposed to exclude foreigners of any nationality who seemed likely to become successful agriculturalists … It is admitted that additions to the population of our cities and towns by immigration [are] undesirable from every standpoint and such additions do not in any way whatsoever contribute to the object which is constantly kept in view by the Government of Canada in encouraging immigration for the development of natural resources and the increase of production of wealth from these resources.[1]

Sifton's public pronouncements on the types of immigrants he did not favour were no less blunt. Speaking in the House of Commons during a debate on the merits of American versus Canadian immigration policy, he said:

> I do not think we need to disturb ourselves by a comparison between the volume of immigration to the United States and the volume to Canada. If our friends will undertake to make an analysis of the figures, they will find that out of a total immigration to the United States last year of 648,743, there were only 8,168 farmers and 80,562 farm labourers. Practically all the rest were mechanics and labourers of the same common class, people who congregate in cities, and cannot in any sense of the word be held to be persons who will become producers and citizens of a valuable class.[2]

In other words, Canada would actively court suitable farmers and farm labourers, no matter what their ethnic or national origin. Agriculturalists were to have priority over every other class of immigrants.

In fact, urban dwellers were to be discouraged because Sifton did not want to see immigration swelling Canadian towns and cities, for if this happened they would invariably develop many of the problems that he observed in their American counterparts.

If he thought necessary, this resolute minister would even use the existing legal framework to restrict the entry of those immigrants he thought unsuitable for prairie settlement. Such an occasion arose in 1898 when

Clifford Sifton as he appeared in 1917.

National Archives of Canada, PA 28125

he ordered a railway car of Italian labourers returned to New York, using for this purpose the toughly worded Alien Labour Act, passed the previous year.

Enacted at the request of Canadian unions and in response to similar American legislation, it was designed to prevent aliens from entering Canada as contract labour. Three years later an amendment prohibited Canadian employers from advertising for labour in American newspapers and outlawed completely the entry of non-American foreign workers via the United States.

Canadian labour leaders rejoiced at this new development, but before the year was out the CPR imported hundreds of American strikebreakers with little trouble, simply because enforcement of the legislation was left up to complainants and unions could ill afford the legal costs.

In the federal election of 1896, Sifton hinted at the policies that he would adopt as minister of the interior when he outlined his views of the problems faced by Manitoba:

> Since 1882 the progress of Manitoba has been disappointing; it has not developed as it should have done if a proper policy had been developed at Ottawa. The land policy of the Government alone was enough to kill

any new country. Today the great need is to have as Minister of the Interior one who will grapple with this question in an intelligent vigorous way. It was useless to spend thousands of dollars in bringing immigrants here when there was no proper means of locating them. What was needed was a study of the agricultural needs of the country, the problem of education, and the settling of the vast quantity of vacant land.[3]

As soon as he took up his new appointment, the young dynamo moved swiftly to attack these problems. With all possible speed, he abolished the Winnipeg-based Dominion Lands Board, convinced that its fumbling and insensitive administration of Dominion lands had been one of the principal causes of western stagnation. Henceforth, overall policy and decision-making would be centralized in Ottawa, where Sifton had replaced Conservative appointees in key positions with his own Liberal appointees. No longer would his ministry be a department of "delay and circumlocution", as he once characterized the Department of the Interior. The elimination of the Dominion Lands Board headed the minister's list of priorities, but it was not alone in claiming Sifton's immediate attention. A year later, in 1898, he swept away still more red tape when he made the regulations of the Dominion Lands Act simpler and more flexible, thereby enabling immigrants to secure their promised homesteads more quickly.

Next, he mounted an assault on the land grants system as it applied to railways. In the 1880s, the federal government had attempted to defray the costs of opening up the West by granting millions of acres of alternate sections of land to the railways for a dual purpose: to serve as collateral for railway bonds and for sale to help meet construction expenses. The railways, however, had selected only a small portion of these huge tracts for sale to individuals and companies, leaving large blocks of land in the prairie West closed to free homesteading. With his customary determination, Sifton abolished the land grants system and pressured the railways — chiefly the CPR — into choosing their granted acreage, thereby freeing the remaining lands for general settlement. Such was his success that the land problem had virtually disappeared by the time of his resignation in 1905.

THE HARD SELL

Equally important, Clifford Sifton became an aggressive salesman for his pet project. "In my judgment", he observed in 1899, "the immigration work has to be carried on in the same manner as the sale of any commodity; just as soon as you stop advertising and missionary work, the movement is going to stop."[4] The Macdonald government had relied chiefly on its offer of free homesteading land; the completion of the CPR; the efforts of colonization companies; and the perceived exhaustion of free or cheap land in the United States to ensure a steady influx of newcomers to Canada. As a result, it had neglected promotion. Sifton, by contrast, launched an aggressive advertising campaign, employing methods that, although not new, had more vigour behind them. Countless pamphlets in several languages flooded Great Britain, the United States, and Europe. His department underwrote the production of "editorial articles" for insertion in foreign newspapers, articles, as Sifton observed, "referring to Canada and incidentally giving information about Canada of such nature as an English paper would be willing to publish and would consider to be interesting to its readers, and also not doing any injury to the present administration."[5] Canadian exhibits were mounted at fairs, exhibitions, and public displays in Britain, the U.S., and Europe. Foreign journalists were wined and dined on guided tours across the West and successful homesteaders were encouraged to visit their homelands, for Sifton believed that the most effective advertising was done by individual contact.

Sifton also stressed new fields for soliciting immigrants. One of these was the United States. While the Conservatives had generally regarded the great republic to the south as merely a competitor for immigrants, Sifton saw it as a vast reservoir of potential new settlers. Previously the Canadian government had concentrated on repatriating former Canadians living south of the border. Now, under Sifton's direction, the Department of the Interior rapidly expanded its network of American offices and agents and pulled out all stops in its attempts to attract experienced American farmers with capital. It is estimated that between 1901 and 1914 nearly a million immigrants entered Canada from the States, many of them returning Canadians, and about one-third of them newcomers from Europe — Germans,

National Archives of Canada, C09671

A Canadian government wagon advertising the bountiful West in Great Britain.

Icelanders, Hungarians, and Scandinavians who had originally settled in the American West but now sought better land for their children.

Although land was still available in large pockets across the western half of the United States, there was nevertheless the disquieting perception in rural America that the frontier had closed and that American land expansion was coming to an undeniable halt. It was a belief fuelled by the observations of the noted American historian Frederick Jackson Turner.

Addressing the American Historical Association in 1893, Turner claimed that American development could be explained by the existence of an area of free land, its continuous recession, and the westward advance of American settlement. By 1893, however, claimed Jackson, there were no longer inexhaustible supplies of land. An era in American history had ended, the frontier had vanished.[6] However, if there was a "psychological closing" of the frontier in the United States, there was both a "psychological" and a "material opening" of the frontier in Canada. In a sense the frontier had merely shifted northward to the Canadian prairies.

Some of the Americans responding to the advertised attractions of the Canadian West were members of groups founded on a religious basis. Notable among these parties were Mormons who headed north from Utah to join the small colony started in 1887 by Charles Ora Card in southern Alberta. With these pioneers came a knowledge of irrigation techniques that would prove invaluable in developing the dry lands of the Palliser Triangle.

Sifton's campaign was so effective that Americans constituted the largest immigrant group in the newly formed provinces of Alberta and Saskatchewan. There, they were enthusiastically welcomed, most Canadians regarding Americans as a sterling addition to the young society then taking shape. The *Lethbridge Herald* summed up current feeling when it wrote:

> This class of immigration is of a top-notch order and every true Canadian should be proud to see it and encourage it. Thus shall our vast tracts of God's bountifulness ... be peopled by an intelligent progressive race of our own kind, who will readily be developed into permanent, patriotic, solid citizens who will adhere to one flag — that protects their homes and their rights — and whose posterity ... will become ... a part and parcel of and inseparable from our proud standards of Canadianism.[7]

To Ottawa's chagrin, the Americans took great umbrage at seeing many of their fellow citizens lured north of the border. With typical American spirit, they launched a vigorous counter-attack in an effort to halt or curtail the northern flow. Often this took the form of a virulent newspaper war against Canada. Testifying before the House of Commons Select Standing Committee on Agriculture and Colonization, James A. Smart, the deputy minister in Sifton's department, reported:

> They publish articles in which they decry Canada and praise their own country. They publish letters from people who have gone to the North-west and who have

returned to the United States, in order to prevent further emigration from the United States. It is only a few months ago that I noticed a complaint made at some conference in New York, that some particular parish or district was being practically depopulated by people going to North-western Canada.[8]

Decades later, when Canada was experiencing a large "brain drain" to the United States, Arthur Lower, the distinguished Canadian historian, would fulminate against the lack of effort made by Canadian statesmen to retain Canada's best people, or to persuade them, once they had emigrated, usually to the U.S., to return to this country. If there is one Canadian statesman who does not deserve Lower's reproaches for failing to act on this aspect of migration, however, it is Clifford Sifton. Nobody could have done more to try to woo Canadians living south of the border back to Canada than this aggressive salesman for the West.

Sifton's American campaign, it should be noted, did not seek out black settlers. Unlike prospective white immigrants, blacks received a decidedly cold reception from Canadian immigration agents. Black spokesmen made numerous proposals to Canadian agents regarding group settlement on the prairies, but these were routinely discouraged. Invariably blacks' unsuitability to Canadian conditions, particularly our climate, was cited as the reason for rejection. But colour, of course, was the real obstacle.

IMMIGRANTS IN SHEEPSKIN COATS

Sifton's second new field of recruitment was central and eastern Europe. And it was here that the minister tilled a field rife with controversy and difficulty. Referring to what he looked for in the desirable immigrant, Sifton said in his immortal words:

When I speak of quality I have in mind something that is quite different from what is in the mind of the average writer or speaker upon the question of immigration. I think that a stalwart peasant in a sheepskin coat, born to the soil, whose forefathers have been farmers for ten generations, with a stout wife and a half-dozen children, is good quality.[9]

Immigration Hall, Winnipeg, Manitoba, c 1890–1910.

The North Atlantic Trading Company

Attracting stalwart peasants, who could push back the frontiers of western settlement and furnish seasonal or casual labour when needed, required exceptional measures. This was because most European governments were hostile to emigration promotion; several actually prohibited it. Sifton's department, therefore, entered into special arrangements — usually secret — with shipping agents at key embarkation points. So effective was this approach in helping to engineer a dramatic rise in continental immigrants between 1897 and 1899 that Sifton decided to organize European recruitment even more efficiently. Thus was born the North Atlantic Trading Company, a clandestine network of European shipping agents who agreed, whenever possible, to direct agricultural settlers to Canada in return for a larger bonus. For purposes of the higher bonus, the government would classify persons over twelve, rather than eighteen, as adults. However, Ottawa would only pay for genuine agricultural settlers and the head of each family had to have at least $100 upon arrival.

The choice of countries covered by the agreement is interesting: Russia (probably understood to include Finland), Austria, Germany, Romania, Switzerland, northern Italy, Belgium, Holland, and France. The first four countries were selected because they had been the principal sources of agriculturalists in previous years. France, despite a dismal record of emigration, was included for political reasons while southern Italy was deliberately excluded because of Sifton's disdain for southern Europeans and their mythical inability to meet the challenges of prairie frontier life. Scandinavia was omitted from the line-up because of the government's general failure to obtain immigrants from that part of the world.

This new arrangement was instituted in 1899, thanks largely to the prodigious energy of W.T.R. Preston, a former Liberal organizer in Ontario. Six years later it was abandoned, but not before demonstrating that it had one big advantage over similar plans made by previous governments: it paid only for effective results.

In a further attempt to draw the desired type of European immigrant to the prairies, the government did everything possible to establish bloc settlements of the different ethnic groups. Such settlements, it was thought, could have a powerful magnetic effect and often they did, particularly in the case of groups like the Doukhobors, a Russian peasant sect whose pacifism and simple lifestyle invited brutal persecution and harassment from the Czarist authorities. Fortunately for the dissidents, their plight aroused the sympathy of the great Russian novelist Leo Tolstoy, who used his international connections and literary skills to help them to emigrate. Peter Kropotkin, a prominent Russian anarchist, and Professor James Mavor of the University of Toronto also aided their cause. Acting as intermediary, Mavor persuaded Canadian authorities to admit sect members to Canada and in late January 1899, the first of over 7,500 Doukhobors headed west to settle in what is now Saskatchewan.

There they occupied three large areas in the east-central part of the province with a government promise of freedom from military service and the right to live in communal villages. In 1905, however, public opposition to the activities of a radical wing of the sect would persuade Frank Oliver, Sifton's successor, to confiscate more than half their land holdings on the grounds that their religious convictions prevented the Doukhobors from taking the oath of allegiance to the Crown, necessary to acquire final title to land.

BRITISH IMMIGRATION

During Sifton's years the government continued to promote emigration from Britain to Canada, and this despite the fact that there were relatively few good agriculturalists left to court. Yet the work was deemed politically necessary since English Canadians took it for granted that the government would do everything possible to retain the British character of the country. Up until 1903, Canada's immigration service in Britain had been under the control of the Canadian High Commission, but that year Sifton decided to set up an immigration office in London that was effectively independent of the high commissioner's office. This heralded a significant increase in British immigration. In 1900, fewer than 1,200 Britons entered Canada. Five years later the annual number had soared to above 65,000, exceeding the numbers of new settlers arriving from the United States.

Most of these newcomers were individuals who emigrated to Canada on their own in search of a higher standard of living and freedom from the rigidities of the British class structure. The ranks of these unsponsored immigrants included not only people of modest means but also individuals with substantial funds, which were often invested in large-scale farming or ranching ventures in Western Canada. Many of these well-off middle- and upper-class Britons had struck out for Canada because employment was difficult to obtain in the overcrowded and highly competitive professions in Britain and emigration seemed the only answer to maintaining their and their children's lifestyle in a rapidly changing world. For these people Canada became the chosen destination thanks largely to the efforts of emigration and booking agents, the aggressive campaigns mounted by colonization companies, and the seductive message conveyed by promotional material extolling the attractions of the various provinces for "gentlemen emigrants."[10]

Not all these well-heeled British immigrants received a warm welcome in their adopted country. In fact, there was widespread resentment against those who expected special treatment in the "colony". Not infrequently, employment ads in western newspapers included the words "No English Need Apply". And when a London reporter, H.R. Whates, covered the immigration boom for the London *Standard* in 1905 he was bluntly informed by Canadians: "The Englishman is too cocksure; he is too conceited, he thinks he knows everything and he won't try to learn our ways."[11]

Among the great influx from Britain were poor immigrants who had been assisted by charitable organizations eager to rid the United Kingdom of paupers and help them to get a fresh start in the colonies. The Salvation Army, which was established in Canada in 1882, was one of the many philanthropic organizations that became involved in the immigration boom. In 1902, it opened a recruiting office in London, England, and before long it was sending chartered shiploads of the "deserving" poor of Great Britain to Canada. By 1914, the "Army next to God" had assisted 150,000 such people with emigration to Canada.[12] The Army's immigration program was not without controversy, however. Indeed, it excited outright hostility on the part of organized labour, which charged that the Dominion government was paying the Army bonuses for "agriculturalists" who soon became industrial workers.[13]

THE HOME CHILDREN

Conspicuous in the ranks of the British poor were thousands of slum children who were dispatched to this country by well-meaning philanthropists, philanthropic rescue homes, and parish workhouse schools in what seemed to be the ideal solution to a two-pronged problem: what to do with tens of thousands of children from the slums of Britain who faced a bleak future there and how to meet the soaring demand for cheap labour on Canadian farms.[14] Once in this country most of the boys — many of whom were eight, nine, and ten years of age — were located on farms where they apprenticed as agricultural labourers. Girls were sent to smaller towns or rural homes to work as domestic servants.

A Group of Barnardo boys who arrived at Marchmont House, April 1922.

At a time when few British emigrants were indentured in their overseas destinations, nearly all these child immigrants were apprenticed shortly after their arrival in Canada. Moreover, unlike other nineteenth-century British newcomers, most of these young immigrants found themselves on their way to Canada before they had reached the legal age of consent. They all came without their parents, despite the fact that perhaps only one-third of them were orphans. And during the Sifton era these children of paupers, widowed or sick parents, and families who had fallen on hard times arrived in unprecedented numbers.

Although British children had been dispatched to farms in Lower and Upper Canada in the 1830s, the movement really traces its beginnings to 1868 when two women brought parties of children to Ontario in the wake of the last great London cholera epidemic. They were Maria Susan Rye, the feminist daughter of a noted London solicitor, and Annie Macpherson, a Quaker. Rye, Macpherson, and her sister, Louisa Birt of Liverpool, along with Thomas Barnardo of London and other like-minded activists, had all come to view emigration as an effective means of aiding children from the poorest and most crowded districts of Britain's teeming cities. Soon several other charities joined them in setting up Canadian branches and the movement was given new impetus.

This program of uprooting British children and dispatching them to rural Canada for their own good was not without its critics, even in its early years. Harriet Beecher Stowe, for example, roundly condemned

Maria Susan Rye for shipping little girls like cattle to foreign markets. And in Canada itself, the movement was attacked on economic grounds. In the House of Commons, on March 20, 1890, Liberal James Somerville asked the Macdonald government:

> Is it the intention of the Government to continue the system of paying $2 each for children brought out here? I see by the Auditor-General's Report that the following, amongst other sums, were paid last year for this purpose: Barnardo Home, Peterboro, $1,322; E.A. Bilborough, Belleville, $244 ... Now, as I understand, in a large number of places in Ontario ... the parents of children have great difficulty in finding employment for them, and many children who have grown up are unable to find employment in consequence of the influx of emigrant children, who are hired out to farmers and others in the towns and cities.[15]

The movement did, of course, continue because Canadian governments and the public supported it, furnishing grants-in-aid, transportation subsidies, and an unending supply of applicants for the children's services. In all, about 100,000 children would be packed off to Canada before the program officially ended in 1939 with the closing of the last distribution home in Toronto.

Although there are many names closely associated with this unique immigration program, the one most familiar to Canadians was probably that of Irish-born Thomas John Barnardo, known everywhere that he went as "Dr. Barnardo", although he had never completed his medical studies. Born into a Dublin family of modest means in 1845, he headed to London in 1866 to train as a medical missionary for China. This move would prove to be the turning point of his life because shortly after his arrival he found himself deeply affected by the discovery of homeless waifs sleeping in the city's alleys and on roofs. Rejected for missionary work in China, Barnardo gave up all plans to be a physician and vowed to make his life work among these children of the streets. To this end, the authoritarian trailblazer established the first of numerous

Barnardo homes for destitute children, a boys' refuge in London, in 1870. Before long the first contingent of Barnardo children was dispatched to Canada, where it was thought they would grow up to be devout, industrious adults thanks to doing healthy work far from the temptations of city life.

Most of the approximately 30,000 Barnardo children who came to Canada led anonymous lives, but not so George Everitt Green, a young agricultural labourer from England. After his death Canadians would know more about him than about any of the other "home children" sent to Canada. Only seven months after his arrival at an Ontario farm, in 1895, young George Everitt Green was dead — his limbs gangrenous, his frame emaciated, and his body covered with sores as a result of cruel treatment at the hands of his spinster employer.[16] The inquest and trial that followed caused such a sensation that in 1897 the federal and Ontario governments introduced legislation designed to prevent such a calamity from ever happening again.

Even more far-reaching action was taken after three home children committed suicide in the winter of 1923–24. Following these tragedies a parliamentary delegation journeyed from Britain to Canada to interview immigration officials, social workers, representatives from women's, labour, and farm organizations, and the child immigrants themselves. As a result of its findings the delegation declared that in the future children who emigrated to Canada should be of working, i.e., school-leaving, age. Taking its cue from this report, the Dominion Immigration Branch ruled in 1925 that no children under fourteen years of age who were not accompanied by parents would be admitted to Canada for the next three years. In 1928, the ban was made permanent.

The movement received still another setback when the Canadian economy slid into depression and the labour movement stepped up its opposition to the program. However, it was only with the arrival of the last Barnardo children in July 1939 that the movement of home children to Canada officially came to an end. It had been a remarkably long-lived program but ultimately it ground to a halt because Canadians and Britons were no longer willing to see young children separated from their parents and sent to work in distant lands, no matter how salubrious the setting.

THE BARR COLONY

During the waning years of the Sifton era, though, it was not the thousands of British home children being sent to Canada that captured Canadians' attention but the remarkable odyssey of the Barr colonists. They were the central players in the one attempt made to establish a British settlement in Western Canada during this period: the Barr Colony, named after an impractical visionary, the Reverend Isaac Barr.

Canadian-born Isaac Barr was an Anglican clergyman who was fascinated by the flamboyant career of Cecil Rhodes, the British imperialist and diamond merchant. He even dreamt of joining the famous man in a colonizing venture, and in pursuit of this dream he left a Washington, D.C., parish for London in January 1902. When Rhodes died in March of that year Barr was brought up short in his plans to serve "the Empire" by founding an overseas colony. However, he revived his lofty goal when he learnt of the Reverend George Lloyd's interest in organizing the settlement in Canada of unemployed British workers and soldiers demobilized from the Boer War.

The two Anglican clerics joined forces to found a colony of almost 2,000 Englishmen, most with no farming experience, in a remote location in present-day Saskatchewan. Barr handled nearly all the administrative arrangements: persuading the Canadian government to reserve a block of land for the settlers; collecting settlers' fees; purchasing supplies; and arranging for transportation. But unfortunately for the colonists the ardent imperialist was no organizing genius and things began to go wrong the day the *S.S. Lake Manitoba* sailed in 1903. After a rough ocean voyage — in a ship equipped to handle about 550 passengers — the settlers arrived in Saint John, New Brunswick, to face countless delays and numerous baggage inspections. Finally, they boarded three filthy immigrant trains with no overnight accommodation for the five-day trip to Saskatoon.

Saskatoon, where a tent city was erected to receive the settlers, was another disappointment. Local merchants charged exorbitant prices, there were baggage mix-ups, and the inept preparations for their arrival fanned the flames of dissension. As a result, by the time that the group arrived in Battleford — after a 300-kilometre wagon trip with no guide to lead them — the surviving colonists were prepared to take strong action against Barr. During a meeting held in a trailside marquee they voted to depose him as their leader. At the same time they also voted to rename the venture "Britannia Colony". To head it, the settlers elected the Reverend George Lloyd, who had accompanied the group as chaplain, and a committee of twelve, soon dubbed the "Twelve Apostles". Barr moved to the United States and then to Australia, where he continued to nurse dreams of settlement in the far corners of the British Empire. Re-named Lloydminster to honour the man who had won the settlers' confidence, the Barr Colony survived and grew. When the railway came to the settlement in July 1905 its success was assured.

Slavic Immigrants working for the Ontario and Rainy River Railway.

Not surprisingly, the comic-opera trials of the Barr colonists triggered considerable criticism of Sifton, whose department had handled the venture. One MP, Haughton Lennox, for example, saw fit to remind the government that:

> The fertility of the west, the vast inducements the west
> offers to immigrants will attract a tide of immigration
> quite fast enough for the settlement of the country, if we

pursue such a line that when these men come in they will not be disappointed of their reasonable expectations. There is nothing, to my mind, more important than that when there is immigration aided and authorized by the government or by any person occupying a senior or quasi official position, there shall be no picture of the west more glowing than the circumstances permit of. [17]

Immigration to British Columbia

The prairies were not alone in attracting a large influx of immigrants during the Sifton period. British Columbia, which had launched its organized existence as an outpost of the British empire only decades earlier, was also a magnet for immigrants. Admittedly, the volume of this immigration did not begin to approach the volume of that to the prairies, but, nevertheless, it was impressive.

Among the British newcomers who flocked to Canada's most westerly province were retired businessmen, farmers, and the younger sons of aristocratic families. Their attention was first aroused by advertising material that described the joys of farming in interior valleys speckled with jadegreen and Prussian-blue lakes filled with trout. Inspired further by the enthusiastic reports of Lord Aberdeen, the governor general, well-off British immigrants purchased fruit farms and ranches in the Okanagan Valley, where the Scottish aristocrat had extensive properties. [18]

These years also saw the arrival of the Japanese, who began to settle in southwestern British Columbia in 1900. Other non-British immigrants included such disparate groups as the Sikhs and the Norwegians. Sikhs (members of the reformist religion that originated about 1500 in the Punjab on the Indian subcontinent) began arriving in British Columbia in 1904.

The first group became interested in the province after learning about its possibilities from a detachment of Sikh soldiers who returned home by way of Canada after attending Queen Victoria's Diamond Jubilee in 1897. Between 1904 and 1908, some 5,000 Sikhs arrived in the province, where most found work in the lumber mills or in the logging camps. [19]

For their part, most of the Norwegians came from other parts of North America, notably from the American Middle West. During the Sifton years their ranks included a group of newcomers who established a co-operative settlement at Bella Coola on the B.C. coast. According to the colony's constitution and by-laws the settlement's purpose was to "induce moral, industrious and loyal Norwegian farmers, mechanics and businessmen to come to Bella Coola and to make their home here under the laws of British Columbia."[20] The colony succeeded in attracting about 300 Norwegians between 1896 and 1898.

Thanks to vastly improved economic conditions, the completion of the CPR, and Sifton's aggressive immigration policies, immigrants poured into Canada during the Sifton period. In a swelling tide they arrived from Great Britain, the United States, and dozens of other countries, mostly in central and eastern Europe. Especially spectacular was the growth of groups from central and eastern Europe, notably those of Ukrainian, Polish, Romanian, Hungarian, and Russian origins.

In 1897, total immigration reached a mere 21,716 — of which 11,383 arrived from Britain, 2,412 from the U.S., and 7,921 from "other countries". By 1901, the overall figures had rocketed to 55,747, and the largest group, 34 percent, now came from "other countries", compared to 33 percent from the U.S. and 22 percent from Britain. In 1903, another dramatic increase took place, with 138,660 entering in numbers almost equally divided among the three sources.

By far the largest group from central and eastern Europe were the Ukrainians, the collective name applied to Slavs from regions of the Austro–Hungarian and Russian empires in eastern and southern Europe. It is clear that some Ukrainians (or Galicians, as they were commonly called) settled in Canada before the closing years of the nineteenth century, but the arrival of the symbolic first Ukrainians, in September 1891, heralded the start of massive Ukrainian emigration to this country. The first wave occurred in 1896 after Dr. Josef Oleskow, an agriculturalist, had toured Canada under the aegis of the Department of the Interior. Convinced that Canada was a country of promise, he set about organizing groups of immigrants, the first of which, 107 in number, arrived at Quebec in May 1896. Eventually this trickle of individuals became a stream of thousands, with some 22,363 Ukrainians arriving in Canada in 1913, the peak year for Ukrainian immigration.[21] For the most part peasant farmers from Galicia, Poland, and Bukovina, Romania (both provinces of the Austro–Hungarian Empire), they settled in the more northerly parkland of the prairie provinces because the prime land had already been taken up by American, British, German, and Scandinavian settlers and because they wanted wood for fuel and for building materials.

Since Canada received substantial numbers of good agricultural settlers from Europe during this boom period, it is safe to say that Sifton's policies met at least one of their chief objectives. In other respects, however, they failed miserably. Popular image to the contrary, approximately 70 percent of the newcomers obtained work in industry and transportation — and not entirely by accident: a host of Canadian companies and business associations actively promoted the importation of unskilled immigrant labour. Thousands of the immigrants who came to this country from southeastern and central Europe became either part-time or full-time industrial workers. Of these many went to work for the railway companies, then engaged in a frenzy of construction. In 1904 alone, some 3,000 Italians arrived in Montreal, where they helped to swell the ranks of unemployed Italian Montrealers, then numbering between six and eight thousand. When construction of the Grand Trunk Pacific, Canadian Northern, and National Transcontinental main lines began in earnest two years later, their numbers increased dramatically.

Organized labour, of course, took a very jaundiced view of such developments. In 1900, for example, James Wilks, one of the vice-presidents of the Trades and Labour Congress, wrote to Laurier mentioning the impact of an influx of Finns and Scandinavians from Minnesota upon the Canadian labour market and beseeching the government to enforce the Alien Labour Act. As far as the congress was concerned, only rigorous enforcement of this law would prevent Canada from being inundated with "ignorant, unfortunate … non-English-speaking aliens", who would do irreparable damage to the community.[22] It is not surprising that many new arrivals in Canada, particularly those from eastern and central Europe, found work in industry because settling on the land in Canada was then, as now, an expensive business and few immigrants had the necessary capital to take up farming right away. Temporary employment in railway construction, mining or lumbering was absolutely essential for most prospective farmers. However, many of those immigrants who entered the agricultural force as wage labourers soon left it entirely to work elsewhere. But still the government persisted in promoting the immigration of agriculturalists. To the end of his days Sifton clung obstinately to his cherished belief that the only good immigrant was an agricultural immigrant.

GROWING DISCORD ON THE PRAIRIES

Unfortunately, even the good agricultural immigrants from Europe posed problems for Sifton and his policies because in Western Canada newcomers from central and southeastern Europe raised a groundswell of hostility. Excellent farmers they might have been, but in the eyes of many westerners this did not qualify them as desirable settlers. Only those newcomers who assimilated readily into the dominant Anglo–Saxon society, and did not seriously threaten it, were welcome. On the Prairies hatred focused mainly on two groups, the Ukrainians and the Doukhobors. Between 1897 and 1899 the Ukrainians consistently equalled or outnumbered the combined totals of American and British arrivals in Winnipeg, the gateway to the West. The year of the largest influx was 1899, when under 6,000 Americans and Britons were swamped by 6,914 Ukrainians and 7,400 Doukhobors. It did not matter that less than half the total of immigrants to Canada in most years (and usually far less than half) were other than British in origin. What did matter was what was happening in Winnipeg. And from this vantage point concerned westerners saw sizeable pockets of unassimilable ethnic groups establishing themselves across the West. The result was a heated debate about "Canadianization" and a cry for a more selective immigration policy, both of which would figure prominently during the years when Frank Oliver, Sifton's successor, and his deputy minister, William Scott, were making their imprint on Canadian immigration policy.

— CHAPTER 6 —

Forging a New Immigration Policy

FRANK OLIVER

FRANK OLIVER'S APPOINTMENT AS MINISTER of the interior and superintendent of Indian affairs on April 8, 1905 presaged significant changes in Canadian immigration policy. For although Oliver and Clifford Sifton were both Liberals and newspaper publishers skilled at using the press to publicize their views, they differed markedly in their approach to immigration. Frank Oliver, in fact, had been one of the severest critics of Sifton's policies, which he attacked both in the Liberal Party and in his fiery Edmonton newspaper, the *Bulletin*.

Like Sifton, Oliver was a transplanted easterner who had migrated west when a young man. Born of English and Irish origins in Peel County, Canada West, in 1853, he left high school to pursue a career in the printing trade. This took him first to Toronto, where he worked in the composing room of George Brown's reformist newspaper, *The Globe*, and then to Winnipeg, where he had a stint at the Manitoba *Free Press*. From Winnipeg, he struck out by ox brigade in the spring of 1876 for Fort Edmonton, an isolated settlement on the upper reaches of the North Saskatchewan River.

Edmonton became his home and it was here that the nascent politician founded the *Bulletin*, the first newspaper to be published in what is now Alberta. With his election to the North West Council in 1883 Oliver embarked on a political career that saw him become a participant first in Territorial politics (1883–96) and then in federal politics (1896–1917). He was appointed to Sifton's portfolio on the recommendation of Sifton himself, who, despite his personal dislike of

Oliver, recommended him for this coveted cabinet post, citing his "long service and capacity."[1]

As soon as he became minister, Oliver moved quickly to make Canadian immigration policy more selective and to forge the machinery necessary to carry out this new policy. Clifford Sifton's policy had been selective in the sense that it promoted the immigration of farmers and farm labourers above all other types of immigrants. It was not selective, however, as regards the origins of these agriculturalists. Since Sifton saw immigration through the most pragmatic of lenses, what mattered to him above all else was the ability of new immigrants to become good farmers and farm labourers, not their ethnic origin. Although ethnic and cultural factors could not be ignored, they took second place to the ability of newcomers to strengthen Canada's agricultural base. In any event, Sifton believed that central and eastern Europeans would eventually be assimilated into English Canadian society through their experience on the land.

Frank Oliver.

Oliver, on the other hand, saw things differently. For him the ethnic and cultural origins of prospective immigrants took precedence over occupation. In a not too veiled reference to the difficulty that Anglo-Canadians had accepting such newcomers as Ukrainians, the MP observed:

National Archives of Canada, C4650

> The filling up of the North-west with settlers … is not merely a question of furnishing a market for the manufacturers and traders of the east. It is not merely a question of filling that country with people who will produce wheat and buy manufactured goods. It is a question of the ultimate results of the efforts being put forward for the building up of a Canadian nationality so that our children may form one of the great civilized

nations of the world, and be one of the greatest forces in that civilization. This can never be accomplished if the preponderance of the population should be of such class and character as will deteriorate rather than elevate the conditions of our people and our country at large.[2]

In Oliver's hierarchy of desirable settlers for the West, newcomers from eastern Canada occupied the top rung. British immigrants, who arrived as "ready-made citizens", ranked next, closely followed by American settlers. Whether British immigrants hailed from the British countryside or from Britain's teeming towns and cities was of little consequence to the MP, who did not share Sifton's strong antipathy to immigrants from urban centres. Indeed, the minister preferred Britons from the towns and cities to agriculturalists from central and eastern Europe. Canada could tolerate Britons who were not farmers, but as for those "stalwart peasants in sheepskin coats" who violated the prevailing social mores, that was another matter. At one point, before he learned to temper his public criticism, the MP had even castigated Slav immigrants for being a "millstone" around the necks of Western Canadians.[3]

THE IMMIGRATION ACT OF 1906

In his determined attempt to lay the free-entry policy officially to rest, Oliver quickly embarked on a revision of Canadian immigration legislation. Two acts capped his legislative program, the first being the Immigration Act of 1906, which extensively consolidated and revised all immigration legislation dating from the implementation of the primitive 1869 statute respecting immigration. Distributing immigration propaganda in countries from which Canada wished to recruit immigrants was one thing. But denying entry to Canada to "undesirable" individuals from these same countries was quite another matter. In order to do this, Oliver's department had to have the necessary legislation.

Accordingly, the 1906 act provided for the following: a definition of "an immigrant"; the barring of a broad spectrum of individuals, including prostitutes and their procurers, anyone who was mentally retarded, epileptic, insane, or afflicted with a contagious disease, and any individual "who was deaf and dumb or dumb, blind or infirm unless he belonged to a family accompanying him or already in Canada"; the establishment of a greatly enhanced immigration service, to include controls along the Canada–U.S. border; the deportation of prohibited immigrants (by the transportation company that had brought them to Canada) and immigrants who, within two years of their arrival, had become a charge upon public funds or had been an inmate of a jail, hospital, or charitable institution; and, most important of all, the drawing up of regulations "necessary or expedient for this Act according to its true intent and meaning for the better attainment of its objectives", and, in particular, decreeing the amount of "landing money" immigrants must have in their possession.

When describing the proposed legislation, Bill 170, Oliver informed the House that it provided the means "for controlling immigration generally and respecting undesirable immigrants, which did not exist in the old Bill"[4] Thanks largely to the clauses dealing with exclusion and deportation, this new act would become the first legal mechanism for enforcing a policy of selective, i.e., restrictive, immigration.

Admittedly there had been, since 1869, laws prohibiting certain kinds of immigration and since 1889 laws permitting designated classes of immigrants to be returned whence they came. The 1906 act, however, significantly increased the number of categories of prohibited immigrants and gave official sanction to the deportation of undesirable immigrants.[5] Now that the deportation process was enshrined in legislation, a small coterie of government officials could legally employ an administrative procedure to deport newcomers according to the functionaries' own extralegal and informal system of justice. And in the years to come immigration officers would, in fact, expel thousands of both foreign-born individuals as well as naturalized Canadian citizens from Canada, using an arbitrary procedure that did not even recognize rights normally accorded to criminals. The numbers of deportees were such — 825 in 1908 — that by March 1908 three full-time and two part-time officers were employed by the Immigration Branch for this purpose.[6]

Bill 170 inspired considerable debate in the House, much of it concerning its definition of an immigrant and its provision for the imposition of a head tax on immigrants. When all the technicalities are swept aside, though, the discussion reveals two underlying views about the general direction that immigration policy should take. Among those who argued for a raising of immigration barriers was the provincial chief of the Conservatives, Frederick Monk. The son of an English-Canadian father and a French-Canadian mother, but a man who was nevertheless more French than English in his outlook, Monk said: "We should exercise more prudence in the choice. What is fifty years in the life of a nation? It is nothing; and in building up our nation we should aim to have the best kind of men, men who would be prepared to maintain here the institutions of a free people. I do not at all agree with the principle that our ambition should be to fill up the country."[7]

W.M. German, the Liberal member from Welland, on the other hand, lobbied for a completely open-door policy. "The United States wanted to fill up their country with people and they did so; we want to fill up our country with people — Let the people come. They may not in all cases be desirable, but we will endeavour to lead them in the proper paths and make them desirable when we get them here."[8] Not surprisingly, this position found favour with economic nationalists such as the archetypal capitalist and CPR president, Sir William Van Horne. Voicing chagrin over the new direction being taken by Canadian immigration policy, Sir William, an American immigrant, declared:

National archives of Canada, PA 30820

Interior of a typical immigrant's home in Western Canada, 1900-1910.

> What we want is population. Labour is required from the Arctic Ocean to Patagonia, throughout North and South America, but the governments of other lands are not such idiots as we are in the matter of restrict-

ing immigration. Let them all come in. There is work for all. Every two or three men that come into Canada and do a day's work create new work for someone else to do. They are like a new dollar. Hand it out from the Bank and it turns itself in value a dozen or more times a year.[9]

THE IMMIGRATION ACT OF 1910

The second milestone in restrictive immigration legislation was reached in 1910 when Parliament passed "An Act Respecting Immigration" (Chapter 27 of 9-10 Edward VII), otherwise known as the Immigration Act.[10] Unlike the previous act, it conferred on the cabinet virtually unlimited discretionary powers allowing it to issue orders-in-council to regulate the volume, ethnic origin, or occupational composition of immigration destined for Canada.

Frank Oliver explained his government's thinking behind the bill's exclusion provisions to his fellow MPs:

> We want to be in such a position that, should occasion arise, when public policy seems to demand it, we may have the power, on our responsibility as a Government, to exclude people whom we consider undesirable. If this power is given to the government, then the Government can be held responsible should there be a sudden influx of an undesirable class of people. We cannot tell at what time, or under what circumstances, there may be a sudden movement of people from one part of the world or another, and we want to be in a position to check it, should public policy demand such an action.[11]

Although the new act did not bar any specific group of immigrants on the basis of racial, ethnic, or national origin, it provided the Immigration Branch with the necessary machinery to encourage some immigrants and to restrict or virtually exclude others. Section 38, for example, provided the cabinet with the requisite authority to prohibit the entry of "immigrants belonging to any race deemed unsuited to the climate or requirements of Canada." [12] This new and sweeping designation would not be banished from the statute books of Canada until 1978, although by 1967 all vestiges of discrimination had been removed from immigration regulations. The section of the act outlining prohibited classes (Section 3) also contained a significant new addition: all charity cases who had not received written authority to emigrate to Canada from the superintendent of immigration at Ottawa or the assistant superintendent of emigration for Canada in London. [13] This clause was inspired by the large number of impoverished British immigrants who had arrived in Canada in 1907, a year of economic downturn, with the assistance of charitable organizations, eager to rid Britain of paupers and to provide them with a new start in Canada. In 1908, 70 percent of the deportations from Canada were British immigrants, many of them undoubtedly destitute and inexperienced would-be farmers who had landed in Canada the year before.

The act of 1910 also added provisions for deportation on the grounds of political and moral instability, thereby paying homage to the American practice of excluding immigrants for immorality or political beliefs. The political provisions were found in Section 41, which classified as an undesirable immigrant any non-Canadian who:

> advocates in Canada the overthrow by force or violence of the government of Great Britain or Canada, or any other British dominion, colony, possession or dependency, or the overthrow by force or violence of constituted law and authority, in same, or the assassination of any official of the Government of Great Britain or Canada or other British dominion, colony, possession or dependency, or of any foreign government, or shall by word or act create or attempt to create riot or public disorder in Canada. [14]

The conditions and types of offences subject to deportation as well as other principal features of the deportation process were set out in the act of 1910. Although subsequent legislation would refine procedures, the legal framework for deportation as outlined in this act would remain substantially unchanged until well after the Second World War (and in some respects up to the present time).[15]

Despite the drastic nature of its exclusion provisions and the virtually unlimited discretionary powers that it conferred on cabinet, the act of 1910 did not provoke a heated and prolonged debate in the House of Commons. It incited more debate than did its predecessor, the Immigration Act of 1906, but nevertheless there was no major disagreement with its principles. As William Scott, superintendent of immigration from 1903 to 1924, later observed, "The discussion which took place upon the bill showed that Canada, in common with other young countries, whose natural resources attract the residents of the overcrowded communities of Europe, is fully aware of sifting 'the wheat from the chaff' in the multitudes who seek her shores."[16]

Subsequent to the act, orders-in-council were passed regulating and amplifying its provisions. One of these (P.C. 924, May 9, 1910) levied a tax on all immigrants, the figure varying according to the season of the year. This last tax raised a storm of protest in Great Britain because it required that each immigrant, male or female, have $25 in addition to a ticket or the funds necessary to travel to a pre-determined destination in Canada. In a press conference in London later that year, William Scott defended the new regulation, insisting that $25 was a reasonable amount for a skilled labourer to have in his possession when embarking for Canada.[17]

CANCELLATION OF THE NORTH ATLANTIC TRADING COMPANY CONTRACT

Frank Oliver's legislative program was supplemented by other measures. In an effort to trim the numbers of newcomers arriving from eastern, southern, and central Europe, for example, the minister, in 1906, cancelled the North Atlantic Trading Company contract with its system of bonuses for agriculturalists from designated European countries. While he was inclined to be less selective as regards British immigration, Oliver was prepared to move in just the opposite direction where

Continental European immigration was concerned. In the future if "Sifton's pets" wanted to emigrate to Canada, they would have to do so on their own initiative. They would not be lured to these shores by a clandestine organization of European shipping agents paid by Ottawa to attract agriculturalists. Or, in the words of William Scott, "In the end the Minister of the Interior claimed the company was devoting too much attention to the southern and eastern countries, and too little to the northern countries. This, he held, was in violation of the agreement, and in 1906 he gave notice terminating the agreement."[18] The abrogation of the North Atlantic Trading Company contract did not spell the end of Continental bonuses, however. On March 1, 1907, less than four months after the agreement's cancellation, the Department of the Interior began to pay selected European booking agents a bonus for both adults and youngsters from one to eighteen years of age, who came to Canada to engage in farm work or railway construction or who had worked for at least one year as a farmer, gardener, carter, "railway surface man", navvy or miner.[19]

Although the agreement's demise was deplored by Laurier and Sifton, it was applauded by most parliamentarians, irrespective of party label. One of these was Frederick Monk, who always took a keen interest in immigration questions. When contrasting the unpopular contract and Canada's policy of unchecked entry of Continental Europeans with American immigration policy, the MP noted, "In the United States... they do not encourage immigration. There is a law forbidding advertising or giving any bonuses on immigrants and the strictest possible rules are enforced against inducing immigrants to come from Europe to America."[20]

Any government attempt to choke off or curb immigration from southern, central, and eastern Europe was welcomed by organized labour, which was frequently in the van of anti-immigration efforts. Labour, of course, has always entertained fears about the impact of surplus workers on unionization and Canadian wage levels. But in these years it also harboured a deep dislike of newcomers from eastern, southern, and central Europe, a distaste that it shared with the majority of middle-class Canadians. In 1906, for example, a trade unionist publication, the Toronto *Tribune*, reacted to the arrival of thousands of central and southern Europeans that year with the stinging observation, "The

commonest London loafer has more decency and instincts of citizenship than the Sicilian, Neapolitan, Croat or Magyar."[21] Echoes of these
sentiments would later find expression in the fulminations of labour
leader S.R. Berry, who, in 1910, protested to Frank Oliver about "the
sudden influx of immigrants whose habits of life and moral characteristics are repugnant to Canadian ideals."[22]

INCREASING BRITISH IMMIGRATION

The same year that he cancelled the North Atlantic Trading Company
agreement, Frank Oliver took steps to increase British immigration, convinced that Canada had to reinforce her British heritage if she was to
become one of the world's great civilizations. To boost the numbers of
newcomers arriving from Britain, he raised the bonus paid to British
booking agents who sold tickets to British farmers, farm labourers, and
domestics, and had new immigration offices opened in Exeter, York, and
Aberdeen. The following year the Immigration Branch adopted an even
more aggressive approach to immigrant recruitment: it appointed 100
government agents and paid
each one a two-dollar bonus
for every British agricultural
labourer recruited and placed
in Ontario or Quebec.[23]

It is noteworthy that
immigration from the British
Isles soared from 86,796 in
the fiscal year ended March
31, 1906 to 142,622 in the fiscal year ended March 31,
1914.[24] And, although there is
no conclusive evidence, one

Immigrants skipping on the
SS Empress of Britain *on its*
way to Canada, 1910.

Department of Mines and Resources/LAC C009660

National Archive. of Canada, C9652.

Scottish immigrants for domestic service, Quebec, c. 1911.

Canadian Pacific Limited, Corporate Archives, neg. no. A6201

can probably ascribe part of this increase to the bonuses awarded to British shipping and Canadian government agents. Immigration figures reveal, for instance, that while in 1900–1901 the United States received over four times as many immigrants from the British Isles as did Canada that year, in 1906–1907 the U.S. received over 7,000 fewer British immigrants than did the Dominion.

Homeseekers' Fares to Western Canada.

Period	To Canada	To U.S.A.
July 1, 1900 to June 30, 1901	11,810	45,546
July 1, 1901 to June 30, 1902	17,259	46,036
July 1, 1902 to June 30, 1903	41,792	68,947
July 1, 1903 to June 30, 1904	50,374	87,590
July 1, 1904 to June 30, 1905	65,359	137,134
July 1, 1905 to June 30, 1906	86,796	102,193
July 1, 1906 to June 30, 1907	120,779	113,567[25]

WILLIAM SCOTT AND AMERICAN IMMIGRATION

Frank Oliver's enthusiasm for British and American immigration was shared by the superintendent of immigration, William Duncan Scott. An able and energetic administrator, "Big Bill" Scott was deeply involved in the running of the Immigration Branch during the years that he was at its helm. As a result, immigration policy and the machinery for implementing it closely reflected, if they did not actually embody, his views regarding the kinds of prospective immigrants that Canada should solicit and the kinds that she should discourage.[26]

Since he was a cultural nationalist like Frank Oliver, William Scott set great store by the ability of prospective immigrants to conform to the fixed WASP values and institutions of Anglo-Canadian society. In defining what constituted an undesirable immigrant, the senior bureaucrat observed, "… undesirable immigrants are those who will not assimilate with the Canadian people, or whose presence will tend to bring about a deterioration from a political, moral, social or economic point of view."[27]

Because they adapted most readily to Canadian conditions and were, by and large, agriculturalists who understood Canadian conditions, Americans headed the immigration superintendent's list of desirable immigrants.[28] But while Scott and probably most other Canadians gave them top billing, there were some who did not want to see a large influx of American settlers, believing that the flag invariably followed massive immigration. For reinforcement of their views, they had only to point to a bold declaration made in *Reminiscences*, published in 1910 by the influential political commentator and former Oxford University history professor, Goldwin Smith. In this work, Smith, a long-time advocate of political and economic union with the United States, cheerfully predicted, "The Northwest will be American."[29]

As an enthusiastic champion of American immigration, however, Scott entertained no fears of "Americanization." Dismissing such concerns as not only parochial but also groundless, he declared, "If Americanization means the progressiveness of the American will be copied by the Canadian, the more rapid the Americanization the better."[30]

When Scott wrote this, in 1912, Americans were continuing to stream across the border in ever increasing numbers, bringing with them new populist political ideas, and welcome capital and leadership qualities. Every state in the Union was represented in this influx, with perhaps the largest number of arrivals coming from Oregon, Washington, Montana, and Idaho. Reporting to Ottawa in 1910 on the swelling number of American immigrants, W.J. White, the inspector of United States agencies, wrote: "There is now in all parts a 'land hunger,' an anxiety and a tendency to go 'Back to The Farm,' and there is everywhere the greatest unrest I have known amongst the people of the cities and smaller towns to get on land, and to make a living from the soil. I believe that our work in the States has been largely responsible for this."[31]

ATTEMPTS TO EXCLUDE BLACK AMERICAN IMMIGRANTS

When it came to prospective American settlers, however, the Immigration Branch under Scott continued to solicit only white farmers, especially those farming on the Prairies and in the Midwest states. As was the case during the Sifton years, no attempt was made to recruit black agriculturalists, for blacks were widely regarded as being cursed with the burden of their African ancestry. Even the distinguished social gospel clergyman, J.S. Woodsworth, quoted in his book *Strangers within Our Gates* an article from the popular American magazine *Chautauquan* to the effect that the "very qualities of intelligence and manliness which are essential for citizenship in a democracy were systematically expunged from the negro race through two hundred years of slavery."[32]

Canadians prided themselves on being removed from the racial troubles that had developed in their neighbour to the south following the collapse of Reconstruction in the southern states. And the Immigration Branch was bent on keeping Canada free from such racial tensions. Writing in 1912, shortly after some American blacks had succeeded in making it to the Canadian West, William Scott observed: "The Negro problem which faces the United States, and which Abraham Lincoln said could be settled only by shipping one and all back to a tract of land in Africa, is one in which Canadians have no desire to share. It is to be hoped that climatic conditions will prove unsatisfactory to those new settlers, and that the fertile lands of the West will be left to be cultivated by the white race only."[33]

Not only did the Immigration Branch not solicit American black immigration, it effectively throttled it by discouraging private schemes for black settlement and by instructing its agents in the United States to withhold assistance from individual blacks who wanted to emigrate to Canada. Partly because of such measures, the black population on the Prairies, consisting of 98 persons in 1901, climbed to only 1,524 by 1911.[34]

Black immigration to the Canadian West had hitherto aroused little concern on the part of white Canadians. In 1910, however, when rising anti-black sentiment in the newly created state of Oklahoma threatened to prompt a large migration of Negroes north to Canada, Canadians took alarm. On hearing rumours that sizeable numbers of blacks were headed for the Edmonton area, the citizens of Alberta's capital mounted a strong protest against Negro immigration. A petition, organized in 1911 by the local board of trade and representing approximately 14 percent of the population, urged the federal government to act immediately to prevent any more blacks from immigrating into Western Canada.[35]

The issue of the Oklahoma blacks and the resulting Negro backlash in Western Canada played directly into the hands of those Immigration Branch officials who wanted to see the Canadian border sealed to black immigration. Up to that point the quasi-official policy of Negro immigration restriction had served to discourage significant numbers of blacks from settling in Western Canada. But now, it was thought, legislative action was necessary. In 1911, therefore, steps were taken to have Canada acquire the first racial exclusion ordinance in the Western Hemisphere.

That March the assistant superintendent of immigration, Edward Robinson, wrote to Frank Oliver suggesting that provisions in existing immigration legislation be used to pass an order-in-council prohibiting the admission of blacks. The minister agreed to the recommendation and dispatched a note to that effect to the governor general in council (i.e., the cabinet). The recommendation was never implemented, however. In September a general election threw the Liberals out of office, and to all appearances the "crisis" of black immigration passed. In the future, immigration authorities would have recourse to other methods to keep blacks out of Canada.[36]

THE VANCOUVER RIOT OF 1907

As it was, other events had conspired to shove Frank Oliver further along the path of selective immigration. One of these was the Vancouver riot of September 1907 and developments surrounding it. The riot itself, which resulted in extensive damage to buildings occupied by Orientals, was a spontaneous outburst, precipitated by a rock that a youngster hurled through the window of a Chinese store following a mammoth anti-Asiatic parade.

Although it ignited spontaneously, the rampage had complex origins. Indeed, its principal roots lay deep in racial tensions which had been building steadily and which had reached new heights in the summer of 1907. The cause was an upsurge in Asian immigration, particularly Japanese immigration, to British Columbia. In July alone over 2,300 Japanese arrived in the province, far more than had been anticipated under a voluntary agreement concluded earlier between Canada and Japan to restrict the number of Japanese immigrants destined for Canada.

With the soaring of Japanese immigration to unprecedented levels, increasing numbers of West Coast whites became convinced that the Japanese had become the leading Oriental threat to their province. Like the Chinese, the Japanese had always been regarded as unassimilable. Following Japan's recent victory over Russia in the Russo-Japanese War, however, the Japanese image acquired another and more frightening dimension. Growing numbers of white British Columbians now began to view the Japanese immigrant as loyal to Japan, aggressive and eager to further Japan's expansionist aims.[37]

As alarm mounted over the Japanese influx, daily comment appeared in the press on the Japanese "invasion." Accompanying this were demands by the Vancouver Trades and Labour Council for measures to curb the rising immigrant tide. The council was not content with just this action. It also formed the Asiatic Exclusion League to promote agitation. Subsequently, the league, which by then had cut all ties with the council, staged the anti-Asian parade, which preceded the riot.

Following the riot the Laurier government found itself in the nearly impossible position of trying to placate British Columbia and Japan simultaneously. In response to the province's insistent demands that Asian immigration be halted, the government sent Rodolphe Lemieux, postmaster general and minister of labour, to Tokyo to urge Japanese officials to implement more vigorous emigration controls. After a month of negotiations, an agreement was reached whereby Japan would voluntarily limit the emigration of Japanese to Canada to 400 a year.

As part of this same initiative, the government dispatched Mackenzie King, Lemieux's deputy minister of labour, to Vancouver to investigate and settle Japanese claims for damages. In his capacity as a one man royal commission, the future prime minister conducted a series of hearings and then awarded $9,000 in compensation to Japanese riot victims. Chinese riot victims, who had suffered more damage, were later awarded $26,000.

After settling the Japanese claims, King set about probing the origins of the recent Oriental influx. His report, which examined Japanese immigration in detail, exonerated the Japanese government from major blame for the problem and instead attributed the crisis to high immigration from Hawaii and the activities of immigration companies based in Canada.

King concluded that immigration should be banned by way of Hawaii, that the practice of importing contract labour should be forbidden, and that the remaining number of Japanese newcomers should be carefully limited. He also implied that immigration from India should be discouraged.

THE CONTINUOUS JOURNEY REGULATION

In 1908, shortly after Lemieux concluded his negotiations in Tokyo, the Laurier government introduced what would become a new and important amendment to the Immigration Act. Known as the "continuous journey regulation", it stipulated that all immigrants to Canada were required to come directly from their country of origin or citizenship by a continuous journey on a through ticket purchased in that country. By means of this ingenious device, the government succeeded in choking off immigration from India — there being no direct steamship service from that continent to Canada — and in shutting the door on the Hawaii route for Japanese immigration. Effective restriction, it seems, did not require that Canada resort to the distasteful and increasingly unacceptable practice of designating "undesirable immigrants" by race or nationality in immigration regulations.

The continuous journey regulation and subsequent barriers to East Indian immigration would not go unchallenged. On May 23, 1914, 376 prospective East Indian immigrants arrived in Vancouver harbour on board the *Komagata Maru*, a ship hired by a wealthy Sikh merchant and contractor from Hong Kong, Gurdit Singh. For two months the vessel lay in harbour with its human cargo while the legality of a federal exclusion order was tested in provincial courts. Eventually the Supreme Court of British Columbia upheld the order and on July twenty-third, with the local citizenry cheering it on, Canada's HMCS *Rainbow* escorted the steamer to sea. It returned to Asia minus just a handful of passengers, previous residents of British Columbia allowed to land by the federal government.

ESTABLISHMENT OF A BORDER INSPECTION SERVICE

In a further attempt to make Canadian immigration policy restrictive and selective in comparison to Sifton's, Frank Oliver, in 1908, used provisions in the Immigration Act of 1906 to institute an immigration inspection service on the Canada–United States border. Other than the quantum leap in immigration during these years, it is unclear just what decided Oliver to take this action at this particular time, unless it was the economic recession of 1907–1908 and unremitting pressure from local governments. In any event, in April 1908, the Immigration Branch inaugurated an inspection service along the American frontier, starting with thirty-seven points of entry in the Central Border District, which stretched from Toronto to Sprague, Manitoba.[38]

Reflecting the bias of a typical English-speaking Canadian of his era, Border Inspector H.G. Herbert of the Central Border District reported in June 1910:

> It must be remembered that the neighbouring republic has enormously increased and is increasing its population by the immigration of people whose racial customs and habits of thought are entirely unsuited to the conditions and requirements of Canada. These enter the United States with comparative freedom and, attracted in considerable numbers towards our country by its superior advantages, attempt to enter Canada at the "back door", so to speak.[39]

When he wrote his observations, H.G. Herbert was probably acutely conscious of the formidable workload that he and his fellow inspectors had to discharge because of the very small budget under which the service then operated. So tight was the budget in these first years that no provision was made for office accommodation or detention facilities of any kind. Hard-pressed immigration inspectors and customs officers, who also took on immigration duties, had to conduct much of their work under extremely trying conditions in depot waiting rooms, on ferry docks, and on railway platforms. And the work could be dangerous. This same Inspector Herbert was shot to death on a Windsor–Detroit ferry by an individual refused entry to Canada.

The Reality

Frank Oliver and the Liberals may have aspired to a more selective immigration policy, but belief had it that Canada's prosperity required a large dose of immigration. So, despite the introduction of restrictive immigration legislation, people continued to pour into the country. In 1906, the influx exceeded 200,000; in 1911, the year the Liberals were toppled from power by the Conservatives, over 300,000. Two years later, in 1913, immigration soared to a record figure of 400,810.

The Liberal and Conservative governments did succeed in dramatically reducing immigration from Asia, but they failed to staunch the flow from central and eastern Europe. For, although both governments' stated goal was to attract agriculturalists to Western Canada, the fact remains that Canadian railway companies, manufacturers, and resource extraction industries needed, and clamoured for, a large pool of labour to supply the goods and services required by the new settlers. Responding to the demands of the ever vociferous and powerful business lobby, the government of the day opened the floodgates still wider, admitting in the process increasing numbers of unskilled and semi-skilled labourers in the period 1911 to 1913.

A German immigrant family arriving in Canada, c. 1911.

National archives of Canada, PA 10254.

FROM OVERSEAS

Year	Unskilled and Semi-Skilled Labourers	Farming
1906	33,585	32,278
1907	62,583	36,724
1908	16,666	20,779
1909	17,193	23,870
1910	28,694	55,233

Year	Unskilled and Semi-Skilled Labourers	Farming
1911	50,411	58,186
1912	63,743	60,515
1913	101,065	53,756[40]

THE NEW SOCIETY

Between 1896 and 1914, some 3 million newcomers came to settle in Canada. In the ten-year period from 1901 to 1911 the Canadian population rocketed by 43 percent and the percentage of foreign-born in the country as a whole exceeded 22 percent. Almost overnight, it seemed, immigration from Great Britain, the United States, Europe, and Asia had transformed the country, particularly Western Canada, into a polyglot society.

But this transformation was not without its tensions, as public debate raged over the assimilability of those immigrants whose language was incomprehensible, whose religion was strange, and whose education lacked a grounding in even the fundamentals of parliamentary democracy. James Shaver Woodsworth, the well-known Ontario-born Methodist minister, social reformer, and pacifist, was one of many Canadians who expressed these concerns. In his case they were sharpened by his experience with newly arrived immigrants whom he served as superintendent of All People's Mission in Winnipeg's North End in the early years of this century. Prominent social reformer that he was (Woodsworth played a distinguished role in virtually all the reform movements of the pre-First World War era and later went on to become founding leader of the Co-operative Commonwealth Federation), Woodsworth came to share the prevailing belief that if newcomers were to become good Canadians they had to embrace Anglo-Canadian Protestant values and become part of a Christian society in English-speaking Canada. In his well-known work *Strangers within Our Gates*, published in 1909, he argued: "We, in Canada, have certain more or less clearly defined ideals of national well-being. These ideals must never be lost sight of. Non-ideal elements there must be, but they should be capable of assimilation. Essentially non-assimilable elements are clearly detrimental to our highest national development, and hence should be vigorously excluded."[41] In other words, immigration should be controlled when it causes social problems or conflicts with what are perceived to be the goals of national life. But in any event, all immigrants admitted to this country should be capable of being assimilated into mainstream Anglo-Canadian society. And for Woodsworth, as for most of his compatriots, the principal instrument of "Canadianization" was the public school. As he expressed it, "The public school is the most important factor in transforming the foreigners into Canadians."[42] "Too great emphasis cannot be placed upon the work that has been accomplished and may — yes, must be accomplished by our National Schools."[43]

It was not only English-speaking Canadians who were alarmed by the transformation that Canada's population was undergoing. There were also French Canadians who voiced misgivings about what was happening. As immigration figures soared to new heights, these observers wondered what their future would be in a Canada where the overall relative size of the French-Canadian population was decreasing, and in the West where the numbers of French Canadians were being overtaken by those of several other ethnic groups.

In Quebec, Henri Bourassa was the barometer for many of the concerns of these French Canadians. During his first years in Parliament the celebrated journalist and politician had supported Sifton's immigration policy, but when he realized that immigration was shifting the balance of Canada's population, Bourassa began to lash out at the newcomers to the West and the Laurier government. Writing from the comfort of his study, he described the new arrivals on the Prairies as strangers who had contributed nothing to the building of Canada and who had made no sacrifices to the cause of national unity.[44] On another occasion, this time in Parliament, he even went so far as to berate the Liberals for changing "a providential condition of our partly French and partly English country to make it a land of refuge for the scum of all nations."[45]

So many newcomers arrived from Continental Europe in the years immediately before the First World War that the Anglo-French consensus of nineteenth-century Canada was permanently transformed. Although they were most noticeable in the Prairie provinces, the new arrivals also had a decided impact on society in the rest of Canada. In this sense they heralded the dramatic changes that immigrants would make to post–Second World War Canada. But before that buoyant period of immigration lay three decades of "immigration doldrums".

— CHAPTER 7 —

Immigration Doldrums

Hard on the heels of the most exuberant years in Canadian immigration history came the most inglorious period, the three decades between 1915 and 1945. War, recession, uneven prosperity, grim depression, and then another world war, each in its turn helped to create antipathy to immigration and to throttle the movement of newcomers to Canada.

The First World War heralded the first of several precipitous declines in immigration during these troubled decades. In 1915, immigration plunged to an all-time low of 36,665, with three-quarters of the immigrants that year arriving from the United States. The following year immigration increased to 55,914, and in 1917 to 72,910. Then it slumped in 1918, the year the war ended, to 41,845. The following year it soared to 107,698.[1]

THE FIRST WORLD WAR AND FOREIGN-BORN CANADIANS

Besides cutting short the movement of immigrants to Canada, the First World War created difficulties for many foreign-born Canadians, not just Germans, who had previously ranked high on the list of desirable newcomers. Other "enemy aliens" who had once been citizens of Germany or the Austro-Hungarian Empire — Hungarians, Poles, Romanians, Czechs, and Ukrainians — also became objects of intense hostility on the part of Anglo-Canadians. Many Ukrainians, for example, were interned and almost all were disenfranchised.

Shortly after the outbreak of war the federal government took upon itself unprecedented authority with the passage of the draconian War Measures Act, designed to give Ottawa emergency powers to deal with real or apprehended war, invasion, or insurrection. Nowhere was the blanket character of the act revealed more clearly than in the provisions of clause 6, which allowed the cabinet to make orders and regulations regarding a wide variety of subjects, including "arrest, detention, exclusion and deportation". Before the war's end this provision was invoked in the internment of some 8,579 enemy aliens,[2] a relatively small number, however, when it is realized that over 80,000 such individuals had been registered. The insignificant number of enemy aliens incarcerated during the war in no way reflects, though, the depth of anti-alien sentiment felt by much of the Canadian population.

As a result of the tedious and often irresponsible pre-war debate over the naval issue, many Canadians had come to regard "foreigners", especially German immigrants, with misgiving and distrust, if not outright hostility. A Toronto newspaper even went so far as to recommend on August 7, 1914, that alien immigrants be subject to a rigid system of registration and curfews. Then it concluded with the hysterical injunction: "Anyone disobeying these orders to be court martialled and shot as a spy."[3]

Wartime rumours of the imminent invasion of Canada by large numbers of German–Americans and alarming reports of activities in the German–American communities of several American cities only served to heighten Canadian anxiety about "foreigners" in their midst. Then there was the incautious statement made by a Winnipeg prelate, Bishop Nykyta Budka. On July 27, 1914, while the world anxiously awaited Austria's response to the assassination of the Archduke Francis Ferdinand, the bishop urged his Ukrainian parishioners to remember their duty to the Austro–Hungarian Empire if war should occur and to go to the defence of the threatened fatherland. In a second pastoral letter Bishop Budka affirmed his loyalty to the British Empire, but his initial statement was not forgotten during the early months of hostilities.

In the early months of the war the Borden government urged the public to adopt a policy of tolerance and restraint towards enemy aliens, but nevertheless harassment of them increased as the hostilities continued. Toronto gave birth to the Anti-German League in 1916; and, in

Ontario's capital, the dean of Trinity College declared that the $500 head tax on Chinese immigrants should be doubled for future German immigrants, and their families denied entry to Canada. Southwest of Toronto, in Berlin, a prosperous city where persons of German ancestry made up almost three-quarters of the city's population, anti-German feeling ran so high that a statue of Kaiser Wilhelm was pulled down and heaved into the lake in Victoria Park. Later, in 1916, the city's name was changed to Kitchener.

As the war dragged on, censorship of the foreign-language press became far more vigorous than that of its English and French counterparts. Still, this was not enough to satisfy certain parties who urged a total ban on such publications. When the Great War Veterans' Association registered loud complaints against what they saw as government leniency, and when a government investigator reported an upsurge in Bolshevist sentiment, the Borden administration resorted to more severe measures. On September 25, 1918, it passed an order-in-council making it an offence to print, publish, or possess any document in "an enemy language" without a licence from the secretary of state. This was followed three days later by a ban on a number of "foreign" organizations and the meetings of other groups that employed enemy languages.

Eclipsing even these measures, however, was the Wartime Elections Act of September 1917, which was invoked in the 1917 federal election. It disenfranchised people who were of enemy alien birth or who customarily spoke an enemy alien language, and who had become naturalized British subjects after March 31, 1902.[4] A blunt weapon designed to eliminate the opposition of "enemy aliens" to conscription, it dramatically altered the political balance in Western Canada. Like other anti-"enemy alien" measures, it was a powerful reflection of the anti-foreign sentiment that would spill over into the post-war years and help to nurture the growth of an influential anti-immigration lobby.

Despite all the demands made on it by the war effort, the government did not banish immigration from its official agenda during the First World War, even during the darkest, most harrowing days of this conflict. In June and July 1917, for instance, the Borden administration piloted through a bill to exempt Chinese clergymen and students from the $500 head tax. Explaining the government's position, William James

Roche, minister of the interior and superintendent general of Indian affairs, said:

> At present students are admitted into Canada by paying a head tax of $500, but upon producing proof of having attended an educational institute recognized in Canada, they are refunded the head tax when leaving the country. Considerable objection to the payment of the head tax has been made on behalf of Chinese students entering Canada. Chinese students are allowed free entry into the United States for the purpose of attending educational institutions ... At the earnest request made by quite a number of persons in Canada during the last few years, we have decided to include Chinese students in the class exempted from the head tax. In the existing Act, clergy-men are not specifically included in the class exempted; this, I believe, was an oversight, because clergymen's families have been admitted free of head tax.[5]

The passage of this legislation was followed, on October 29, 1917, by the creation of the Office of Immigration and Colonization, by Order-in-Council P.C. 3073. By means of this device the Immigration Branch of the Department of the Interior was transformed into a separate department of the public service. The following spring statutory authority for the new department was provided by Statute 8-9 George V, chapter 3, assented to April 12, 1918.

One might have expected that the elevation of the Immigration Branch of the Department of the Interior to full departmental status would have stirred some discussion in Parliament, but this was not the case. When the relevant order-in-council was passed by Robert Borden's newly formed Unionist government in the autumn of 1917 it prompted no comment in the House of Commons at all. Only when the enabling legislation was before the House the following spring was some interest evinced in the subject. Among those who spoke on the issue was Daniel Mackenzie, a Liberal, who voiced strong objection to the establishment of a new department. The Nova Scotia MP observed that the old machinery of the

Department of the Interior had been able to handle all the demands posed by immigration during the palmy days of the Laurier government and he wondered why it did not satisfy present requirements. The MP continued:

> Now that we have no immigration or homestead entries to speak of, I cannot, as an outsider though a member of this House, understand why, at this stage, and at this time, under war conditions, when every dollar should be saved and when everything should be avoided that involves the expenditure of a dollar except for the purposes of war, we are establishing this new department … I think that it is only fair to the country, and fair to the Government, that it should be pointed out that we have no explanation why this new department was created … It would appear to me the trouble was this: the Prime Minister wanted a new government; he wanted to take in new blood, and he would not take it in without making places for it, and his heart was too tender, and he was too much attached to his dear old friends of the dear old times to have them removed, and therefore he took his carving knife and he began to cut and carve the departments in order to make room for his friends … I strongly protest against this creation or splitting of departments when the business of the country does not require it, merely for the purpose of feathering a nest for foreign birds that wish to go into the Government.[6]

It is possible that honest, dour Robert Borden was motivated by the considerations alluded to by Mr. Mackenzie. But it is much more likely that the government anticipated a resurgence of immigration after the war, indeed, a return to pre-war levels. Events, of course, would belie these optimistic expectations.

The conclusion of hostilities in Europe found the European economy in shambles and destruction widespread. Canada could have responded to the situation by opening its doors to Europe's homeless and dispossessed. Instead, this country began to erect one roadblock after another to immigration from that part of the world. The anti-foreign sentiment of the war and pre-war years played no small role in this. But also Canadians, like their neighbours to the south, had succumbed to a "red scare" following the Russian Revolution of 1917. As a result, they took a jaundiced view of accepting European immigrants lest they bring with them dangerous ideologies in addition to their foreign languages and strange lifestyles. In any event, Canada was not about to welcome immigrants because of the widespread unemployment that followed the war.

With the conclusion of hostilities, thousands of demobilized soldiers were thrown onto the labour market at a time when business and industry were undergoing a painful conversion to a peacetime economy. The result was widespread unemployment accompanied by mounting disillusionment with a peace that had seemed to promise so much but that appeared to introduce nothing but hardship. Given these conditions, it is not surprising that nativist sympathies resulted in pressure for the dismissal of foreign workers to make way for Canada's "heroes". Fearing that returned veterans would embrace socialism if their employment needs were not met immediately, organizations such as the British Columbia Employers' Association declared that they were prepared to dismiss enemy aliens and offer their jobs to returned soldiers. In a demonstration of where its sympathies lay, the International Nickel Company, located in Sudbury, Ontario, dismissed 2,200 of its 3,200 employees, the overwhelming majority of whom were foreigners.[7]

THE WINNIPEG GENERAL STRIKE

Soaring inflation gave rise to a wave of labour unrest, which rolled across Canada in 1918 and 1919, exacerbating fears of an international Bolshevik conspiracy. Nothing did more to inflame anti-foreign sentiment and fears of a revolution than the Winnipeg General Strike of 1919, in which European workers figured prominently. What had begun as a dispute between management and labour in the building and metal trades over wages and collective bargaining escalated into a general strike called by the Winnipeg Trades and Labour Council for May fifteenth. Within hours almost 30,000 workers had forsaken their jobs and headed for the streets. Overnight, the prairie city split into two camps and soon virtually all industrial activity, as well as many municipal functions, ground to a halt.

On one side of the strike stood the Central Strike Committee. In fierce opposition was the Citizens' Committee of One Thousand, composed of Winnipeg's leading Anglo-Canadian businessmen, manufacturers, and professionals. As self-appointed defenders of the "Canadian way of life," they resolved to crush the radical labour movement in Winnipeg and flush aliens out of the community.

J.S. Woodsworth, newly converted to socialism, and William Ivens, another Protestant clergyman, painted a picture of God's paradise on earth while addressing enthusiastic gatherings of strikers in the language of the King James Bible. But there were other crowd-pleasers who peppered their oratory with eloquent exhortations from Karl Marx. The mere invocation of Karl Marx's name was enough to awaken the worst fears of the Citizens' Committee of One Thousand. With the backing of the city's leading newspapers, the committee pronounced the strike a revolutionary conspiracy led by a small group of "alien scum". None of the available evidence validated this charge, but nevertheless the committee used it as an excuse to block any conciliatory efforts made by the strikers.

Acting on the advice of hard-liners Arthur Meighen, minister of the interior and acting minister of justice, and Gideon Robertson, minister of labour, the federal government threw its support behind the employers. Federal employees were ordered back to work and on June twenty-first a crowd of strikers was charged by the North-West Mounted Police. Later that "Bloody Saturday" federal troops occupied city streets, thereby effectively crushing the strike, which left a long-lasting legacy of bitterness and unrest across Canada.

During the full fury of the strike, June 6, 1919, assent was given to legislation that made the Immigration Act even more restrictive. To previous grounds for deportation, outlined in Section 3, the amended act added a host of new ones, including such conditions as "constitutional psychopathic inferiority" and "chronic alcoholism." Entry to Canada was made more difficult by revisions to Section 3, providing for the barring of any "persons over fifteen years of age, physically capable of reading, who cannot read the English or French language or some other language or dialect" and by alterations to Section 38, which, in its amended form, prohibited the entry of prospective immigrants because of "their peculiar customs, habits, modes of living and methods of holding property". Equally significant was the redrafting of Section 41, which, in its second revision (An Act to amend an Act of the present session entitled "An Act to amend the Immigration Act"), added to the list of undesirables: Every person who by word or act in Canada seeks to overthrow by force or violence the government or constituted law and authority in the United Kingdom of Great Britain and Ireland, or Canada ... or who without lawful authority assumes any powers of government in Canada ... or who is a member of or affiliated with any organization entertaining or teaching disbelief in or opposition to organized government.

Such a person was liable to deportation.[8] Deportation, an arbitrary administrative proceeding, was deemed just the weapon necessary to deal with the Winnipeg General Strike leaders in the absence of suitable provisions in the Criminal Code. Or so thought hard-liners in the government, who spearheaded the draconian revisions to Section 41 when Robert Borden was in France signing the peace treaty. In its final form, Section 41 was invoked in the arrest of key foreign-born "anarchists and Bolsheviks" involved in the radical ferment that figured so prominently in Canada in 1919. On June seventeenth, ten of the leading Winnipeg General Strike leaders — "foreigners" and British-born alike — were arrested in Winnipeg and rushed to the nearby federal penitentiary at Stony Mountain, where they were later joined by three others who were alleged to have conspired with them. Such an outcry greeted news of the incarceration of six impeccable Anglo-Saxons, however, that the Borden government backed down and announced that it did not plan to use Section 41 against the British-born agitators either in Winnipeg or elsewhere. Later, eight of the British-born leaders, including William Ivens, were tried by jury while the aliens were subjected to deportation hearings before a board of inquiry. J.S. Woodsworth, who had also been arrested, was given a separate trial along with labour leader R.J. Dixon. Ultimately only one leader, Oscar Schoppelrie, was deported; not because he had violated Section 41, but because he had crossed the Canada–United States border illegally three years previously.

Less fortunate was a group of aliens arrested in Winnipeg on June 21, 1919. Most of these men were denied the formal deportation hearings provided for under Section 41. Instead they appeared before a Winnipeg magistrate who ordered all of them interned in a camp at Kapuskasing, Ontario. Subsequently, they were deported in secret.[8]

In June 1919, the government also used the revised Immigration Act to bar entry to various European immigrants. Under the authority of Section 3 it issued an order-in-council excluding all persons who then were, or had been, enemy aliens during the war. That same day the government also issued, under the authority of Section 38, an order-in-council prohibiting the entry of Doukhobors, Mennonites, and Hutterites, because of "their peculiar customs, habits, modes of life and methods of holding property, and because of their probable inability to become readily assimilated or to assume the duties and responsibilities of Canadian citizenship within a reasonable time after their entry."[9] In 1918, Hutterites, driven north from the United States by anti-foreign sentiment, had established ten colonies in the Calgary and Lethbridge areas of Alberta and six in Manitoba west of Winnipeg. But now they, along with members of other pacifist sects, were barred from settling in Canada until June 1922, when the regulation was rescinded by the newly elected Liberal government of Mackenzie King. Taking advantage of a more tolerant view of unorthodox sect members, some 20,000 Russian Mennonites settled in Canada between 1923 and 1929. Like their predecessors, these Russian Mennonites were exempt from military service, but unlike the earlier Mennonite immigrants, they were not allowed to settle in blocs.

The revisions made to the Immigration Act in 1919 and the order-in-council issued under its authority signalled a dramatic shift in Canadian immigration policy. Whereas, prior to the First World War, economic considerations had reigned supreme, now a prospective immigrant's cultural and ideological complexion weighed most heavily in the selection process. This resulted in immigrants from the white Commonwealth countries, the United States, and, to a lesser extent, newcomers from the so-called preferred countries (i.e., northwestern Europe) being welcomed and the celebrated agriculturalist of the Sifton regime being relegated to the bottom rung of the ethnic preference scale employed by immigration authorities in the selection of immigrants.

By the Chinese Immigration Act of 1923, all Chinese were barred entry to Canada except members of the diplomatic corps, children born in Canada to Chinese parents, students, and merchants who had a minimum of $2,500 invested in a business for at least three years and who were prepared to invest at least $2,500 in a business in Canada. (The day on which this piece of legislation replaced the Chinese Immigration Act of 1885 — July 1, 1923 — became known to Canadian Chinese as "Humiliation Day".) To tighten the screws of restriction still further, the act prohibited the landing of Chinese anywhere in Canada except at the ports of Vancouver and Victoria in British Columbia. It has been estimated that only about twenty-five Chinese entered Canada between the passage of the act and its repeal in 1946.[10] As might be expected, the entry of other Asians continued to be severely restricted.

The opposition to immigration from central and eastern Europe was promoted by leading educators, journalists, and politicians, who took the view that immigrants from that part of Europe resisted assimilation into mainstream Canadian society and that encouraging their immigration only led to the "balkanization" of Canada. J.S. Woodsworth, by no means a strident nativist, voiced concerns that he had on the question when he observed in the House of Commons in 1923:

> I am not one who thinks that the Ukrainian people are undesirable settlers. There are some 300,000 of them in the West, and they have on the whole made good, especially when they were settled on anything like decent land … During the war it began to dawn upon us in Canada, as it did in the United States, that this talk about all these people going into the melting pot was a lot of nonsense. As they said in the States, they may be put into the melting pot, but they refuse to melt; and unless we are careful in this country we shall have a Balkanized Canada.[11]

R.K. Anderson, the Conservative MP from Halton, Ontario, echoed the prevailing view on the most desirable type of immigration when he informed the House of Commons that same year: "It is certainly desirable that we should get increased population in this country. We need immigrants of the right class, and I would say that immigrants should be preferably of British stock and that they should be sound physically and sound mentally. These are the chief desiderata in an immigrant."[12]

COURTING BRITISH IMMIGRANTS

When the economy became more buoyant in 1923 the federal government once again began to recruit British immigrants. Since the idea of land settlement still held sway in the 1920s, immigration officials targeted Britons prepared to farm. Some of these prospective agriculturalists were brought to Canada by colonization programs made possible by the Empire Settlement Act. Passed in 1922 by the British Parliament, it provided for cooperation between the British and Dominion governments and public authorities or private organizations in a variety of settlement schemes that offered reduced transportation fares and in some cases agricultural training to immigrants intending to settle on farms.

On of the fruits of this legislation was the "3,000 Families Scheme", so called because it provided for the settlement in Canada over a period of three years of 3,000 British families. The first wave of these settlers arrived in this country in 1925 with a guarantee of financial aid from the British government for the purchase of farm equipment and the promise of assistance from the Canadian government in the form of financing for farm purchases, placement on farms, and practical instruction in agriculture.

The program excited a lot of editorial comment, both in the United Kingdom and Canada. In the U.K. most leading newspapers were quick to lavish praise on it, but in Canada opinion was more divided. The Regina *Leader*, for example, observed: "It is doubtful if a more attractive means of stimulating emigration from Great Britain could be presented."[13] The Montreal *Star*, however, was more sceptical, noting, "It is to be hoped that the new agreement is not merely the trumpet of the heralds announcing the oncoming of a new army which is to be found only in the phantom form."[14]

Unfortunately, the programs inaugurated under the Empire Settlement Act did not result in impressive numbers of Britons taking up farming in Canada. All told, an estimated 130,000 came to Canada between 1925 and 1931 under various agreements spawned by this act, and of this number less than 10 percent, according to the 1931 census, were found to be farmers.[15] The program's relative lack of success can perhaps be explained by the situation of the English farmer, which was summed up trenchantly in 1922 by the still forceful Clifford Sifton. In a letter to the well-known Canadian editor John Dafoe, the former minister of the interior wrote, "The farmer class in England will not emigrate; they are doing too well …"[16] In all likelihood, though, the reason for the program's lacklustre results was to be found in the scheme's promotion of land settlement at a time when the urbanization of native-born Canadians was proceeding at an accelerated rate. In any event, British immigration received its greatest encouragement not from land settlement schemes but from the reduced transportation fares made possible by an agreement between the British and Canadian governments and the transportation companies, signed in December 1925.

Left: Canadian Pacific Limited, Corporate Archives, neg. no. 4320
Right: Canadian Pacific Limited, Corporate Archives, neg. no. 4312

One of those transportation companies was the Canadian Pacific Railway. When it established its Department of Colonization and Development in 1916, the company embarked on a more comprehensive settlement policy, initially designed to promote the settlement of unoccupied lands in the West held by speculators and farmers.[17] So impressive were the results of this policy and its earlier settlement efforts that by 1924 it could boast that it had been responsible for settling some 55,000 families on 30 million acres of prairies.[18] The 1920s, however, failed to reproduce the buoyancy of the earlier settlement period for the CPR. A severe recession in Canada and a drought of unprecedented magnitude in the West brought hard times to agriculture on the Prairies and in British Columbia. Nevertheless, during these difficult years the company continued to maintain its colonization department, which boasted both a publicity branch and an exhibits branch.

JEWISH IMMIGRATION

Between 1919 and 1925, the admission of newcomers to Canada was restricted for the most part to immigrants from Canada's traditional source countries. But there were some notable exceptions. One involved the Russian Mennonites, the other Jews. In 1920, for example, 150 Jewish war orphans were brought from the Ukraine to Canada largely through the efforts of Lillian Freiman, the tireless philanthropist wife of well-known Ottawa merchant A.J. Freiman.[19] Then, three years later, the Canadian government agreed to admit a significant number of Jews from Romania on compassionate grounds. These were Jewish refugees who had fled from the Ukraine to Romania between 1918 and 1920, and who had later been ordered to leave their adopted country by the Romanian government. The Jewish Colonization Association appealed to Ottawa to admit 5,000 of these refugees and declared that it was prepared to shoulder their transportation and settlement costs. In response to this entreaty, the federal government gave its approval to the undertaking and agreed to grant entry to 100 families a week. Some 3,040 refugees actually arrived in Canada before the government pulled the plug on the project and terminated it.[20] Although there were many obstacles to their entry, approximately 48,500 Jews were admitted to Canada between 1920 and 1930, accounting for 3.9 percent of the total immigration during this decade.[21]

The framers of Canadian immigration policy believed, in 1919, that sufficient numbers of white English-speaking agriculturalists and industrial workers could be obtained either in Canada or from the United States and Great Britain. In arriving at this conclusion, however, they failed to take into account the sweeping changes in American immigration legislation that had been introduced in 1921 and 1924 to reduce sharply the number of immigrants allowed into the United States from continental Europe. Since no move was made to impose quotas on the entry of native-born Canadians, the way was paved for a significant increase in the north-south exodus and a corresponding decrease in the Canadian labour pool.

When increased numbers of Canadian agricultural and industrial workers began to flow southward, Canadian employers, particularly those in labour-intensive industries, began to sound the alarm. Sir Joseph Flavelle, who had turned his meat-packing company, the William Davies Company, into the British Empire's largest pork-packer, was one of those Canadian businessmen distressed by the new turn of events. In a letter to an English banker in 1924 the millionaire financier provided a cogent analysis of the situation:

> Until the United States adopted the policy of strict limi-
> tation of immigration of all except native born
> Canadians, we always welcomed the promise of great
> activity in the United States because it was followed some
> months later by somewhat similar conditions in Canada.
> During the last two or three years, however, ... with
> increasing activity, and sectional or general shortages of
> labour, important numbers of Canadians are attracted to
> the United States. The trouble is, our loss is chiefly in men
> between twenty-five and thirty years of age.[22]

The concerns of Canadian businessmen were also shared by many farmers, and together they joined the transportation and mining interests in lobbying for a more liberal immigration policy. Clifford Sifton set the tone for the new appeal when he declared in 1922 that 500,000 "stalwart peasants" were required in Western Canada. These people, he urged, should be brought immediately from "Central Europe, particularly from Hungary and Galicia."[23]

THE RAILWAY AGREEMENT OF 1925

In response to this pressure, the King government gradually removed most of the barriers erected against large-scale European immigration, starting in 1923 with the repeal of the regulation that restricted the entry of immigrants from Germany and her wartime allies. The real breakthrough came in September 1925 when Ottawa, in a stunning abdication of federal responsibility, signed an agreement with the CPR and Canadian National Railways giving them control over the recruitment of "bona fide" European agriculturalists. To meet Canada's labour requirements, the arrangement allowed the railways to recruit immigrants from those countries previously designated "non-preferred" by the Department of Immigration and Colonization. Thus, thanks to the Railway Agreement, prospective immigrants from Estonia, Latvia, Lithuania, Poland, Russia, Hungary, Czechoslovakia, Yugoslavia, Romania, Austria, and Germany were placed on the same footing as those from Western Europe.

Because they were bent on ensuring themselves a steady supply of cheap foreign workers, the railways flagrantly ignored many of the provisions of the agreement, often bringing to Canada immigrants when there was no guaranteed farm employment and calling temporary harvest work year-round employment. Nevertheless, despite widespread opposition to its terms from churches, trade unions, and organized farmers and mounting evidence of the railways' flagrant violation of the agreement, the arrangement remained in force until 1930, when soaring unemployment forced its cancellation. Ironically, while it was in effect, Canada received a higher proportion of newcomers from the "non-preferred" countries than from those countries from which it was supposed to be encouraging immigration![24] Moreover, few of these immigrants from central and eastern Europe still resided on the Prairies in 1931. According to a study conducted in 2000 by Bryon Lew, the majority of them had drifted south, moved to the cities, or returned to their homeland.

THE DEPRESSION'S IMPACT ON IMMIGRATION

If the Railway Agreement of 1925 paved the way for a surge in immigration from continental Europe, the Great Depression of the 1930s had just the opposite effect. In fact, no single development, other than the Second World War, did more to choke off immigration to Canada than this economic calamity. In August 1930, when the Depression was well under way, the federal government passed an order-in-council that suspended immigration from Europe, except for those immigrants who had sufficient capital to establish and maintain themselves on farms, and the wives and minor children of family heads already resident in Canada. This was followed, in March 1931, by the notorious Order-in-Council P.C. 695, which permitted only the following categories: British subjects and American citizens with sufficient capital to maintain themselves until employment was secured; agriculturalists with sufficient means to farm in Canada; farm labourers with guaranteed employment; any individual engaged in the mining, lumbering, or logging industry with assured employment in one of these industries; and the wives and unmarried children of adult males legally resident in Canada. As a result of such stringent provisions, immigration plummeted from 1,166,000 in the decade 1921 to 1931 to only 140,000 between 1931 and 1941.[25]

There can be no question that Ottawa's restrictive legislation reflected Canadian opposition to immigration, for Canadians everywhere took the view that immigrants threatened scarce jobs in an economy that saw almost a quarter of the labour force unemployed in 1933. Not only prospective immigrants but immigrants already established in Canada became targets of opposition. Among those who felt the brunt of such hostility were foreigners employed on a reforestation project near North Bay, Ontario. In May 1931, they roused the anger of area residents, who claimed that Canadian workers had "to stand around and starve while foreigners get the first privilege."[26] Equally unwelcome were immigrant workers thrown out of work or engaged in radical protests.

Not infrequently they became victims of the deportation provisions of the Immigration Act.

Deportations

All immigrants who had not lived in Canada long enough to obtain domicile and, ideally, citizenship could be deported if they no longer held a paid job, or got into trouble. Deportation could take place formally, under the auspices of the Department of Immigration and Colonization (after December 1936 the Department of Mines and Resources) or it could occur informally, outside the legal framework. An immigrant thrown out of work, for example, might apply to a municipality for relief and the municipality would then report the immigrant to the department, thereby setting in motion the legal deportation process. Alternatively, the municipality could refuse to grant welfare, thereby leaving the immigrant with little choice but to deport himself or herself.[27] Throughout the "hungry thirties" the deportation weapon was often used to relieve municipalities, employers, and the state of unwanted foreign workers, who had become surplus, useless, or obstreperous. According to estimates, Ottawa returned some 30,000 immigrants, largely public charges, to Europe between 1930 and 1935 by means of the deportation process.[28] Their ejection from Canada did not fail to arouse the sympathies of concerned Canadians, however. Among those most afflicted by their predicament were deportation officers. At least two serving in the western region became severely depressed and of these one later committed suicide.[29]

Closing the Door to Refugees

Even as many forlorn, despairing immigrants were being returned to Europe (some later returned to Canada and made notable contributions to Canadian life), other Europeans were clamouring to get into this country. These were refugees who had managed to escape the engulfing Nazi tide and now sought a new life in this country. Although they could bring badly needed skills and talents to the Canadian community, refugees were certainly not welcomed by the federal government, or by large numbers of Canadians. When she was most required to show compassion, Canada shut herself off from the world and strenuously fought any attempt by desperate refugees, especially Jewish refugees, to breach the wall of restrictive legislation erected by P.C. 695 of March 31, 1931, which barred access to most potential immigrants, and the Continuous Journey Regulation (P.C. 23 of January 1919), and the Contract Labour Regulation (P.C. 23 of January 1914). Under no circumstances was this country prepared to create a special humanitarian classification for the entry of refugees and to make a distinction between them and ordinary immigrants.

Canada's anti-refugee stance found expression not only in the stringent enforcement of certain immigration regulations but also in its refusal to let the *S.S. St. Louis* dock at a Canadian port when she sought in vain in the spring of 1939 to find a country of asylum for her desperate human cargo. The 936 passengers — 930 of them Jewish refugees — had embarked on "the voyage of the damned" on May 13, bound first for Cuba, where they were denied entry, and then for the United States, where American authorities dispatched a coast guard cutter to shadow the liner and make sure that not a single frantic passenger swam to shore. In Canada, forty-four well-known Torontonians sent a telegram to Mackenzie King urging the Canadian government to provide a sanctuary for the homeless exiles, but their request was turned down. Having exhausted all her options, the *St. Louis* returned to Europe, where almost certain death awaited the majority of her passengers.

Canada's indifference to the plight of refugees also found expression in this country's position vis-à-vis the Evian Conference. The brainchild of Sumner Welles, Franklin Roosevelt's secretary of state, the conference brought together thirty nations in the summer of 1938 to discuss the worsening refugee situation in Europe. One of the reluctant participants was Canada, which dawdled for months before accepting the American invitation to attend. The stalling tactics of King and his cabinet are easily explained: Canadian officials realized all too well that attendance at this gathering implied an interest in helping to alleviate the refugee problem by lowering immigration barriers and admitting sizeable numbers of Jews. And Canada, like most other countries, was not prepared to do this. That shrewd politician, Mackenzie King, may have wanted to act on humanitarian grounds, but as always he was loathe to ignore political realities. And one of these was Quebec's attitude towards refugees in general and Jewish refugees in particular.

Anti-Semitism was rife throughout Canada, but nowhere did it show a more overt and ugly face than in Quebec, thanks to a revival of French-Canadian nationalism, the influence of the Roman Catholic Church, and the impact of the Great Depression. Many a French language newspaper, from moderate organs such as *Le Devoir* to ultranationalist ones such as *L'Action*, sounded dire warnings against Canada's opening its doors to Jewish refugees. French-Canadian MPs and such Quebec organizations as the St.-Jean-Baptiste Society were equally vociferous.

In the view of Ernest Lapointe, King's minister of justice and Quebec lieutenant, admitting Jewish refugees would only play into the hands of the right-wing Union Nationale (led by Maurice Duplessis) and further weaken Quebec's Liberal Party, which had been thrown out of office by the Duplessis forces in 1936. And since King firmly believed that the Liberal Party had to remain a national party, he listened to the advice of Lapointe and like-minded colleagues. Canada therefore delayed in replying to the American invitation to attend the Evian Conference. Finally this country agreed to participate, but having done so it resolved to make no promises or commitments. Canada's participation in the conference's proceedings would be minimal. As it turned out, the Canadian government need not have worried that it would have to adopt a more liberal immigration policy because of Canada's participation in the conference. Despite lofty statements of principle, the delegates at the French resort town of Evian accomplished little of any significance.

FREDERICK CHARLES BLAIR

One of those senior mandarins who advised against Canada's participation in the Evian Conference was Frederick Charles Blair, director of the Immigration Branch of the Department of Mines and Resources (responsibility for immigration was assigned to the Department of Mines and Resources when that department was created in 1936). Thomas Crerar was nominally in charge of immigration after the

Liberals' return to power in 1935. But the one-time prairie radical, now minister of mines and resources, was not particularly interested in immigration. As a result, nearly all decisions relating to this contentious issue were left to F.C. Blair. A dedicated, inflexible civil servant of Scottish descent, Blair was the perfect instrument of the government's anti-immigration policy. Although he could recommend the issuance of special permits, the immigration director rarely did so, believing that immigration should be discouraged whenever possible. To make matters worse for prospective immigrants, Blair disliked Jews, and by extension, refugees, since he equated the label "refugee" with Jew. Refugees seeking entry to Canada therefore faced a formidable bureaucratic obstacle in the person of this long-serving civil servant.

Frederick Charles Blair (left) and C.A. Collins following investiture at Government House, 1943.

Blair's attitude was undoubtedly shared by some of the immigration officers serving overseas, but, contrary to the picture painted by many historians, there were numerous officers on the firing line in Europe who did their best to help Jewish refugees wanting to come to Canada. Maurice Mitchell, who eventually became director of operations for the Foreign Service of Manpower and Immigration, recounted, with some bitterness, how immigration officers he knew responded to the plight of Jewish applicants for special permits:

> Naturally, we were very sympathetic towards these unfortunate people and we tried to help in the only way legally allowed to us, which was by helping them in making an "appeal" to the Department against the decision which we had rendered and seeking a special permit. Every day we came across people who had money readily available in the United States, who had business experience, and who would have established a business in Canada which would have given employment to Canadian residents. We made it a point always to submit their appeals to Ottawa. A continuous stream of these appeals flowed across the Atlantic and sometimes we were successful. Frankly, it seems rather ludicrous to me in recent years that so much has been written about the cold-heartedness of the Department at this time. The thousands of letters which had been written by us to plead with the Department have been used as proof of our unwillingness to assist![30]

If the government, whether Liberal or Conservative, influential civil servants like F.C. Blair, and a large part of the Canadian population wanted to deny entry to refugees in the 1930s, there was a select group of Canadians who wanted to see immigration barriers lowered. They included leading spokesmen for the Jewish community, prominent members of the Protestant churches, newspaper editors and commentators in English-speaking Canada, the Co-operative Commonwealth Federation, particularly its leader, M.J. Caldwell, and various pro-refugee organizations.

THE CANADIAN NATIONAL COMMITTEE ON REFUGEES

Foremost among the leading non-sectarian refugee lobbies was the Canadian National Committee on Refugees and Victims of Political Persecution, later shortened to the Canadian National Committee on

Refugees (CNCR). It was founded by the League of Nations Society in Canada, which was spurred to organize for a new struggle by the pogroms of Europe in the autumn of 1938 and by the aftermath of the Munich settlement, which saw a large chunk of Czechoslovakia surrendered to Hitler and some 80,000 anti-Nazi residents fleeing for their lives.

Under the chairmanship of Cairine Wilson, Canada's first woman senator and the society's president, the CNCR mobilized to lobby for a more liberal immigration policy and to champion the refugee cause. In pursuit of its goals, the organization would encounter unrelenting opposition from the King government and public indifference or hostility to refugees. Ultimately it did not succeed in bringing about a dramatic change in government immigration policy in the pre-war and Second World War years, but it did perform valuable work in helping to settle individuals and families in Canada; in raising public awareness of the refugee question; in prodding the government into admitting refugees from the Iberian Peninsula in 1944; and in assisting anti-Nazi Germans, Italians, and Austrians, transported from Britain to Canada in the summer of 1940 and then interned in Canadian prison camps.

When refugees did succeed in breaching Canada's immigration wall during the 1930s, they were usually well supplied with skills and money. Thomas Bata, the Czech-born industrialist and later head of the Bata shoemaking empire, was one such refugee. Just a few days before German troops invaded his homeland, Bata, then aged twenty-four, fled to Switzerland. From there he made his way to England, where he sought permission to emigrate to Canada and establish his shoemaking business. When the CNCR became aware of Bata's case, it went to work orchestrating pressure on the Canadian government to admit the Czech industrialist. The committee's efforts bore fruit, for eventually Thomas Bata and eighty-two of his key Czech workers settled outside of Frankford, Ontario, where they laid the foundations of a business that would become an international success story. It was estimated that refugees like Bata established fifty-six industries in Canada between 1939 and 1942, industries producing goods valued at over $22 million and employing close to 5,000 people.[31]

Groups of lesser-known Czech refugees were also admitted to Canada in the months following the Munich Pact signing and the Nazi occupation of Czechoslovakia. Some of these were Germans from the heavily industrialized Sudeten, who, because of their Social Democratic affiliations, fled Czechoslovakia and made their way to Britain. Here their cause was taken up by the Labour Party, which asked Canada to admit some of these skilled industrial workers.

In response to the Labour Party's intervention, the Immigration Branch asked CPR and CNR agents in Britain if they would determine if the Germans would make good settlers. When the agents delivered a positive assessment, the Canadian government obtained a guarantee from Whitehall that it would pay $1,000 per family to cover the costs of transportation and other expenses. For its part, the Canadian government agreed to accept 1,200 families. It then asked the western provinces for their support in the projected resettlement scheme. Only British Columbia and Saskatchewan agreed to cooperate, and it was in remote areas of these two provinces — St. Walburg in northeastern Saskatchewan and the Tomslake region of northeastern British Columbia — that 303 families and 72 individuals made their way before the outbreak of the Second World War.[32]

Another sizeable group of refugees that succeeded in gaining entry to Canada in these years was made up of Poles, some 800 in all. Five hundred of these newcomers went to work as skilled engineers and technicians for the Canadian armaments industry. But, whereas their arrival did not excite controversy, plans to admit an undisclosed number of refugee families from the Iberian Peninsula did. When Thomas Crerar announced on November 2, 1943 that Ottawa intended to admit some refugees from this part of southwestern Europe, he ignited a storm of protest from anti-refugee interests, who feared that the government's timid scheme heralded an unchecked flow of immigrants to Canada and capitulation to pressure from the Jewish lobby. One of the most strident and cynical notes was struck by Maurice Duplessis, now opposition leader in Quebec. At a rousing pre-election rally he charged that provincial and federal Liberals would allow the "International Zionist Brotherhood" to settle 100,000 Jewish refugees in Quebec in return for election financing.[33] Notwithstanding the furor created by Duplessis's absurd charges and the general anti-refugee climate, the government did go through with its plans and almost 450 refugees, who had fled from Nazi occupation to the Iberian Peninsula, arrived in Canada in 1944.

THE "ACCIDENTAL IMMIGRANTS"

By far the most colourful refugees to make it to Canada in this period were the so-called "accidental immigrants". These were some 2,500 enemy aliens — for the most part German and Austrian nationals, many of them highly educated Jews — who had been living in Great Britain when war erupted. Regarded as dangerous security risks by the British authorities, they were interned in Britain, then transported in the summer of 1940 across the submarine-infested Atlantic to Canada, where further imprisonment awaited them.

The Canadian government agreed to receive these male civilian internees in the belief that it would be assisting hard-pressed Britain by accepting custody of a number of "potentially dangerous enemy aliens". Canadian authorities were therefore astonished to see a large assortment of teenage boys, university students, priests, and rabbis step ashore at Quebec. Despite their misgivings, however, the Canadians proceeded to place them all in camps that resembled maximum security prisons. And it was here that scientists, theologians, musicians, teachers, artists, and writers, among others, would be forced to bide their time for months to come.

Fortunately for these prisoners the British government soon realized that it had done a possible grave injustice to many of the internees and

Soccer team at an internees' camp near Fredericton, New Brunswick.

National Archives of Canada, PA 104569

initiated steps to have them released. By July 1941, arrangements had been made for 700 genuine refugees to return to Britain and for the remainder to be housed in three camps designated only for refugees. Eventually those remaining in camp were released when sponsors could be found to guarantee their maintenance. By the autumn of 1943, when the last refugee camp closed, over 1,500 inmates had returned to the U.K.; others had departed elsewhere or stayed in Canada. Later, still others would emigrate to the United States.

In 1945, Canada reclassified its one-time prisoners as "Interned Refugees (Friendly Aliens) from the United Kingdom" and invited them to become Canadian citizens. Nine hundred and seventy-two chose to do so, thereby providing their adopted country with one of her most remarkable pools of foreign-born talent.[14] Many, in fact, would go on to make outstanding contributions in such fields as music, theology, science, university teaching, literature, and the dramatic arts.

GUEST CHILDREN FROM GREAT BRITAIN

The summer that saw civilian internees sent to Canada also saw an influx of British guest children arrive on Canadian shores. Some came under private schemes, but by far the largest number arrived courtesy of a government-financed evacuation program.

Even before hostilities erupted in 1939, some concerned Canadians had urged Ottawa to admit large numbers of British children in the event of an outbreak of war. A few Canadians had even lobbied the government to grant entry to refugee children from the Continent, most of whom were Jews. Senator Cairine Wilson and the CNCR, for example, had petitioned Ottawa to have 100 of these youngsters brought from Britain, where they were then living, to Canada for adoption or guaranteed hospitality. After tireless lobbying by the committee, the government finally granted permission for such an undertaking, but it coupled its permission with three pages of stringent regulations. As a result, only two children were adopted under the scheme and proponents of the project abandoned their efforts in the summer of 1940.

Dr. W.A.B. Douglas, author and official historian of the Department of National Defence, before he retired from the federal government, was one of 7,730 British "guest children" dispatched to Canada in 1940 and 1941. The son of a widowed mother, he sailed on one of the last available passenger liners for North America in July 1940. Once arrived in this country, he stayed with friends of his mother, a well-to-do Toronto family.

Alec's mother missed him terribly, of course, and when it seemed obvious that a German invasion of England was no longer imminent, she searched for a way to get him home. This became possible when in 1943, with several other boys, he was able to take passage on HMS Pursuer, an auxiliary aircraft carrier, as a "guest of the British Admiralty". He did so on the understanding that if the war was still raging when he reached the age for military service he would join the Royal Naval Volunteer Reserve. As it happened, the war was over before he reached military age, his mother had married a Canadian army chaplain in 1945 and had sailed to Canada as a war bride in 1946. Consequently, after leaving school in 1947, Alec set off to join his parents in Canada, sailing on the Acquitania, as a "military dependent" — the only male military dependent among hundreds of war brides. When Alec arrived by train in Montreal from Halifax he was welcomed by a Red Cross representative who, assuming he had been born after his mother's second marriage, said to him in some astonishment, "You're supposed to be twins!"

Alec was 11 in 1941 when he penned a letter to his mother on New Year's day. In this missive, he waxed ecstatic about

— continued

The scheme to evacuate British children to Canada under government auspices seemed to offer more promise. Its beginnings can be traced to the spring of 1940 when the German war machine was poised for an assault on England and war hysteria was mounting in Britain. Against this backdrop, T.A. Crerar proposed that Canada admit at least 10,000 children between the ages of five and fifteen. The British government would pay for their transportation to Canada and they would be cared for by Canadian families at no cost to their parents.

To implement the government-assisted scheme, a British-appointed board received applications, examined individual cases, classified the youngsters, and then arranged for them to be sent by ship to Canada, the costs of their crossing being defrayed by the British government. In Canada the children were taken to provincial clearing centres, where provincial authorities took charge, and through the Children's Aid Society or other child welfare organizations, placed the youngsters in carefully selected homes.

All told, some 1,500 children

were brought to Canada under government sponsorship during that fateful summer of 1940. The program was abruptly terminated, however, after the *S.S. City of Benares* sank on September 14, 1940 with the loss of 73 children and it became evident that it would be too difficult to obtain warships for convoy duty.[35]

— continued from previous

the mid-day meal served in the city home of his Canadian friends, reporting, "In the morning we stayed indoors then had a marvelous lunch of roast DUCK and CHICKEN. Then we had a super pudding. Out here we call it dessert. Then we all wished for the new year's happiness and drank a toast of Madeira wine." (Source: Dr. W.A.B. Douglas).

THE PLIGHT OF THE JAPANESE CANADIANS

In Canada itself probably no other people experienced so much hardship and upheaval because of the war as the Japanese Canadians. Their ordeal began on December 9, 1941, the day after the Japanese bombed Pearl Harbor. Within hours of that attack the Canadian government ordered the impounding of fishing boats operated by Japanese–Canadian fishermen and the registration of all Japanese aliens with the RCMP. The worst blow was delivered in February 1942. Although defence officials did not regard them as a security threat, the government ordered the expulsion of some 22,000 Japanese Canadians from a 100-mile swath of the Pacific coast. Thus began a process that saw a visible minority uprooted from their B.C. homes, stripped of their property, and dispersed across Canada.

The majority of these people were relocated in the interior of British Columbia, often in detention camps in isolated ghost towns and sparsely settled areas. The remaining Japanese Canadians were sent out of British Columbia altogether, to Alberta, Manitoba, and Ontario to fill labour shortages in the sugar beet fields there. Unlike their counterparts in the United States, Japanese Canadians would be forced to remain in detention camps until the end of the war. Then, after the conclusion of hostilities, about 4,000 of them would surrender to pressure and leave Canada for Japan under the federal government's "repatriation" scheme. Of these, more than half were Canadian-born and two-thirds were Canadian citizens. Decades would elapse before Japanese Canadians

Tak Toyota and LAC C046350

Relocation of Japanese Canadians to camps in the interior of British Columbia in the 1940s.

received redress for the harsh treatment meted out to them. Concluded in 1988, the settlement that the Association of Japanese Canadians negotiated with the federal government provided, among other things, for compensation of $21,000 for each Japanese Canadian whose civil rights had been violated between 1942 and 1949.[36]

The conclusion of Second World War hostilities would signal the end of three inglorious decades of slow immigration and the subordination of humanitarian considerations to anti-Semitism and economic priorities. It would also set the stage for a renewed interest in welcoming newcomers and a great upsurge in immigration.

CHAPTER 8

Immigration's Post-War Boom
(1947–1957)

CANADIAN IMMIGRATION POLICY CONTINUED TO be highly restrictive in the first couple of years following the Second World War. Fashioned during the Depression, notably by the infamous P.C. 695 of March 21, 1931, it made few, if any, concessions to humanitarianism. Nevertheless, in the months following the war's end, proponents of a more liberal immigration policy had good reason to expect that immigration barriers would soon be lowered and that in no time at all Canada would become a land of hope and opportunity for thousands of Europe's war-weary and oppressed. For one thing, the high unemployment of the Great Depression and the profound feelings of economic insecurity that had haunted Canadians during that harrowing decade were but bitter memories. In their place was an industrial complex in transition from a wartime to a peacetime economy and a growing demand for skilled and unskilled workers.

The Canadian government's demonstrated sympathy for European refugees and displaced persons was another factor that augured well for the development of a less restrictive immigration policy. As an indication of its interest in Europe's homeless, the government had donated substantial funds to agencies involved in post-war rehabilitation and reconstruction, notably the United Nations Children's Emergency Fund (UNICEF) and the United Nations Relief and Rehabilitation Administration (UNRRA). Developments such as these seemed to presage the immediate lowering of Canada's immigration barriers and the admission of many Europeans to this country.

Events proved, however, that a more generous immigration policy was not just around the comer. For two years Mackenzie King's government stubbornly rejected an increase in immigration, invariably citing two factors to justify its position: the possibility of a post-war recession, such as the one that had followed the First World War, and a lack of suitable passenger vessels to transport people from Europe to Canada. Initially a shortage of ships did force authorities to assign top priority to repatriating Canadian servicemen and their dependents who were overseas. But with the return of these men and their dependents to Canada and the availability of more ships, this particular argument for continuing to pursue an exclusionist immigration policy crumbled. It would appear that by the summer of 1946 the real obstacle to getting immigrants from Europe to Canada was a lack of immigration officers, not a dearth of transport.[1] As for the possibility of a post-war recession, it never materialized. By and large, the conversion of the wartime economy proceeded quickly and with comparatively little dislocation.

The Pro-immigration Lobby

While the government steadfastly resisted the idea of increasing immigration, a growing number of Canadians, representing a variety of interests, spoke out in favour of lowering immigration barriers. A more generous immigration policy, argued these advocates, meant a larger population and therefore a larger market, more economies of scale, and greater productivity, i.e., continuing expansion of the Canadian economy. Increased immigration, they noted, would also enhance national security, because immigrants would occupy uninhabited regions of Canada, thereby making this country less tempting to overcrowded, aggressive states. For their part, knowledgeable parliamentarians pointed to the example of Australia, which had established a separate department of immigration in 1945 and was now zealously developing an ambitious immigration program.

Such a rosy scenario did not go unchallenged, however. A predictable cautionary note was sounded by the Canadian Congress of Labour, which insisted that immigration be planned, "not left to the hit-or-miss, catch-as-catch-can, Micawberish methods of the years before 1914." Continued the congress, in its brief to the Senate Immigration and Labour Committee, "We cannot afford to expose Canadian workers to the constant threat of having their standards undercut by immigrants who must take any kind of job at any wages and under any conditions to avoid sheer starvation."[2]

THE EUROPEAN REFUGEES

The whole question of Canada's exclusionist immigration policy was thrown into sharp relief by the presence of over a million displaced persons and refugees languishing in crowded European shelters maintained by United Nations agencies. The most significant in terms of numbers were the displaced persons, who had been uprooted from or displaced in their homelands by war. Some of these were concentration camp survivors, while others were individuals who had been dispatched to labour camps in Germany and Austria. Among those driven from their homelands were many who refused to be repatriated to Communist regimes.

Another Perspective on Immigration: *Increased immigration had many propo-nents in the post-World War II years, but the well-known Canadian historian, Arthur Lower, was not one of them. Raised in an Ontario town with a high degree of ethnic homogeneity, he stood firmly in the anti-immigration camp. When Lower headed the students' Conservative Party at the University of Toronto in 1913, the Party advocated restricted immigration. And thereafter, the historian consistently attacked the presumed benefits of immigration.*

Lower derided those boomsters who confidently predicted that Canada's population was destined to climb to the hundreds of millions and questioned the proposition that European immigrants were, or had ever been, necessary for Canada's economic development. As he saw it, this country's economic growth depended principally on foreign demand for its staple exports and the availability of land for settlement, not on immigration. He concluded that not even the periodic large influxes of immi-grants during the nineteenth and twen-tieth centuries had enabled Canada's population to grow faster than it might have done by natural increase. Although 3,230,000 immigrants had entered Canada between 1901 and 1921, just under 2 million people had left it.

Lower contended that immigrants with inferior standards of living had sim-ply displaced native-born Canadians who headed for the United States in larger numbers than might have been the case had there been no immigration. In other words, there was a Gresham's Law of immigration at work: cheap men drive out dear men. (Carl Berger, The Writing

— continued

— continued from previous

of Canadian History: English Historical Writing Since 1900, 2nd edition [Toronto: University of Toronto Press, 1986], 128-130.) The historian was no less sceptical about the positive role played by immigration in the immediate post-World War II years. Writing in Maclean's Magazine in 1949, he declared, "Despite the fact that you can hardly pick up a newspaper without being told Canada should bring in 500,000 immigrants a year, or that she should double her population in the next few years, I'm going to argue that mass immigration is both unwise and unpractical." (Arthur Lower, "The Myth of Mass Immigration," Maclean's Magazine, May 15, 1949, 68.) And he proceeded to do just that.

Refugees, by strict definition, were all those people who had fled totalitarian regimes before the outbreak of the war and those who, starting in the second half of 1945, had left East European countries that had come under Communist control. No matter what their designation, though, all these individuals were virtually refugees without a country, home, material possessions, or future. In the words of the illustrious Canadian editor who lobbied for an increase in immigration, B.K. Sandwell, they were "like prisoners in a great, dark, airless room which [had] fifty different doors, the doors of admission to fifty different countries where they could build their lives afresh; but every door [was] locked, barred and bolted."[3]

Demands for a more humane immigration policy multiplied as increasing numbers of Canadians, reacting to the plight of the displaced persons and refugees, called for the prompt admission of these people on the grounds of simple human decency. In response to appeals from their constituents, many of whom represented ethnic organizations, members of Parliament called on the government to admit Europe's homeless.

When estimates for the Immigration Branch were being reviewed in the House of Commons on August 27, 1946, for instance, Liberal David Croll, then a staunch advocate of increased immigration, observed:

> May I say to the Minister it is heartening to see that the vote has been considerably increased this year. I do not know whether he has made provision for sufficient money to carry him through. I had hoped that he would increase the vote even more than he did, and I am sure the committee would agree to it in

order to ensure that he had sufficient money to carry
out fairly bold plans. However, I rose to remind him
and the government that immigration in this country is still a front-page topic and will remain so until
such time as we do something definite about it.
There are no groups, or no organization [sic] or representative bodies, in fact very few individuals in this
country, who do not think we need more people. We
need them now.[4]

Even the Senate, to which Croll was later elevated, embraced the
immigration issue. Eager to examine prevailing views on immigration,
it reconstituted its lapsed Standing Committee on Immigration and
Labour in 1946. The first witness to appear before the Senate committee was the director of the Immigration Branch, A.L. Joliffe, who made
it quite clear that the government had no intention of reopening
immigration offices in Europe until the remaining Canadian servicemen and their dependents had been brought back to Canada. He
acknowledged, however, that the government was reviewing the whole
question of immigration policy, including the issue of displaced persons and refugees.

Among the groups that lobbied most forcefully before the committee for a liberalized immigration policy was the Canadian National
Committee on Refugees (CNCR). Appearing before the committee in
his capacity as honorary chairman of the CNCR, B.K. Sandwell made a
pitch for the age-old doctrine of sanctuary, declaring:

> The obligation to grant sanctuary is not, and never was,
> unlimited. The nation has the right to protect itself
> against excessive influx of population, against disease,
> against ethical and political ideologies hostile to its
> own. But the obligation to grant sanctuary still exists,
> the need for sanctuary is greater than ever before in his-
> tory, and the nation which ignores this obligation will
> suffer as all nations ultimately do which ignore the fun-
> damental moral obligation, the debt which man and

nations owe to the human being at their gates simply because he is a human being.[5]

In a brief that it presented to the committee, the CNCR decried the government's selfish and exclusionist immigration policy and punctured the old argument that immigration causes unemployment. The CNCR also made several recommendations, among which was a request that Canada state her policy on displaced persons without waiting for decisions from the United Nations. When it comes to immigration policy, declared the refugee organization, Canada should distinguish between two categories of immigrants: (a) general immigrants and (b) refugees and displaced persons. Having done this, it should assign top priority to the admission of displaced persons and refugees as opposed to other European immigrants.[6]

In its widely acclaimed report, the Senate committee stated categorically that "of all the witnesses heard not one opposed the general principle of immigration into Canada" and that "All were agreed that Canada, as a humane and Christian nation, should do her share towards the relief of refugees and displaced persons."[7] Equally important, the committee strongly condemned the government for having a "non-immigration policy" dedicated essentially to exclusion, and recommended that the Immigration Act and regulations be revised to provide for the selection and admission of the most desirable immigrants to Canada. The parliamentarians also urged the government to reopen immigration offices in Europe in order to begin processing applications as soon as possible, and to take steps to admit as many qualified agricultural and industrial workers to Canada as the country could successfully absorb.[8]

The widespread enthusiasm that the report's recommendations generated in the Canadian press and the dismay felt by many MPs over government inaction on immigration helped to fuel the momentum for change. So did the requirements of the labour market and mounting pressure from ethnic organizations, religious groups, transportation companies, and federal public servants. Among the latter were Canadian diplomats who were acutely aware of the desperate conditions in Europe and who wanted to see machinery established to resettle some of Europe's displaced persons in Canada.[9] Six years would elapse before the government enacted a new immigration act, but in the meantime it slowly opened Canada's doors to Europe's homeless.

MOVES TO LIBERALIZE IMMIGRATION POLICY

The first tentative steps in this direction were taken on May 28, 1946 when cabinet passed P.C. 2071, which allowed residents of Canada, who were capable of caring for them, to sponsor the admission of first-degree relatives in Europe plus orphaned nieces and nephews under sixteen years of age. That same month the government also made provision for Canadian officials to accept identity and travel documents instead of passports from displaced persons. Then, two months later, in July, Mackenzie King and his cabinet colleagues responded to a request from Britain, which sought help in resettling Polish Free Army veterans, who had been placed under British military command after Poland's surrender in 1940 and who refused to be repatriated at the end of hostilities to a homeland occupied by the Red Army.

Initially Canadian authorities rejected the idea of accepting Polish soldiers as immigrants. When it was realized, however, that they could help to offset a grave shortage of agricultural workers in Canada, the cabinet approved a resettlement program that involved Britain furnishing the shipping and paying the transportation costs. Anticipating the "bulk labour" schemes developed in the following years, the government passed an order-in-council in July 1946, providing for the admission of some 3,000 Poles from General Anders's army. By the terms of the standard contract, each veteran was required to serve on a farm for one year, after which he was free to renew or discontinue his contract. The majority of workers decided not to continue this arrangement after their term was up and migrated to Canadian cities in search of better-paying jobs.

CANADIAN WAR BRIDES

Among the other notable newcomers in these early post-war years were war brides who had married members of Canada's fighting forces. Between 1942 and 1947, close to 48,000 of them arrived in this country (over 44,000 came from England), many with tiny babies in their arms and toddlers clinging to their skirts. Relatively few war brides came before the cessation of hostilities. They only began arriving in significant numbers when the RMS *Mauritania*, carrying 943 women and children docked at Pier 21 in Halifax on February 10, 1946.[10] Although most of the war brides and their approximately 22,000 offspring settled in Canada's towns and cities, some made their homes in the countryside or remote regions of this vast land.

That autumn another step was taken. On November 7, almost a year after the American president had made a similar offer, Mackenzie King announced in Parliament emergency measures to aid the resettlement of European refugees and displaced persons in cooperation with international refugee agencies. Some four months later this theme was taken up by J .A. Glen, the minister of mines and resources, who recommended in a memorandum to cabinet that admissible relatives include displaced persons and that special provision be made for the admission of persons under group labour movements.

A NEW POLICY ON IMMIGRATION

All these pressures and recommendations finally culminated in a landmark statement on immigration that the prime minister read to the House of Commons on May 1, 1947. It was a typical Mackenzie King exercise in that it offered something for everybody and managed to sound somewhat progressive at the same time. In other words, it testified to the fact that King was nothing if not the consummate realist when it came to Canadian political affairs. Responding to those who advocated a more liberal immigration policy, the prime minister declared that "The policy of the government is to foster the growth of the population of Canada by the encouragement of immigration."[11]

But to appease those Canadians who entertained doubts about an increase in immigration, he stressed that the number of new arrivals would be related to the "absorptive capacity" of the Canadian economy, which would change from year to year. Just precisely what the wily politician meant by "absorptive capacity" is not known. Over the years, however, statements by ministers and others have repeatedly reasserted this goal of immigration: to allow enough immigrants to enter the country to meet domestic labour shortages but not enough to disrupt the Canadian labour market.

Besides making a pitch to those Canadians concerned about an increase in immigration, King sought to pacify those opposed to Oriental immigration. He did this by defending Canada's right to discriminate, stating that the racial and national balance of immigration would be regulated so as not to alter the fundamental character of the Canadian population. There would be no large-scale immigration from Asia, but in deference to the United Nations Charter the Chinese Immigration Act of 1923 would be repealed, and Chinese residents of Canada, not already Canadian citizens, could apply for naturalization.

According to the prime minister, applicants from the "old" Commonwealth countries and the United States would continue to receive preferred treatment in Canadian immigration policy. He then outlined the one breakthrough concession that advocates of a more humane immigration policy had been hoping for:

> Canada is not obliged as a result of membership in the United Nations or under the constitution of the international refugee organization, to accept any specific number of refugees or displaced persons. We have, nevertheless, a moral obligation to assist in meeting the problem, and this obligation we are prepared to recognize.
>
> The government is sending immigration officers to examine the situation among the refugee groups, and to take steps looking towards the early admission of some thousands of their number.[12]

Notwithstanding its vagueness, King's statement paved the way for hundreds of thousands of Europeans to enter Canada in the next decade. For the first time since the turn of the century, a Canadian government had decided to use immigration as an instrument to expand the Canadian population and economy. Today we may not regard this as a bold move, but at the time it represented a watershed in Ottawa's approach to immigration policy. For never again would Canada's doors be almost completely closed to immigrants seeking a better life, or to refugees fleeing political or religious persecution.

National archives of Canada, PA 123476.

The Dutch ambassador, Dr. J.H. van Roijin, accompanied by Mrs. Van Roijin, greets Dutch immigrants as their ship docks in Montreal, June 1947. Photo by George Hunter, National Film board collection.

In a commendable move, the government decided to admit displaced persons before an international agreement was reached on the resettlement of hundreds of thousands of Europe's homeless. Taking independent action, it passed an order-in-council on June 6, 1947 authorizing the entry of an initial 5,000 non-sponsored displaced persons. With this breakthrough, the movement of displaced persons and refugees to Canada began in earnest. Subsequent orders-in-council, passed between July 1947 and October 1948, would provide for the admission of an additional

45,000 of these people, many of whom would later sponsor European relatives. The door had at last been opened to thousands of continental Europeans who did not have relatives in Canada to sponsor them.

Five mobile immigration teams were dispatched to Germany and Austria in the summer of 1947. Composed of immigration, medical, security, and labour officials (the Department of Labour now had a voice in selecting prospective immigrants), these teams went from one displaced persons' camp to another, interviewing large numbers of desperate people living out of suitcases or, where possible, the trunk of a car. In a sense they resembled itinerant "head hunters", only their mission was to select able-bodied refugees "like good beef cattle, with a preference for strong young men who could do manual labour and would not be encumbered by aging relatives", to use a description employed by that eminent Canadian, the late John Holmes.[13]

An individual's potential value to the Canadian economy was not the only criterion employed by the Canadian immigration teams when making their selection. Ethnic origin was also central to the screening process. Acting on instructions from Ottawa, the Canadian officials routinely rejected Jewish applicants, even though the Jews had been the most abused victims of the Fascists.[14] A person's political and ideological views were also taken into account. The RCMP was responsible for conducting security clearances, and went to great lengths to prevent "undesirable" individuals from entering Canada. But since the force had a strong right-wing bias, the label "undesirable" was all too often applied to applicants regarded as left wing in their sympathies, Communists being the ultimate pariahs during the Cold War. In fact, the whole question of who constituted a possible threat to Canada's security would stir up controversy at least until the 1970s.[15]

These immigration teams later earned warm praise from Dr. Hugh Keenleyside, who was deputy minister of the Department of Mines and Resources from 1947 until 1949 and a key figure in the resettlement of displaced persons in Canada. Speaking to an audience at Dalhousie University in November 1948, the highly respected Keenleyside praised the work of these early immigration officers and then observed: "I think it is not an exaggeration to say that the achievement of bringing to Canada something over 50,000 DPs between July 1947 and November

1948 under the conditions that existed in Germany during that time, and in spite of the transportation difficulties which had to be overcome, is as remarkable a performance as anything to be found in the history of immigration to Canada."[16]

IMMIGRATION OF BALTS TO CANADA

Among the first displaced persons selected by Canadian immigration teams sent to the United Nations-run camps in Austria and Germany were Balts, who, along with other Nordic peoples, ranked high on Canada's list of preferred immigrants. Generally speaking, the Balts were Estonians, Latvians, and Lithuanians who had found themselves caught between German and Soviet forces in the Second World War, opposing Soviet occupation of their respective countries in 1940, the German invasion that followed, and then the advance of the Russian forces in 1944. When the Russians were advancing on Estonia in 1944, thousands of Estonians fled their homeland by sea for Sweden and Germany. Of those who remained in Estonia, some later effected a dramatic escape to Canada.

Between 1948 and 1950, groups of these illegal immigrants, numbering in total almost 1,700 people, made their way by small, often unseaworthy, boats to Canadian ports, where ad hoc immigration inspection machinery was set up to process them. The government granted entry to nearly all of the intrepid, would-be immigrants, waiving current immigration regulations to admit each newcomer by a special order-in-council.[16] Large numbers of other Estonians, usually displaced persons, would follow the "boat people" to Canada in the next couple of years thanks to the liberalization of Canadian immigration policy. Their transportation and method of entry would be far more conventional, however.

REFUGEE LABOUR

Humanitarianism undoubtedly played a role in Canada's decision to admit large numbers of non-sponsored displaced persons, such as the Estonians in Germany and Sweden. But without question it was eclipsed by a less noble and more pragmatic motive, namely, Canada's need for additional workers to serve the unquenchable needs of its expanding economy. The fact that displaced persons admitted under the orders-in-council were selected on the basis of their employment skills attests to this. Indeed, many displaced persons who entered Canada in these years did so under the "bulk labour" scheme, whereby potential employers in the logging, mining, or lumbering industries forwarded applications to the Department of Labour requesting that a certain number of labourers be brought to this country under prearranged contracts covering wages and basic living conditions. Shortly after its introduction in 1947, the program was expanded to include other types of labourers and specialized agricultural workers, such as the sugar beet farmers who settled with their families in Western Canada.

One of the leading boosters of this scheme was the legendary C.D. Howe, himself an American immigrant and the principal architect of the Canadian war effort. When Canada was converting to a post-war economy, Howe became an outspoken advocate of increased immigration, including the immigration of displaced persons. As minister of reconstruction and supply, and acting minister of mines and resources, he directed a stream of requests to cabinet for the admission of skilled and unskilled European workers — craftsmen for the clothing industry, woodworkers, men suitable for work in heavy industry, lumber camps, and construction, and people for domestic work in homes, hospitals, and similar institutions.

Not surprisingly, the bulk labour movement excited criticism from both pro- and anti-immigration forces. In a May 28, 1947 editorial, the *Globe and Mail* summed up the sentiments of many of the program's critics when it assailed the government for a bankrupt immigration policy that allowed "employers to recruit labour on a plan of semi-servitude utterly at variance with Canadian notions of human rights and freedoms." From a different end of the political spectrum, representatives of the Canadian labour movement and the Co-operative Commonwealth Federation (the forerunner of the New Democratic Party) lashed out at the scheme for undercutting wage rates and threatening to displace Canadian workers from their jobs.

When press reports began to appear about the program's abuses, M.J. Coldwell became one of its harshest critics. Rising in the House of

Commons on June 2, 1947, the forceful and dignified CCF leader launched into a lengthy attack on the government for allowing Canadian industrialists to hand-pick displaced persons in Europe for employment in Canada. What roused Coldwell's ire so much was the blatant violation of Section 2 of the Alien Labour Act that this practice represented, and the rank exploitation to which the "contract" labourer was sometimes subjected.

As it turned out, a prime example of an exploitative employer was to be found among the CCF chieftain's fellow MPs in the House of Commons, for their ranks included the notorious Ludger Dionne. The owner of the Dionne Spinning Mill Company at Saint-Georges-de-Beauce, south of Quebec City, he had attracted a torrent of adverse publicity after recruiting 100 Polish girls to work in his mill for two years at rock-bottom wages. As the *Globe and Mail* so aptly noted, though, it was not the enterprising Mr. Dionne who should have been the target of Canadian indignation. It was the Canadian government that deserved to be "charged, censured and compelled to annul its arrangements" with the MP "if this country's reputation [was] not to be damaged."[17] Speaking to the same theme, the Saskatchewan school teacher and CCFer Gladys Strum observed: "I do not think it improves our standing in the united nations [sic] to have appearing in our daily papers reports which sound like descriptions of scenes from *Uncle Tom's Cabin*, which remind one of the old slave market where girls were put up at auction with someone looking at their muscles and someone else looking at their teeth."[18]

Notwithstanding the heated attacks against it, the bulk labour movement began to lose momentum in the summer of 1948 after President Harry Truman prodded Congress into passing the Displaced Persons Act, which made the United States the preferred destination for many of Europe's homeless. This, coupled with the emptying of the camps in Europe, contributed to a downturn in immigration. When the available supply of manpower could no longer keep up with the insatiable demands of the Canadian labour market, the government was forced to the conclusion that further action was required: measures that would allow more people into Canada and at the same time ensure the right kinds of immigrants.

Its response was the more liberal P.C. 2856 of June 9, 1950. This measure replaced all former orders-in-council and amendments; maintained the preference for British, Irish, French, and American immigrants; and expanded the admissible classes of European immigrants to include any healthy applicant of a good character who had skills needed in Canada and who could readily integrate into Canadian society.

In practice this meant that the following groups became eligible for admission to Canada: relatives of any degree sponsored by residents of Canada; agriculturalists, professionals, entrepreneurs, domestics, and nurses' aides; other workers nominated by Canadian employers; and workers who had been approved by the immigration settlement service or by the Department of Labour. Blacks were still considered inadmissible unless they came under the preferred-class designation or were the spouses or minor children of Canadian residents. A prospective black immigrant from Barbados, the granddaughter of a Canadian citizen, was actually refused admission to Canada in 1952 on the grounds of climate. Justifying his refusal, the minister responsible, Walter Harris, declared that newcomers from countries like Barbados "are more apt to break down in health than immigrants from countries where the climate is more akin to that of Canada."[19]

The year 1950 not only saw the government lowering immigration barriers another notch or two, it also saw the establishment of the Department of Citizenship and Immigration with Walter Harris as its first minister. No longer was immigration to be the responsibility of a multifunction department whose other activities bore little relation to immigration. Instead, responsibility for immigration was assigned to a newly created ministry, which had two major branches, the Immigration Branch and the Citizenship Branch. Such a move was considered essential if immigration was to receive the recognition and attention that it warranted. Politicians, however, have never sought the Citizenship and Immigration portfolio. For them it has always held the danger that new measures might lose them votes among ethnic groups in their constituencies, or that immigration itself might get out of control and become a political battleground.

Close on the heels of these developments in 1950 came a further liberalization of regulations, which enlarged the admissible classes of Asiatics to include the husbands of Canadian citizens and unmarried children up to the age of majority. Regulations also eased the way for German nationals to enter the country. This development resulted in large part from pressure exerted on the government by Canadian German ethnic organizations and by church groups, such as the influential Canadian Christian Council for Resettlement of Refugees (CCCRR), an umbrella organization representing Lutheran, Mennonite, Baptist, and Roman Catholic groups of predominantly Germanic origin. It had already assisted thousands of ethnic Germans to come to Canada and would aid many more in the next few years.

The door was widened still further when agreements were signed in 1951 with the governments of India, Pakistan, and Ceylon, whereby Canada agreed to accept limited numbers of their citizens as immigrants, over and above any who might be accepted under the regulations governing the entry of Asiatics.

THE 1952 IMMIGRATION ACT

The long-awaited new Immigration Act was finally passed in 1952, but not before some interested observers voiced their hopes for the legislation. One of these was Alistair Stewart, the MP for Winnipeg North. Addressing the House of Commons, he expressed a principal concern of many immigration advocates when he said that he hoped the new bill would foreshadow "an immigration policy in Canada."[20]

As it turned out, the new act, which came into effect on June 1, 1952, did nothing to satisfy Mr. Stewart's hopes for the development of a coherent immigration policy. But in its major provisions, this act did simplify the administration of immigration and it did define the wide-ranging powers of the minister and his officials regarding the selection, admission, and deportation of immigrants.

Concerning the selection and admission of prospective immigrants, the act vested all-embracing powers in the governor-in-council (i.e., the cabinet) to prohibit or limit the admission of persons by reason of such factors as nationality, ethnic group, occupation, lifestyle, unsuitability with regard to Canada's climate, and perceived inability to become readily assimilated into Canadian society.[21] Included in the act's basic provisions was one that authorized the granting of loans to immigrants to cover the costs of transportation and expenses en route. This last provision was put to good use the following year when the government implemented the Assisted Passage Loan Scheme to aid Europeans who had skills urgently needed in Canada but who could not pay the full costs of transportation to this country.

Much more significant, however, was the provision of the act that vested a large degree of uncontrolled discretionary power in the minister and his officials. It would have far-reaching, often negative, implications for Canadian immigration. But when used creatively and responsibly, it could be an invaluable tool in assisting desirable and/or humanitarian immigration. As John Manion, who was deputy minister of employment and immigration from 1977 to 1979, later remarked, "While they [the Immigration Act of 1952 and Regulations] facilitated the entry of carefully selected people, after due process, God help those who had not followed due process or encountered one of the statutory provisions, or were otherwise found wanting."[22]

Among those ministers who employed the act to good purpose was J.W. Pickersgill, the flamboyant, fiercely partisan Liberal who abandoned an academic career for a stint in the federal public service and then politics. When he was minister of citizenship and immigration (1954–57), Jack Pickersgill demonstrated clearly that he was prepared to use his ministerial powers to make fundamental changes in immigration policy. On different occasions, for example, he announced that he would waive immigration regulations and approve the admission, under minister's permits, of epileptics whose condition could be controlled by drugs, tubercular cases, and people who had a previous history of mental illness, provided these cases posed no danger to the community and were adequately sponsored.[23]

The Palestinian Refugees

It was while Jack Pickersgill was minister of citizenship and immigration that Canada took the bold step of admitting some Palestinian Arabs displaced as a result of the Israeli-Arab war in 1948. In 1955, when the idea for such a scheme was conceived, there were over 900,000 such refugees living in Lebanon, Syria, Jordan, and Gaza, where they

National archives of Canada, PA147725.

*J.W. Pickersgill (right) with Dean of faculty of forestry engineering
at the University of Sopron, Montreal, 1957.*

served as pawns in inter-Arab machinations and posed a dangerous
threat to the delicate political balance in the Middle East.

The resettlement of these refugees abroad was nothing if not a politically explosive issue in the Middle East. Canada's participation in any such
operation, therefore, meant that she risked incurring the wrath of Arabs,
who might charge that it was part of a Zionist plot to deprive Palestinian
refugees of UNRRA care and their right to return to Palestine.[24]
Nevertheless, in 1955, a young official at the Canadian legation in Beirut,
where UNRRA had its headquarters, approached that agency and obtained

its cooperation in arranging for a selection of Palestinian refugees to be interviewed by a Canadian immigration team.[25]

The following January a Canadian immigration mission visited Lebanon and Jordan, and from among 575 applicants presented to it by UNRRA it chose ninety-eight who were "apparently well qualified to become Canadian citizens." Eventually this number was trimmed to thirty-nine heads of families and their dependents and it was this group that set out for Canada in the summer of 1956. To the surprise of Canadian officials in Beirut, the operation did not trigger nearly as much opposition as they had anticipated from sources in the Arab world.[26]

Canada's acceptance of Palestinian refugees in this period has attracted little, if any, attention from historians. By contrast, this country's admission of close to 40,000 Hungarian refugees in 1956–57 has invited extensive coverage. What is sometimes overlooked, however, is how ingeniously Mr. Pickersgill and his officials used the 1952 Immigration Act's discretionary powers during this exciting chapter in Canada's immigration history.

The Hungarian Refugees

Canada's response to the Hungarian refugees represents one brief period of glory in the post-war Liberal government's handling of immigration and one of the few times in Canadian history when Canadians have wholeheartedly welcomed immigrants. The speed with which the Louis St. Laurent government acted, and the generous admission program that it launched, were not solely the result of government initiative, however. They can be attributed directly to the pressure created by the Canadian public, whose sympathies had been aroused by the plight of over 200,000 Hungarians fleeing their homeland after the brutal crushing of the Hungarian uprising by Russian tanks in November 1956.

Moved by the graphic depiction of the uprising and its defeat on television and by broadcast accounts of the General Assembly proceedings in New York, Canadians found themselves overcome with compassion for the liberty-seeking Hungarians. Among French Canadians this compassion, reinforced by sympathy for their Roman Catholic co-religionists, even succeeded in banishing traditional fears of immigration.

Besides, the Roman Catholic Church, in 1952, had officially expressed the view that "any regulations that would restrict, in an arbitrary manner, the emigration of ... refugees from persecuted lands would be contrary to the fundamental principles of justice and true peace."[27]

As the revolution unfolded, the coffers and facilities of Austria, where most of the refugees fled, became so taxed that an SOS soon went out for help. Among those Western nations that came under increasing pressure to accept some of the refugees for permanent resettlement was Canada. Fortunately for the refugees' cause this country was still experiencing a booming economy. The Canadian industrial complex, successfully converted from a wartime to a peacetime economy, was surging ahead, its momentum fuelled by increasing world trade, massive development projects, a growing population, and an expanding domestic market for manufactured goods. Only one short-lived economic downturn darkened the horizon in this period and that occurred in late 1955. At the time of the Suez crisis, which also unfolded that autumn, the economy was again buoyant and most Canadians were hard pressed to find economic reasons why they should not welcome more immigrants.

Important as economic factors were in creating the right climate for increased immigration, however, it was ultimately the Canadian public's reaction to events in Hungary that triggered the Canadian government's open-door policy in relation to the Hungarian refugees.

As is so often the case with such occurrences, the Hungarian uprising of October and November 1956 caught Ottawa and the Canadian public off guard. On November 6, 1956, after receiving news of developments in Austria, the minister of citizenship and immigration instructed Canada's immigration office in Vienna to hire additional staff, and to assign top priority to applications from Hungarians wishing to emigrate to Canada. At this juncture, however, none of the normal immigration procedures and provisions were waived or altered.[28]

In the view of many Canadians this rather cautious approach was not enough. Pressure steadily mounted outside the government and Parliament for a more energetic response. As a result of this lobbying, Ottawa decided to simplify all immigration procedures. Then, in the last week of November, Pickersgill initiated steps to charter a ship and aircraft to bring the first influx of refugees to Canada. Finally, the long-awaited breakthrough came. On November 28, two days after Parliament convened in a special session to debate the Hungarian and Suez situations, the minister of citizenship and immigration announced his government's intention to proceed with a generous admission program, the chief feature of which was free passage for all those Hungarian refugees who met this country's admission standards.

Jack Pickersgill, "commandant" of the Hungarian refugees' operation, flew to Austria after the House of Commons adjourned on November 29. In Europe, thanks to the discretionary powers vested in him by cabinet, he made a number of important "on the spot" decisions relating to the implementation of government policy, decisions all designed to facilitate the movement of refugees.

While all this was going on, the government had to cope with 108,989 British immigrants spurred to emigrate by the Eden government's inept handling of the Suez crisis, which had erupted just before the Soviet invasion of Hungary. Because of the large number of Britons and other Europeans headed for Canada, the Canadian government eventually launched an airlift program designated the "Air Bridge to Canada" or the ABC scheme. During the opening months of 1957 over 200 chartered flights brought nearly 17,600 immigrants to Canada, including many Hungarians, most of whom were young people.

Among the Hungarians was a sizeable group from the Faculty of Forest Engineering at the University of Sopron, some 350 students, professors, and families. The first group of this kind to emigrate to Canada, they travelled in a "freedom train" from Halifax to Vancouver, eliciting rousing receptions at stops across the country. Thanks to initiatives taken by Pickersgill, the forest faculty was incorporated into the University of British Columbia, where it functioned as the Sopron Division of the Faculty of Forestry until 1961. Another group associated with the University of Sopron's Faculty of Mining Engineering, approximately 150 people, went to the University of Toronto, where they were assimilated into a variety of faculties.

Never before had such a large number of refugees arrived in Canada in such a short time. Equally significant, the influx of Hungarians actually succeeded in uniting the House of Commons briefly on an immigration issue, a truly remarkable feat. The movement was also noteworthy for the degree of successful planning and management that it prompted on the part of Pickersgill's department; the collaboration that it obtained from the provinces and voluntary welfare groups; and the large number of young people and students that it contained.

Summing up the planning and management involved in the operation, the Department of Citizenship and Immigration noted that it had sole responsibility for the placement of Hungarian refugees and, pending their establishment, for ensuring that they had food and shelter. Through the generosity of voluntary groups and individuals a number of refugees were taken into private homes while others were placed in reception centres across the country. Those requiring medical treatment were cared for at government expense.[29]

In carrying out the resettlement of the Hungarian refugees (approximately one-third were settled west of the Great Lakes, one-third in Ontario and the remainder in Quebec and the Maritimes), the Department of Citizenship and Immigration succeeded in overcoming many restrictions inherent in the system. This would prove to be a breakthrough with far-reaching consequences because it paved the way for immigration authorities to respond more quickly and with more flexibility to later refugee and ordinary immigration movements.

THE DOWNTURN IN IMMIGRATION

Despite a downturn in the Canadian economy, immigration to Canada in 1957 was higher than in any year since 1913–14: 282,164. The influx of 37,000 Hungarian refugees, and the huge number of Britons who emigrated to Canada that year, contributed significantly to this dramatic figure. But there were also other factors at work, including the burgeoning numbers of sponsored immigrants and the strenuous promotion of unsponsored immigration.

As the Canadian economy became more and more sluggish, the newly elected Progressive Conservative government turned off the tap. As a result, immigration dropped off sharply. Starting in 1958–59, it plunged to 124,851, then to 106,928 in 1959–60. Not until 1962 did it turn upward again, one year after British immigration skidded to its lowest level since the war.

THE NEW WAVE OF IMMIGRANTS

Unlike the newcomers in the earlier boom period of Canadian immigration, 1900 to 1914, the new arrivals in the late 1940s and the 1950s were a more heterogeneous body, with a greater diversity of skills and training and widely varied intended occupations, which were by and large more urban than rural in character. They came to a country where, in the picturesque phrases of the Senate Standing Committee on Immigration and Labour, the economy had changed greatly since the early immigrants "laid axe to tree or struck long furrows in the Middle West."[30] By 1957, the end of this post-war boom period in Canadian immigration, Canada, which now included Newfoundland, boasted a population of over 16 million people and ranked as a major industrial nation, with manufacturing providing its major source of income and employment. It was, therefore, the urbanized and industrialized provinces — Ontario, Quebec, Alberta, and British Columbia — that benefited most from this immigration.

During this period Canada invested more effort in recruiting immigrants in the United Kingdom than in any other country. As a result, the U.K. and the United States continued to furnish large numbers of newcomers. But no longer were they the predominant sources of immigrants. Now the majority of Canada's new arrivals were being supplied by continental Europe, especially Germany, Italy, and the Netherlands. In fact, even before the liberalization of Canadian immigration regulations in 1950, thousands of Dutch farm families and single agriculturalists came to Canada under the auspices of the "Netherlands Farm Families Movement," an immigration scheme worked out by the Canadian and Dutch governments.

Although immigration assumed increasing importance from 1950 to 1957, there was still no consensus on the role that it should play in Canadian society. Furthermore, despite being a nation of immigrants, Canadians were by and large reluctant to welcome new arrivals in their midst. As one illustration of this, a 1954 poll revealed that just 45 percent of Canadians looked favourably on immigration. Unlike those opposed to immigration, these outward-looking Canadians shared the views of immigration advocates like the noted Canadian economist Dr. Mabel Timlin. In a 1951 monograph she argued cogently for more immigration, claiming that a larger population would result in greater productivity and hence higher incomes for Canadians.[31]

Part of the widespread opposition to increased immigration was fed by the perennial fear of French Canadians that a flood of new immigrants would undermine their minority position in Canada. In September 1948, the federal government, in the hopes of satisfying French-Canadian members of the Liberal caucus as well as French-Canadian opinion in general, placed French nationals on the same footing as British and American citizens for purposes of entry into Canada. Federal civil servants, however, put the brakes on the new policy, insisting that a large proportion of prospective French immigrants were either former Nazi collaborators or Communists.[32] Partly as a result of this the new policy had little effect.

Notwithstanding the lack of consensus in Canada about the desirability of immigration, there could be no gainsaying the fact that it had made an invaluable contribution in the 1940s and 1950s to the size and quality of the Canadian labour force. It accounted for two-thirds of the labour force's increase between 1950 and 1955 and for almost half the total increase between 1950 and 1960. In fact, many of the new professional and new skilled jobs were filled by immigrants — at an enormous saving in national outlay on professional and educational training in Canada.

Still, there were serious problems associated with this new immigration. One involved the swelling numbers of sponsored immigrants brought here by relatives eager to see them share in Canada's economic opportunities. As luck would have it, however, many of these new arrivals were unskilled and often nearly illiterate, manual labourers from southern Europe, ill equipped to enter the Canadian work force and share in Canada's bounties. Not only did they lack marketable skills, they helped to create a backlog in the processing system. After John Diefenbaker's Conservative government came to power in 1957, attempts would be made to restrict the admissible classes of relatives and thereby control the largely unchecked sponsored movement. This question, and others, however, would remain thorny, volatile issues for years to come.

— CHAPTER 9 —

Major New Initiatives

D URING THE BOOM PERIOD, 1947–57, the Liberals gradually eased immigration restrictions to admit not only unsponsored refugees and displaced persons but ordinary immigrants from a growing number of countries. This was always done, however, with a view to preserving the fundamental character of the Canadian population. Access from countries other than those that belonged to the "old" Commonwealth, the United States, and Europe was severely restricted, because the Liberals, under Mackenzie King and Louis St. Laurent, were not prepared to abolish Canada's racist immigration policy. The nominal credit for this achievement belongs to the Progressive Conservatives, who toppled the Grits in the federal election of June 10, 1957 after a twenty-two-year absence from the government benches.

Nothing that John Diefenbaker and the Conservatives did during their first years in office, however, presaged a bold departure in immigration policy. True, Diefenbaker assigned a vital role to immigration in Canada's development when he was campaigning in the 1957 federal contest. Referring to the illiberal 1952 Immigration Act, "the Chief" announced, "We will overhaul the act's administration to ensure that humanity will be considered and put an end to the bureaucratic interpretations which keep out from Canada many potentially good citizens."[1] He also returned to the subject of immigration in an interview given to a *U.S. News and World Report* journalist, published shortly after the Conservative Party's landslide victory on March 31, 1958. At that time he confidently predicted that Canada's population would reach 40 million in the foreseeable future, provided the federal government pursued a vigorous immigration policy.

"Canada must populate or perish", declared the prime minister in one of his typical, rhetorical flourishes.[2] However, despite public pronouncements such as these to journalists and gatherings of ethnic groups, the combative Saskatchewan lawyer was not really interested in immigration. Nor were most other members of his cabinet. Perhaps because of this, the uninfluential Citizenship and Immigration portfolio was assigned, in May 1958, to someone Diefenbaker mistakenly thought would serve as a caretaker minister. She was

Ellen Fairclough. Photo by A. Roy.

Ellen Fairclough, the vivacious MP from Hamilton, Ontario, who became Canada's first woman federal cabinet minister in 1957 when the prime minister appointed her Secretary of State during his first term in office. A chartered accountant by profession, Ellen Fairclough presided over the fortunes of Citizenship and Immigration for four years and three months, longer than any other minister to date, with the exception of Walter Harris. After leaving the portfolio in August 1962 she went on to become postmaster general but was then defeated in the 1963 federal election.

Attempts to Curb the Sponsored Movement

Regrettably, Mrs. Fairclough's own political fortunes took a drubbing during her first two years at Citizenship and Immigration, largely because of pitfalls triggered by the deepening recession and Ottawa's growing concern about the large influx of unskilled sponsored workers and sponsored family members without paid employment. In 1958, when the number of jobless was mounting steadily in Canada, the newly installed Conservative government slammed the brakes on immigration by means of a new policy designed to prevent visitors to Canada from accepting unauthorized employment. The government also decided that prospective immigrants must apply from their own country for landed immigrant status.

Then, on March 19, 1959, less than a year after Mrs. Fairclough became minister of Citizenship and Immigration, the government embarked on a brave attempt to control the escalating sponsorship movement, made up largely of unskilled Italian relatives from southern Italy. By concentrating on the admission of close relatives of earlier immigrants, Canada had ensured a continuing influx of unskilled immigrants from the south of Italy at the expense of skilled, unsponsored immigrants from the north of the country.[3] It was a situation that Mrs. Fairclough's department wanted to see corrected and it decided to initiate action at a time when Italian immigration was still showing healthy numbers, in 1959. In fact, while total immigration to Canada had declined about 15 percent from 1958 to 1959, Italian immigration had fallen off only about 5 percent, from 27,000 to approximately 25,600.

Without warning, on March 19, 1959, the government issued P.C 1959/310, designed to restrict the admissible classes of close relatives so that individuals no longer admissible as close relatives would be considered together with unsponsored immigrants and the educational level of Italian immigration thereby raised. Amending the immigration regulations contained in P.C. 1954–1351 of September 17, 1954, it stipulated that Canadian citizens or legal residents of Canada could no longer sponsor relatives from Egypt or brothers and sisters and married sons and daughters from any country of Europe, North America, Latin America, Lebanon, Turkey, and Israel. The key clause was the one that restricted the admission of relatives to the immediate family, for its enforcement held out hope that the government could finally curtail the chain migration of unskilled relatives and check the too rapid growth of ethnic neighbourhoods with all their attendant social and economic problems. Control of the sponsored movement, especially as it applied to Italian immigration, was not going to be achieved by this particular device, however.

When the new regulation was announced a month later, a storm of protest arose from the Liberal opposition and Canada's ethnic communities. Especially vocal were the Italian Canadians, who had been sponsoring large numbers of relatives in the post-war period and who were well represented in Mrs. Fairclough's own riding. Defending her government's action, the minister informed the House of Commons that the backlog of sponsored applicants had grown from some 77,158 as of December 31, 1955 to 131,785 as of February 28, 1959. In Italy alone the numbers had soared from approximately 12,000 at the end of 1954 and 23,000 at the end of 1955 to about 63,000 as of February 28, 1959.[4]

Observed the embattled Mrs. Fairclough:

> I may say that if we start now to deal with all the applications, or continue to deal with those applications which are now on hand, at a rough estimate it will take two and one half to three years to handle them. It is possible now to accept as unsponsored applications those which were formerly sponsored. Taking into account these two sets of circumstances I cannot see how the regulation can be called discriminatory, a word which has been bandied about quite a bit lately. I do believe, though, Mr. Speaker, that discrimination existed in the past in that well qualified Italians who wished to migrate to this country had little or no chance of having their applications considered unless they were in the sponsored categories. "Cruel," my hon. friend says. What is more cruel than deliberately to misconstrue and misrepresent the intention of the recent amendment?[5]

In the face of all the uproar and a lack of support in cabinet, Mrs. Fairclough backed down and on April 22, 1959 rescinded the new regulation. Under no circumstances, it seems, would an enraged Diefenbaker brook charges of discrimination against his government, especially when they were mounted in the House of Commons by Ellen Fairclough's Liberal predecessor, feisty Jack Pickersgill. Thoroughly intimidated by the furor that it had aroused, the government abandoned any further thought of early legislative changes to immigration policy. In the fall of 1960, it would announce its intention to produce a new immigration act, but then fail to do so.

With the deleted classes restored, the sponsored movement contin-ued to mushroom until mid-1960, when it became evident that immi-gration from Italy would outstrip immigration from Great Britain for the third consecutive year. When faced by this prospect, Mrs. Fairclough's department renewed its efforts to curb the growth of the sponsored pro-gram. To reduce the numbers, it once again attempted to make adminis-trative adjustments. These called for sponsored relatives to be divided into five processing categories, with married children, brothers, and sis-ters of permanent residents receiving the lowest priority, and for the quality of settlement arrangements offered by the sponsor to be graded. These changes achieved the desired results and remained in effect, with minor modifications, until 1964.

WORLD REFUGEE YEAR, 1959–60

Her department's thwarted attempts, in early 1959, to restrict the number of sponsored immigrants cost Mrs. Fairclough much in the way of polit-ical capital. But despite this, the spirited minister was still prepared to tackle difficult issues and run political risks. In 1959–60, for example, she allowed 325 tubercular refugees and members of their families to be admitted to Canada as part of this country's contribution to World Refugee Year. It was a courageous move, given the fact that Canadian enthusiasm for refugee immigration had abated considerably since the arrival of the Hungarians two years earlier. The presence of die-hard Communists and other undesirables in the Hungarian influx had done much to re-awaken latent anti-immigration sentiment across the country.

Canada's decision to admit the refugees represented a major break-through in immigration policy, for illiberal and strictly enforced Canadian regulations did not, of course, permit the entry of individuals with infirmities, even on humanitarian grounds. Although internation-al agencies had tried repeatedly to persuade Canada to accept more "hard-core" (i.e., unsponsored, disabled, or ill) refugees, this country had steadfastly refused to commit itself to accepting such people.

In opposition to this inflexible attitude were Canadian church and charitable organizations, some newspaper editorialists, and a few members

National Archives of Canada, PA 181041

Ellen Fairclough receives a kiss from a refugee accepted by Canada in World Refugee Year, 1959.

of Parliament. Notable among the MPs was Stewart Fleming, the MP for Okanagan-Revelstoke, who mounted a forceful campaign to have the government accept a portion of Europe's TB refugees. As part of his lobbying efforts, Fleming informed Mrs. Fairclough and the House of Commons that certain UN countries had waived regulations classifying such refugees as inadmissible and had introduced special programs to take care of them.

"Probably the best example of this is the program undertaken by Sweden and Denmark in conjunction with each other, in which they took 200 difficult cases and provided for them under a special program", he reported.[6] Noting that these individuals had been successfully cured and integrated into their local communities, Mr. Fleming continued:

> I would suggest that perhaps Canada is in a better posi-
> tion than most nations to undertake a program on
> behalf of tubercular cases in particular. If my informa-
> tion is correct, the incidence of tuberculosis in Canada
> has been considerably reduced in recent years, so much
> so that in one province at least a sanatorium that had
> been in operation for a great many years has been
> closed, since it is no longer necessary, and other similar
> institutions are operating at less than capacity in other
> parts of the country ... I feel, therefore, that Canada
> should join with Sweden, Denmark, Belgium, France,
> Italy and some of the other countries that have recog-
> nized the difficult situation of these refugees and insti-
> tute on a trial basis ... a program designed to provide
> for the difficult cases and in particular those who are
> suffering from tuberculosis.[7]

Initially, Mrs. Fairclough resisted the idea of admitting hard-core refugees to Canada but eventually she changed her mind. As a result, Canada admitted 325 tubercular refugees and 501 members of their families during World Refugee Year. They were among a total of 6,912 refugees admitted that year, which saw seventy countries intensify their efforts to close down the world's refugee camps and rehabilitate count-less thousands of despairing people without a country. The refugees who arrived in Canada came from many parts of Europe, although the majority were Polish, Ukrainian, and Yugoslavian.

Special humanitarian measures such as Canada's contribution to the UN-sponsored World Refugee Year were among the few bright spots in an otherwise gloomy immigration picture during most of the period Ellen Fairclough was minister of citizenship and immigration. Because of a buoyant economy in Europe, the economic recession in Canada, and the government's efforts to discourage the entry of unskilled workers, immigration fell off drastically in these years, plunging to 71,689 in 1961, its lowest level since 1947. As the Canadian economy continued on its sluggish course, unions clamoured for a decrease in immigration and the government set about reducing the number of immigration officers staffing Canadian immigration offices abroad.

Another sour note was struck by the arrival of soaring numbers of unqualified people, who sought to circumvent the criteria for unsponsored immigrants. After entering Canada as visitors, they contacted influential people or organizations and then applied to stay permanently. This seemingly intractable problem was overshadowed by large-scale illegal Chinese immigration, aided and abetted by a Hong Kong-based industry that purchased and sold false identities. In an attempt to deal with the question of illegal Chinese immigration, the government, in June 1960, announced an amnesty for all Chinese who had entered the country illegally before July 1, 1960. But although many thousands of "illegals" did come forward and declare themselves, the program did not succeed in banishing illegal immigration rings.

During her term as minister of citizenship and immigration, Ellen Fairclough also saw the unwelcome reverse side of immigration come to the fore. Disillusioned by their experiences in Canada, and by the lack of job opportunities here, one in every three or four immigrants either returned to his or her country of origin or emigrated to the United States. Especially worrisome to Canadians was the movement southward of thousands of native-born Canadians, many of whom were well-educated and intelligent members of the professional and business classes. In 1961, an estimated 25 percent of the wage-earners among the 70,553 Canadians who left for the U.S. were professionals and managers.[8] There had always been a large annual exodus to Canada's neighbour south of the border, but what made the issue so significant in the 1960s was the increasingly high proportion of emigrants that this country could ill afford to lose. Doctors, trained businessmen, university professors, and scientists were leaving Canada in greater numbers than ever before. Not until the time of the Vietnam War and race riots in the United States would there be a reversal of this "brain drain" and then it would be only temporary.

Notwithstanding the gloomy immigration scene in the late fifties and early sixties, Ellen Fairclough made a significant contribution to her department during the turbulent years that she was at its helm. One knowledgeable observer impressed by her performance was Prof. David Corbett, the noted Canadian immigration expert. Writing in the *International Journal*, he praised Mrs. Fairclough for her "flexible interpretation of regulations and liberal use of ministerial powers" and applauded the "steady improvement of the Immigration Service and its procedures"[9] under the minister. In addition to these accomplishments, however, was an achievement of even greater significance: a long overdue and radical reform that virtually abolished the White Canada immigration policy.

It was introduced to the public on January 19, 1962 when Ellen Fairclough tabled new regulations in the House that eliminated racial discrimination as a major feature of Canada's immigration policy. Henceforth any unsponsored immigrants who could satisfy the Department of Citizenship and Immigration that they had the requisite education, skill, or other qualifications were to be considered suitable for admission, irrespective of race, colour, or national origin, provided they were able to support themselves until they found employment or were coming to take a specific job. In only one respect did the new regulations retain any vestiges of discrimination and that was in the provision that allowed European immigrants and immigrants from the Americas to sponsor a wider range of relatives. Inserted at the last moment because of a fear that there would be an influx of relatives from India, this clause would be removed five years later in the immigration regulations of 1967.

When the new regulations were implemented on February 1, 1962, Canada became the first of the three large receiving countries in international migration — the others being the United States and Australia — to dismantle her discriminatory immigration policy. In 1975, the United States embarked on a similar course, introducing the Kennedy amendments to the Immigration Act, which came into effect in 1978. Gough Whitlam, the Australian prime minister, abolished the White Australia policy in November 1973 by simply announcing that it was at an end.[10]

The new regulations introduced by Mrs. Fairclough before she left the Department of Citizenship and Immigration were foreshadowed by the Bill of Rights that John Diefenbaker presented so proudly in 1960.

Since the bill rejected discrimination by reason of race, colour, national origin, religion, or sex, the government could no longer justify selecting immigrants on the basis of race or national origin. Moreover, the long-standing discriminatory provisions now seemed anachronistic and untenable in an era when racism was coming under attack.

Among those influential Canadians keenly aware of this was Dr. George Davidson, Mrs. Fairclough's deputy minister and one-time executive director of the Canadian Welfare Council. Realizing that Canada's discriminatory immigration provisions hampered her operations in the United Nations and the multiracial Commonwealth, he and other senior Canadian officials lobbied for their removal. Their efforts bore fruit when the cabinet decided to introduce the new immigration regulations that banished racial discrimination from Canadian immigration policy. With this move, the Diefenbaker government virtually abolished the White Canada policy, a policy that had been clearly sanctioned and pursued by every Canadian prime minister from John A. Macdonald to Louis St. Laurent, the courtly corporation lawyer from Quebec City.

The decision to embody the new immigration policy in regulations rather than in statutes was dictated purely by political expediency. For, as noted earlier, regulations can be implemented quickly, while a new, complex immigration act — something promised repeatedly by the Conservatives — requires time to steer through Parliament. This last point was alluded to by David Corbett, who greeted the new regulations enthusiastically. He congratulated Ellen Fairclough for placing "immigration policy in its proper context as part of foreign policy" and speculated that the new regulations were ahead of public opinion and more liberal than those the minister could have obtained had she tabled a new immigration act.[11]

Certain parliamentarians, however, were far less sanguine about the new policy and the method employed to introduce it. In the House the attack was led, as might be expected, by Jack Pickersgill. Speaking immediately after Mrs Fairclough announced the new regulations, Pickersgill declared:

> The hon. lady has said that the new section 31, which is substituted for section 20 of the existing regulations,

abolishes discrimination. Of course it does nothing of the kind. It substitutes one set of criteria for discrimination for another. I am one of those who think that the words "discrimination" and "selection", as any dictionary shows, mean precisely the same thing, and they cannot mean anything different ... I suggest that what the hon. lady has done is to make it necessary to look at every individual case and compare it with every other case, and that by abolishing some of the convenient general categories she is going to create an administrative problem that it will be absolutely impossible to cope with if we are to have any substantial immigration. Of course, if the pattern of 1961 is to be followed, when we had a net emigration from this country, it is probable that the new regulations are well designed to serve that end.[12]

The method used to introduce the new policy came in for stinging criticism from Leon Crestohl, a lawyer and the Liberal member for Montreal Cartier. Said Crestohl: "I find no precedent for a government dealing so evasively with such a serious matter when a different course had been promised, not only to Parliament but to the people of Canada. The production of a new set of immigration regulations instead of a revision of the Immigration Act is, I consider, an affront to the rights of Parliament, to the press of Canada and indeed to the people of the entire country."[13]

Pickersgill's reference to discrimination was echoed by Charles H. Millard, a former director of the International Confederation of Free Trade Unions. He noted that if Canada recruited only skilled immigrants — the sort of people in shortest supply in Third World countries — she would be guilty of "poaching". He took the position, as did a series of *Globe and Mail* editorials, that Canada should admit a substantial number of unskilled immigrants and assume responsibility for training them. "We maintain a position of doubtful international morality", intoned the *Globe*, "while we rattle around in an empty country while the world's masses cry for living room."[14]

The government's venture into a new era of openness in immigration started to be reflected in immigration statistics in 1963, the year that the economy began to recover. During the first nine months of 1963 immigration from non-European areas increased substantially compared with the same period in 1962. From Africa (excluding South Africa, Rhodesia — now called Zimbabwe — and Nyasaland), 264 (104); from the West Indies 1,132 (427); from the Middle East, 1,995 (1,460) and from South America, 424 (201).[15]

Thanks to the new regulations, coloured West Indians began to enter the country in significant numbers after 1962. Their numbers increased from 1,000 to 2,000 a year before 1962 to between 2,200 and 3,700 from 1963 to 1966, and with the implementation of the points system (described later in this chapter) to almost 8,000 in 1967 and 1968, 14,250 in 1969, and 13,600 in 1970.[16] The West Indians concentrated for the most part in Toronto and to a lesser extent in Montreal, where they worked chiefly in Canada's expanding manufacturing, construction, and service sectors.

"BELL'S RESURRECTION"

Richard Bell, the decisive minister who succeeded Ellen Fairclough in the citizenship and immigration portfolio on August 9, 1962, was a true believer in immigration. Time and time again he sought to persuade his fellow MPs that immigration is a stimulus to the economy and a powerful tool in nation building. "I reject completely any tap on, tap off policy or any attempt to relate long-range immigration objectives to immediate changes in our economic climate," stated Bell on September 25, 1967, over four years after he had left the citizenship and immigration portfolio.[17] Richard Bell was therefore expressing his own enthusiasm for the cause when, as minister, he suggested to a Toronto audience, on November 18, 1962, that annual immigration should be increased to a rate equivalent to 1 percent of Canada's population.[18] Under questioning in the House of Commons the next day, however, he explained that he had made "no statement of new policy, but a simple statement of what are appropriate targets and objectives." New policy or not, Bell decided to inject new vigour into his department. Despite continuing high unemployment and the cabinet's anti-immigration stance, he instructed his department to oil the machinery and re-open the doors to immigration. New staff were appointed to London posts and a senior official was dispatched on a tour of visa offices in Europe with instructions to crank up operations again. Partly as a result of these steps, as well as of an upturn in the Canadian economy, immigration figures began to rise. Richard Bell, the member from Ottawa-Carleton, had presided over a veritable resurrection.

Nevertheless, bold new initiatives had to await the return of the Liberals to office. When they formed a government in 1963 under Lester B. Pearson it was evident that the Canadian economy was undergoing marked change. The quickening pace of technological innovation had resulted in certain acquired skills becoming obsolete and in workers requiring periodic training to keep up with technology. Moreover, despite improved economic conditions, the level of unemployment still remained unacceptably high. Even more disturbing was the impressive number of unskilled, under-educated workers among the unemployed; they constituted the largest single component of this reservoir of unutilized labour.

These harsh economic realities would have a bearing not only on worker training but also on immigration policy. Where the latter was concerned, they led to an increased emphasis being placed on the skills and personal attributes of prospective immigrants and to a determination to control the growth of the large sponsored movement with its disproportionate numbers of unskilled and undereducated workers.

These concerns, coupled with the perennial problem of visitors applying for immigrant status, persuaded the government to undertake a sweeping review of all aspects of immigration. One result was the White Paper of 1966, prepared by the Department of Citizenship and Immigration. Released in October 1966, it was largely a defence of existing immigration policy. "Immigration", claimed the paper, "has made a major contribution to the national objectives of maintaining a high rate of population and economic growth." Despite this expansionist position, however, the paper did propose a tightening of the sponsorship system, a recommendation that was later embodied in new immigration regulations.

The Sedgwick Report, drawn up by Joseph Sedgwick, Q.C., also resulted from the review. A one-man board of inquiry, he was commissioned by the government to study a series of highly controversial deportations and such related problems as those posed by visitors seeking to become landed immigrants. Chief among his recommendations was the one that led to the establishment of a completely independent immigration appeal board. Under the act, which came into force on November 13, 1967, the board was empowered to hear appeals against all deportation orders and, subject only to appeal to the Supreme Court of Canada on questions of law, to cancel or stay deportation for humanitarian and compassionate reasons as well as on legal grounds. The board could also consider appeals by some classes of sponsors whose applications to bring in relatives from outside Canada had been refused by immigration officials.

The Department of Manpower and Immigration

The establishment of the Department of Manpower and Immigration in 1966 was another important structural change instituted by the Liberals in this period. It came into being largely as a result of the government's mounting concern about the lack of unskilled workers in the Canadian labour force and the conviction that manpower development programs could play an important role in training the workers required by Canada's expanding economy. Signalling the government's intention to relate immigration more closely to the needs of the Canadian labour market, Prime Minister Pearson said of the proposed new department:

> The government has also decided that it would be a wise course to place immigration under the same minister dealing with manpower generally. Immigration policy must be administered in the interests of the country and of the immigrants themselves in a context that takes into account the entire position of employment, training and placement in Canada. The association of the various aspects of manpower policies under the same minister should make it easier to implement programs and to implement them more effectively.[19]

Among those who criticized this approach to immigration was Richard Bell, who launched a vigorous attack on the government for its decision to place immigration and manpower under the same minister. Speaking from his experience as a former minister, he deplored the government's intention to submerge immigration in what was essentially a labour portfolio, noting that those branches of the Department of Labour that were to be integrated with immigration had consistently sought a decrease in immigration. Bell, always a staunch proponent of immigration, also pressed home the point that those countries which had separate immigration portfolios were "much ahead, in relation to immigration policy, of those that combine immigration with labour."[20] When he moved in the House to defeat the government's intention to set up a department of manpower and to establish instead a department of citizenship and immigration, relieved of its responsibilities for Indian affairs, he attracted some notable support. Interestingly enough, some of this came from Michael Starr, who was minister of labour for five and a half years during the Diefenbaker era.

Starr began by denouncing the dismemberment of the Department of Labour and then went on to criticize the establishment of a new department of manpower and the separation of citizenship from immigration. In opposing the government's course of action, the MP raised questions that have enduring relevance for any discussion of the role of immigration in Canadian society. Asked Starr:

> Is immigration not important enough to warrant the full-time attention of a minister? Are immigration criteria to be established purely and solely on the basis of the demands of the labour market? … Are we going back to the days when immigrants were allowed in according to the demand for labour? … Surely in immigration other factors have to be considered. Surely the very important humanitarian factors must be considered.[21]

Responding to Bell, Starr, and other critics, Jean Marchand, the minister, replied:

Immigration must surely, but not exclusively, be related in some way to the requirements of the labour market. Besides, when we ask immigrants to come to Canada, we are dealing with men who have relatives here and who want to make a living in our country. I feel that to restrict immigration exclusively to the requirements of the labour market in Canada would make for an inhuman and unacceptable policy. It is not our intention, therefore, to restrict immigration in this manner. Besides, I hope we shall be in a position very shortly to introduce in the house amendments which will no doubt enable the member for Carleton to sleep peacefully and to feel reassured about Canada's future.[22]

While defending the establishment of the proposed department of manpower, Jean Marchand informed the House that he was prepared to accept a suggestion that its name be changed. Accordingly he moved that the new department be known as the Department of Manpower and Immigration. When the motion was carried by unanimous consent, the way was paved for the hybrid department to come into official existence on October 1, 1966.

Jean Marchand's right-hand man in the Department of Manpower and Immigration was Tom Kent, the English-born, Oxford-educated public servant who had been a prominent British and Canadian journalist and a Montreal business executive before joining the federal public service in 1961 as a special consultant to Lester Pearson. During his two-year stint as deputy minister some far-reaching reforms took place in Canadian immigration policy, most notably the introduction of the much-vaunted points system. As the chief force behind its institution, Tom Kent deserves credit for one of the most significant developments in the management of Canadian immigration policy.

When Kent arrived in the de facto Department of Manpower and Immigration in January 1966, he found an imprecisely defined immigration policy and only vague guidelines for implementing it. In brief, this policy sought to promote a flow of immigration in line with the "absorptive capacity" of the country and to facilitate the reunion of families already established here. It also encouraged the acceptance of unsponsored immigrants who could adapt readily to Canadian life and the entry of refugees in such numbers as not to place too great a strain on Canadian resources. In Tom Kent's words, "That was about as definite as the political statement of purpose could be."[23]

THE POINTS SYSTEM

Given this state of affairs and the virtual abolition of the White Canada immigration policy, the deputy minister decided that some objective and fair system had to be devised to select unsponsored immigrants. To date, examining immigration officers had recourse to only one precise criterion when assessing an applicant's suitability: education. Normally eleven years of schooling was a necessary, but not a sufficient, condition. The rest was left up to the immigration officer, whose decision was based on his or her judgment of the candidate's personality and work experience in relation to occupational demands in the intended area of settlement.

But the situation had changed. Race and nationality no longer entered the question and Kent wanted to see an unassailable selection method that did away with caprice and prejudice.

"The problem was not unlike, in principle, that involved in the comparative evaluation of jobs. Why not try similar methods? If we could identify and define the various factors affecting a person's ability to settle successfully in Canada, and attach relative weights to them, then immigration officers would have a consistent basis on which to assess potential immigrants."[24]

With this goal in mind, Kent instructed some senior immigration officials to devise a selection system that would meet these requirements. The widely acclaimed product of their labours was the so-called points system, whereby immigration officers assign points up to a fixed maximum in each of nine categories, including education, employment opportunities in Canada, age, the individual's personal characteristics, and degree of fluency in English or French. As is the case with most examinations, fifty points out of a possible hundred earn a candidate a passing mark.

Ethnic groups and the press reacted for the most part favourably to the government's announcement of the new selection method. But there were detractors. In Parliament, for example, Richard Bell made a pitch for the old "eyeball" system and more flexibility in selection procedures.

> While it is certainly true that the more heavily developed and industrialized regions of Canada may require more skilled and fewer unskilled immigrants, the less developed areas of Canada actually require more unskilled and semiskilled immigrants ... It does not seem to me that the new regulations adopting the points system are adequate or flexible enough to meet this point of view. In many ways I would prefer what I have heard described as the old "eyeball" system. The hon. gentleman from Greenwood was worried that he might not be admitted to Canada if suddenly he were confronted by an immigration officer who, looking him over and applying the points system, sought to describe him. For myself, Mr. Chairman, I like the eyeball system. I believe in the judgment of the individual by the properly trained immigration officer.[25]

Since it dramatically reduces the power of the individual immigration officer to assess intangible qualities in a prospective immigrant, the points system has invited criticism along the lines set out by the late Richard Bell. In common with Bell, these detractors believe that this downplaying of the immigration officer's judgment is a weakness in the system that allows potentially good immigrants to be turned away. Still, because the method is easy to understand and implement, it has, by and large, proven popular with both immigrants and immigration officers.

It should be noted, though, that selection procedures are not the only determinant of what kinds of people come to Canada and in what numbers. Equally important are the location of Canadian immigration services and administrative delay (which has sometimes resulted from the elaborate security screening of potential immigrants by the RCMP).

When Tom Kent took up his duties in the Department of Citizenship and Immigration, Canada's immigration services could cope reasonably well with the normal volume of applicants in the United States, the British Isles, and northern and western Europe. By contrast, in southern Europe and the rest of the world, Canadian facilities did not begin to match the interest shown in Canada as an emigration destination. At the request of Roland Michener, who was then Canada's high commissioner in New Delhi, Kent visited India to investigate the handling of immigration applications. At the High Commission he found a file room stacked high with unopened mail.[26] The points system was incorporated into the new immigration regulations of 1967, which also introduced three other new elements into immigration law:

- the elimination of discrimination based on nationality or race from all classes of immigrants;

- the reduction of the sponsored class to dependent relatives, and the establishment of a new class, nominated relatives, which included sons and daughters of any age or marital status, brothers and sisters, parents and grandparents, aunts, uncles, nephews, nieces and grandchildren likely to enter the work force; and

- the creation of a special provision that allowed visitors to apply for immigrant status while in Canada.[27]

Hard on the heels of the introduction of the new immigration regulations and the establishment of the Immigration Appeal Board came the passage of the Canada Manpower and Immigration Council Act (December 21, 1967). It provided for the setting up of a Canada Manpower and Immigration Council and four advisory boards, three of which dealt with adult occupational training, the adjustment of immigrants, and manpower and immigration research respectively.

As in other areas of life, the introduction of change can have unforeseen consequences. And nowhere is this more forcefully demonstrated than in the implementation of new and untried immigration laws and regulations. Initially, nothing very significant happened as a result of the new regulation permitting visitors to apply for immigrant status while in Canada (Section 34 of the Immigration Regulations of 1967). But within a couple of years it was clearly evident that Canada was receiving a steadily increasing number of visitors from the United States, Latin America, Europe, Asia, the Caribbean, and elsewhere. These newcomers had learned or had been told that the fastest way to circumvent normal immigration procedures was to travel to Canada, apply for landed immigrant status, and, if turned down, submit an appeal to the Immigration Appeal Board. The result was a sizeable backlog of cases before the board. By 1972, the situation had become critical and the Trudeau government was forced to take action.

But by this time, too, Canada had a highly respected and effective minister of immigration, Robert Andras. Not only would he grapple with problems posed by the immigration regulations of 1967, he would initiate an extensive review of Canadian immigration policies and practices, paving the way for the Immigration Act of 1976 and a new chapter in Canadian immigration.

— CHAPTER 10 —

A New Era in Immigration

ROBERT ANDRAS

T HE RAPID TURNOVER IN MINISTERS of manpower and immigration
during the first four years of the Pierre Trudeau administration did not
augur well for a sweeping revision of Canadian immigration policy. Nor
did the seriously troubled Canadian economy of the 1970s — a period
of high unemployment, severe inflation and slow productivity growth,
the fallout from energy price changes in the post-Organization of
Petroleum Exporting Countries (OPEC) world.[1]

Nevertheless, the prime minister paved the way for a dramatic and
sorely needed overhaul of Canadian immigration policy in November
1972 when he appointed Robert Andras minister of manpower and
immigration. Unlike his three immediate predecessors, Allan MacEachen,
Otto Lang, and Bryce Mackasey, Mr. Andras would oversee the production of not just a new immigration act but a radically new immigration
statute. This remarkable achievement can be explained by several factors,
not least of which was the minister's determination to obtain a forward-
looking new act despite the inevitable roadblocks to such a plan. The
cause also owed much to the fact that Robert Andras was an extremely
able minister with a strong voice in cabinet, who took on this challenge at
a time when there was general recognition that change in immigration
policy was long overdue.

A veteran of the Second World War, Robert Andras was president of
four automotive sales and car rental firms in Thunder Bay when he was
first elected to the House of Commons in 1965 as Liberal MP for Port
Arthur. He would be re-elected four more times before retiring from

politics in December 1979 for health reasons. When appointed minister of manpower and immigration with responsibility for the Unemployment Insurance Commission in November 1972, he had already held several cabinet positions, including minister responsible for housing, minister of state for urban affairs, and minister of corporate affairs. Fittingly, his appointment coincided with a period of rapidly increasing immigration. From 122,006 in 1972, immigration would climb to 184,200 in 1973 and then to 218,465 in 1974 before dipping to 187,881 in 1975 and 149,429 in 1976.[2]

Robert Andras, appointed minister of manpower and immigration in 1972.

Photo by John Evans Photo Ltd.

PRELIMINARY REFORMS

From the moment that he took over the manpower and immigration portfolio, Robert Andras realized that reform was urgently needed, not just in immigration policy, which had yet to accommodate the new levels of immigration and to shed outdated concepts, but also in the organization of his department. On both fronts he moved quickly. Where immigration policy was concerned, however, he had to postpone the introduction of a bold new immigration act until he had dealt with some pressing problems associated with the huge backlog of cases facing the Immigration Appeal Board.

The board's plight could be traced directly to a combination of factors working in concert. One was Section 34 of the 1967 immigration regulations that permitted visitors to apply for landed immigrant status within Canada. The other was the passage that same year of the Immigration

Appeal Board Act, which set up a new and fully independent appeal board and gave anyone who had been ordered deported the right to appeal to the board, no matter what his or her status was under the Immigration Act. Together these two developments set the stage for a dramatic increase in the numbers of people applying for landed immigrant status in Canada as travel agents and commercial operators around the world began to appreciate the opportunities furnished by the new legislation. In 1971, 40,000 of the 120,000 who had been accepted for landed immigrant status had applied in Canada, while in 1972 this fraction had risen significantly.[3]

Besides undermining the effectiveness of the selection process abroad, this route to landed immigrant status created a host of problems for the Immigration Appeal Board. Invariably those visitors who were refused landed immigrant status appealed to the board, confident that its case backlog would enable them to enjoy the benefits of legally admitted immigrants for several years, by which time political pressure from the ethnic community and sometimes even from the general public would make it extremely difficult for the government to deport them.

The end result was a staggering backlog of appeals, which sparked public attention in the early summer of 1972 when a visitor facing deportation proceedings committed suicide in Toronto. Jolted by these developments, the Department of Manpower and Immigration increased its field strength and reviewed the cases awaiting an immigration inquiry in an effort to reduce the board's case backlog. Thanks to this review, a majority of applicants were granted landed immigrant status. Still, the problem persisted. In fact, there was a dramatic surge in the flow of self-styled visitors to Canada, undoubtedly because many would-be immigrants, who would not qualify for entry under the points system, anticipated tighter controls in the future.

Accordingly, on November 3, 1972, just days after the federal election, Bryce Mackasey announced that the government had revoked Section 34 of the 1967 regulations permitting applications within Canada for landed immigrant status. This action was being taken, declared the minister, because of mounting evidence that Canada's immigration laws were being "flagrantly abused, particularly by unscrupulous racketeers who take advantage of the innocence and gullibility of many citizens from many countries."[4] Mackasey would shortly resign from cabinet, stung by criticism of his handling of immigration problems and the administration of the Unemployment Insurance Commission.

THE SYSTEM IN DANGER OF COLLAPSE

Such was the situation that greeted Robert Andras when he moved into Mackasey's hot seat in the cabinet changes announced on November 27. In an attempt to prevent the government from losing further control over immigration policy and the immigration program, he introduced additional housekeeping reforms. The first of these new regulations required registration of visitors staying in Canada for more than three months and employment visas for those wishing to obtain a job.

Despite both Mackasey's and Andras's initiatives, however, the fundamental problem inherent in the appeal system remained and new appeals continued to escalate. So daunting was the increase in appeals that in June 1973 Andras estimated that, given the appeal board's existing capacity and the rate at which it was receiving new appeals, the case backlog could reach between 25,000 and 30,000 by the end of the year. "That would mean, very simply", reported the minister, "that many persons who appealed a deportation order could count on a 20-year stay in Canada while awaiting the outcome."[5]

More drastic measures were obviously in order. They were taken on June 18, 1973 when the minister introduced legislation to amend the Immigration Appeal Board Act. Assented to on July 27, 1973, it contained provisions designed to clear up the board's current backlog of cases and to prevent a recurrence of the current crisis. Notable among these provisions was one that abolished the universal right of appeal to those persons to whom Canada had granted immigrant or visitor visas. In a striking departure from previous policy, one of the temporary amendments provided for an adjustment of status for those persons who had lived in Canada continuously (legally or illegally) since November 30, 1972 and who registered with an immigration officer within sixty days of the act's coming into force. These persons could apply for permanent residence and, if their application was turned down, appeal to the Immigration Appeal Board.

Referring to this particular provision, Andras commented: "In plain language, the choice facing all those eligible to apply for adjustment of status is this: Either to come forward within the 60 days allotted with immunity from prosecution, or to remain underground for the rest of their lives in Canada running the constant risk of detection and departure."[6]

The Adjustment of Status program was an amnesty in all but name, although it was never regarded in that light by the Liberal Party.[7] Still, this is not what is significant. What is important is that the new program was widely supported by all political parties. Furthermore, it was a conspicuous success, resulting in some 39,000 people from more than 150 countries obtaining landed immigrant status.[8] Little did observers realize, however, that the crisis that precipitated these reforms was just a small foretaste of a much greater problem that would develop in the 1980s. In that turbulent decade the spiralling numbers of refugee claimants would play havoc with the immigration system and unleash a heated debate about the government's handling of immigration and refugees.

THE GREEN PAPER OF 1975

Important as these reforms were, they only laid the groundwork for the bold new immigration act that Robert Andras and his deputy minister, Allan Gotlieb, had been mapping. Radically new legislation was desperately needed as the realities of modern-day Canada had long since overtaken the Immigration Act of 1952. With roots in the nineteenth century, this statute was an outdated piece of legislation that had been conceived essentially as a gatekeeper's act. As such, it was principally concerned with listing the kinds of people who should be refused admission to Canada, and with outlining mechanisms for controlling the entry into this country or stays of persons who had no legal right to be here or who were considered undesirable. Included in its exhaustive lists of inadmissible classes were archaic and offensive provisions that banned such prospective immigrants as epileptics, imbeciles, individuals who had been convicted of, or who admitted to having committed, any crime involving moral turpitude, homosexuals, and persons with tuberculosis. Moreover, those individuals believed to be subject to removal had their deportation inquiries conducted by Special Inquiry Officers (SIOs), who were often regular immigration officers assigned additional responsibilities. The

SIOs, in other words, were prosecuting attorney, defence attorney, jury, and judge. As noted in chapter 7, the act also contained sections that provided a statutory basis for a discriminatory immigration policy.

By contrast, the statute was silent on the principles that governed the selection of would-be immigrants. It also failed to reflect the fact that Section 95 of the British North America Act (now known as the Constitution Act, 1867) recognizes immigration as a joint federal-provincial area of jurisdiction. In short, this was an act riddled with shortcomings, an act that should have been replaced years before by a statute that spelled out an immigration philosophy, and that recognized modern-day policies and practices and Canada's immigration requirements. Regrettably, previous efforts to produce such an act had failed lamentably.

The repeated attempts made to replace this piece of legislation, coupled with the knowledge that immigration policy divided along immigration constituency rather than political party lines, convinced Robert Andras that genuine reform would remain elusive unless one basic question was answered, namely, "Why do we have immigration to this country?" If a consensus could be reached on the role played by immigration in modern industrial Canada, then perhaps, concluded Andras, this country stood a better chance of getting a decent immigration act.[9]

In his quest to find answers to this fundamental question, Robert Andras invited the provinces and any interested organization to submit briefs. He also spearheaded the establishment of a special task force, charged with detailing the way immigration to Canada was handled, analysing policy assumptions on which the program was based, and outlining policy options. Headed by Richard Tait, a professional diplomat who had been seconded from the Department of External Affairs, it completed its task in the fall of 1974, after spending over a year on the job. On February 3, 1975, the minister tabled its four discussion documents, referred to collectively as a Green Paper, in the House of Commons, thereby setting the stage for an unprecedented nation-wide debate on immigration policy.

As befits a discussion document, the Green Paper of 1975 contained the seeds of controversy. The 1966 White Paper on immigration, written during a period when Canada's economy was surging ahead, had stated categorically, "Immigration has made a major contribution to the

Communists protesting the federal government's Green Paper on immigration policy, Toronto, 1975.

national objectives of maintaining a high rate of population and economic growth."[10] By contrast, the Green Paper, drafted when Canada was reeling under the impact of the energy crisis, renounced such an unequivocal position on the benefits of immigration. Challenging some of the assumptions made by the advocates of substantial population growth and high levels of immigration, it observed:

> To many Canadians, living in a modern industrialized and increasingly urbanized society, the benefits of high rates of population growth appear dubious on several grounds. Canada, like most advanced nations, counts the costs of more people in terms of congested metropolitan areas, housing shortages, pressures on arable land, damage to the environment — in short, the familiar catalogue of problems with which most prosperous and sophisticated societies are currently endeavouring to cope.[11]

Then, after reviewing some of the more conspicuous benefits of immigration, the Green Paper concluded:

But when all the arguments are sifted, it would probably be a not unfair assessment of our understanding of the economic consequences of higher against lower population growth rates for a country in Canada's present position to conclude that the evidence in favour of higher rates is uncertain. Furthermore, the hidden costs that they entail in terms of social strains and the impairment of the quality of life, admittedly extremely difficult to quantify, have thus far tended to be neglected in expert appraisals.[12]

When tabling the Green Paper in the House of Commons, Andras observed:

The green paper acknowledges what we all know, the difficulties in reaching consensus in this field. On the subject of immigration there exist many, and often conflicting views about the right line of policy to adopt. Nevertheless, there are several key elements in the present Canadian policy which the green paper assumes Canada's future approach should safeguard. Canadians will want, I believe, an immigration policy that meets our social, economic and cultural needs, that respects the family, that is free from discrimination, and that keeps the door open to refugees. Our approach to the immigration policy review has been inspired by the conviction that the subject of immigration to Canada needs to be examined in an extremely wide framework.[13]

The minister then noted that immigration policy was not solely a question of procedures and regulations, nor of Canada's economic and humanitarian concerns. What was at stake was nothing less than this country's population, its size, its rate of growth, its distribution and composition. In short, immigration had to be regarded "as an element in a broad demographic or population policy for Canada."[14]

With high hopes that the Green Paper would ignite a lively and constructive debate on immigration policy, Andras pressed for the staging of Canada-wide hearings. Rejecting the advice of his officials, who wanted to see a new immigration act tabled in the House as soon as possible, he announced, "We're going to have a dog and pony show. We'll take this across the country and talk it out."[15]

Fortunately for the minister the Liberal caucus and the opposition parties in the House of Commons strongly endorsed his view that there should be a national public debate on immigration. As a result, a Special Joint Committee of the Senate and the House of Commons was struck in March 1975 to examine the Green Paper and to hold public hearings on it across Canada.

REPORT OF THE SPECIAL JOINT COMMITTEE

Over a period of thirty-five weeks the committee staged nearly fifty public hearings in twenty-one cities from one end of Canada to the other. To the parliamentarians' dismay, some of these meetings were packed by noisy representatives from small extremist organizations, who took fiery exception to some of the positions expressed by the Green Paper. Still, even the rowdiest sessions of these hearings yielded fresh points of view and details of new problems for the committee's consideration.[16] Moreover, no matter how much disruption was caused by groups like the Marxist-Leninist "stage army", every instalment of this political theatre created new interest in immigration and triggered a fresh flow of submissions by mail. From the wealth of information obtained in this nation-wide dialogue and their own investigations, the parliamentarians eventually succeeded in developing a consensus, thereby confirming the similarity of views shared by all Canadian political parties on the fundamental features of Canadian immigration policy. Robert Andras could not have asked for a more forceful vindication of his insistence on public hearings, even if these sessions largely involved only organizations, groups, and individuals concerned with immigration.

After studying all the evidence, the committee concluded that, for demographic, economic, family, and humanitarian reasons, Canada should continue to be a country of immigration. In arriving at this position, the committee turned its collective back on the view contained in 5 percent of all received submissions that Canada should stop all immigration, or at least all non-white immigration.[17] Equally, it rejected the opinion expressed by 14 percent of all the briefs presented to it that Canada should establish an open-door policy.[18] Instead, the parliamentarians concluded that, in an age of greatly increased mobility, Canada could not afford to adopt an open-door policy and should continue to control the annual influx of immigrants admitted to it. In subscribing to such a policy, the committee embraced Newfoundland's argument that "in this time of increasing world populations, rapidly depleting resources and economic uncertainty, ... (immigration) must be brought under control and rationally directed ... to best serve the interests of Canadians." [19]

Having decided that Canada should continue to welcome immigrants in moderate numbers, the committee made sixty-four additional recommendations relating to the shaping of Canadian immigration policy. Nearly all of these were accepted by the Liberal government and later incorporated in the innovative Immigration Act, 1976, so called because it was first presented to Parliament in 1976.

THE IMMIGRATION ACT, 1976

The Immigration Act, 1976, the cornerstone of immigration policy from 1978 until 2001, broke new ground by spelling out the fundamental principles and objectives of Canadian immigration policy. Outlined in Section 3, Part 1 of the act, they included the promotion of Canada's demographic, economic, cultural, and social goals; family reunion; the fulfilment of Canada's international obligations in relation to the United Nations Convention (1951) and the 1967 Protocol relating to refugees, which Canada had signed in 1969; non-discrimination in immigration policy; and cooperation between all levels of government and the voluntary sector in the settlement of immigrants in Canadian society. All the act's other provisions derived from one or more of these national objectives.

Among the act's other important innovations was one that, by its very nature, set it apart from nearly all other federal statutes: a provision that imposed on the government a mandatory responsibility to plan for the future. In this case the act made it mandatory for the minister to consult with the provinces regarding the planning and management of Canadian immigration. After consulting with the provinces and other relevant persons and organizations, the minister was required to make an annual announcement in Parliament concerning the number of immigrants that the government proposed to admit during a specified period of time and to account for the manner in which demographic considerations had been invoked in determining that number. After the act came into effect on April 10, 1978, the government routinely tabled an *Annual Report to Parliament on Immigration Levels.*

Where admission to Canada was concerned, the act recognized essentially three categories of individuals eligible for landed immigrant status: (1) family class, which included the immediate family and dependent children, and parents and grandparents of any Canadian or permanent resident who agreed to provide for lodging, care, and maintenance of his or her family members for a period of up to ten years; (2) humanitarian class, which included (a) refugees who fitted the definition of refugee contained in the 1951 United Nations Convention and the 1967 Protocol relating to refugees (i.e., individuals outside their country of origin who, because of a well-founded fear of persecution based on their race, ethnic origin, nationality, religion, or political persuasion, are unwilling to return to their homeland), and (b) persecuted and displaced persons who do not qualify as refugees under the rigid UN definition but who are members of a specially designated class created by the cabinet for humanitarian reasons;[20] (3) independent class, i.e., individuals who applied for landed immigrant status on their own initiative and who were selected on the basis of the points system.

The inclusion of an identifiable class for refugees, selected and admitted separately from immigrants, was an important innovation in the new act. By providing for such a class, the act explicitly recognized Canada's legal obligations under the UN Convention relating to refugees and its Protocol to protect foreign nationals against involuntary repatriation to countries where they have justifiable fears of persecution, and established criteria for the determination of refugee status. Previously, all government activity relating to the admission of refugees was based on ad hoc decisions and cabinet orders-in-council. The act also addressed the question of individuals already in Canada who claimed to be refugees by establishing the Refugee Status Advisory Committee to determine the validity of refugee claims and to prevent the arbitrary deportation of individuals to countries where their lives and freedoms would be threatened.

Other liberal features of the act included the strengthening of various procedural protections for individuals subject to inquiries (those thought to be subject to removal, for example, had the right to a full and impartial immigration inquiry conducted by specially trained adjudicators who were totally removed from the process of producing evidence) and the tempering of administrative discretion. On the other hand, the act provided the cabinet with sweeping authority to exercise administrative discretion in national security questions.[21]

On balance, the Immigration Act, 1976 was a progressive statute that was generally regarded at the time of its baptism as the best legislation of its kind in the world.[22] And initially it did work well. Before long, however, this statute would be sorely tested by new developments in the fast-evolving immigration field, those surrounding the "refugee phenomenon" of the 1980s.

THE IMMIGRATION REGULATIONS 1978

The Immigration Regulations 1978, which complemented the new act, revised the points system to place greater emphasis on practical training and experience as opposed to formal education. They also expanded the act's refugee provisions and outlined a new, imaginative refugee sponsorship program that involved the public and that established a pattern for the handling of future refugee movements, notably the Indochinese influx in the late 1970s.

NEW FACES IN THE IMMIGRATION QUEUE

As the 1970s unfolded, the changes set in motion by the abolition of racial discrimination in Canadian immigration policy and the introduction of the points system began to assert themselves. While 87 percent of Canada's immigrants in 1966 were of European origin, only four years later 50 percent came from new regions: the West Indies, Guyana, Haiti, Hong Kong, India, the Philippines, and Indochina.[23] Throughout the 1970s and 1980s, newcomers would more often than not be from Africa, Asia, the Caribbean, or Latin America; and they would settle in disproportionate numbers in the lower Fraser Valley, the Vancouver-centred region of British Columbia, the Toronto area, and the greater Montreal region. To even the casual observer in these metropolitan areas, it was readily apparent that visible ethnic and racial minorities were becoming a significant part of Canada's social fabric. By contrast other parts of the country remained virtually untouched by this immigration. In 1986, for example, immigrants comprised less than 5 percent of the population in each of the four Atlantic provinces.

The 1970s also saw a change of emphasis in the types of immigrants admitted to this country. Prior to 1968, almost two-thirds of the newcomers to Canada were admitted in the independent class. Between 1968 and 1977, however, independent-class immigrants (those who meet the stringent requirements of the points system) accounted for only about half of all those accepted by this country. With the slide in the numbers of independent immigrants came a corresponding increase in the numbers of family-class immigrants. After 1978, this class would become the largest category, accounting in some years for approximately 45 percent of all Canada's newcomers.[24]

REFUGEES

The removal of racial and geographical discrimination in Canadian immigration policy and Canada's belated signing of the Geneva Convention relating to the Status of Refugees and its 1967 Protocol paved the way for refugees from outside Europe to apply for, and frequently to gain, admission to this country. As if to signal the import of these changes, Allan MacEachen, then minister of manpower and immigration, declared in 1969, following the arrival of some 11,000 Czech refugees the year before, "Greater attention will be given to the acceptance of refugees for resettlement in Canada from other parts of the world."[25] In the 1970s, the government would be given plenty of opportunity to live up to this promise. For in this decade, Ottawa and the Canadian people would find themselves being tested by their response to the fall-out from the large international refugee movements that became a feature of those years.

The Tibetan Refugees

Expressed intentions were translated into action in 1971–72 when Canada admitted some 228 Tibetans. Along with 60,000 to 70,000 of their fellow country-men, they had fled Tibet after its occupation by China in 1959. Led by their Dalai Lama or spiritual leader, they had sought sanctuary in Nepal, which did not welcome them, and India, which provided them with as much assistance as its limited resources permitted. In 1966, the Office of the UN High Commissioner for Refugees attempted to interest Canada in accepting some of the Tibetans for permanent resettlement. Since the refugees were agriculturalists, the Office of the High Commissioner suggested that they be settled on the land in groups so that their spiritual and cultural needs could be met by their lamas. This proposal was turned down on the grounds that Canadian immigration regulations did not permit group settlement. And there the matter might have rested but for the interest that a later Canadian high commissioner to India, James George, took in the plight of the refugees. In the late 1960s, largely through his efforts, a plan was devised to bring this small number of Tibetans to Canada.

Canada's immigration officials had a lot of qualms about admitting 228 self-described nomads, but Prime Minister Pierre Trudeau supported his high commissioner's view that the Tibetans would adapt quickly and successfully to Canadian life. And indeed, against all odds, they did. In fact, after five years in Canada almost all the adults were gainfully employed and able to feed, clothe, and house themselves adequately.[26]

The Ugandan Asians

Among the newcomers accepted from Africa was a group of well-trained and highly educated Asians who had been expelled from Uganda by Idi Amin's decree of August 1972. Their arrival in this country was initiated by the British government, which issued an urgent appeal to Canada and other countries for assistance in absorbing thousands of luckless Asians about to be deported by Amin's brutal regime. In response to that appeal, Pierre Trudeau's Liberal government decided that Canada would accept 5,000 refugees.[27] However, despite the opposition parties' tacit agreement with this decision, the government moved cautiously. Fearing that there might be a public backlash if the Asians were granted special concessions, it insisted that the refugees be processed on the same basis as other prospective immigrants entering this country. Only when the situation grew more critical, with the approach of the deportation deadline, did the government relax the points system and medical requirements for the Asians. Eventually 4,420 of these refugees entered Canada, arriving on an emergency airlift conducted between October and November 1972. Another 1,278 Ugandan Asians would follow them in the first half of 1973.[28]

Notwithstanding the relatively small numbers of these refugees, there was marked public opposition to the exercise. A poll conducted in December 1972, for example, revealed that only 45 percent of Canadians surveyed approved of the government's decision to accept the Ugandan Asians. Bryce Mackasey, in fact, expressed the view that the government's actions had cost the Liberals at least one seat in the October 1972 federal election.

Small as their numbers were, this influx of Ugandan Asians was largely responsible for the first increase in total Canadian immigration since 1967. Furthermore, despite the Canadian public's less than enthusiastic response to their government's decision to admit the Ugandans, the refugees adapted rapidly and remarkably well to life in this country.

Draft-Age Americans in Canada

American draft dodgers and deserters who fled the United States for Canada during the Vietnam War would ignite even more controversy, some of it provoked by the Canadian government's refusal to grant official support and sanction to the refugees. Draft dodgers were, for the most part, college-educated sons of the middle class who could no longer defer induction into the Selective Service System, while deserters were predominantly sons of the lower-income and working classes who had been inducted into the armed services directly from high school, or who had volunteered, hoping to obtain a skill and broaden their limited horizons. Once in Canada these men had to apply for landed immigrant status and permanent residency; but while draft dodgers, because of their education and skills, were usually successful in obtaining such status, the majority of deserters were not.[29]

As landed immigrants, draft dodgers usually succeeded in continuing their education or in finding skilled and professional work. By contrast, the majority of deserters, because they could not obtain landed immigrant status, remained fugitives, living underground, unemployed and without roots. This only changed after Robert Andras introduced the amendment to the Immigration Appeal Board Act that permitted all illegal visitors to become landed immigrants under relaxed criteria (the so-called Adjustment of Status program).

It is impossible to arrive at hard numbers for the number of draft resisters and deserters who escaped to Canada during the Vietnam War. One well informed source claims that the figure was likely somewhere between 80,000 and 200,000.[30] What is known for sure is that immigration from the United States was high as long as the Vietnam War raged and that, in 1971 and 1972, the United States was the single largest country of immigration. After President Jimmy Carter granted draft resisters who had evaded the draft peacefully an unconditional pardon many returned home (military deserters were not included in the blanket pardon). Probably half of these refugees from the States, however, put down roots in Canada, where they made up the largest, best-educated group of immigrants this country had ever received.

Chilean Refugees

Even more controversial than the American draft dodgers and deserters who escaped to Canada were the over 7,000 Chilean and other Latin American refugees that this country admitted after the violent overthrow of Salvador Allende's democratically elected Socialist-Communist government in 1973. Chilean and non-Chilean supporters of the old regime fled the veritable blood bath directed against them by Chile's new military rulers in the wake of the coup.

Although Canada took them in, she did so grudgingly — at least initially. Ottawa could have adopted a liberal and humanitarian policy towards the refugees fleeing the new Pinochet regime, most of whom were left wing, but chose instead to let ideological considerations out weigh other factors. Under no circumstances did the Canadian government want to risk alienating Chile's new administration and the United States, which had deplored Chile's slide into economic chaos under Allende. Canadian immigration policy had shed its openly racist bias and its blatant favouritism towards certain nationalities, but it still retained its bias against left-wing regimes. The Canadian ambassador to Chile had, in fact, supported the coup and had even gone so far as to predict that Chile's new rulers would turn the government over to civilian authorities as soon as practicable.[31]

Various groups in Canada lobbied for a special program for the Chilean refugees, the Canadian Council of Churches, for example, declaring: "Since these refugees are in danger of their lives, under a very repressive military regime, we have only one option: to do what we can to save these lives. Canada opened her doors to refugees from Hungary, Czechoslovakia and Uganda. If we refuse to open our doors to people who are in danger under another type of political regime, this would mean that we had acted from political rather than humanitarian motives."[32]

Despite entreaties from such compelling voices, the Trudeau government refused to grant any special waivers or to relax normal standards of admission. Thus only a comparatively small number of these Latin American refugees found their way to Canada.

The Boat People

Canada was far more humanitarian in her response to the plight of the "boat people", Vietnamese, Laotians, and Kampucheans, who fled Indochina from the Communist regimes established in the wake of Saigon's fall in 1975. In 1979–80, this country admitted some 60,000 of these refugees, most of whom had endured several days in small, leaky boats, prey to vicious pirate attacks, before ending up in squalid camps in Malaysia and Thailand. Although this was not the largest single refugee group to enter Canada since the Second World War, it represented the highest number of boat people admitted per capita by any country during this period.[33] Their numbers were such that they made up 25 percent of all the newcomers to this country between 1978 and 1981, although refugees normally constitute only about 10 percent of the annual flow to Canada.[34]

The Canadian decision to admit Indochinese refugees as immigrants was made immediately after the fall of Saigon in April 1975. But it was not until 1978 that the movement of the boat people to Canada gained momentum. After waging a valiant struggle with key cabinet colleagues, Bud Cullen, then minister of employment and immigration in the Trudeau government, received approval to offer a home to 600 refugees on the *Hai Hong*, which the Malaysian government had refused permission to dock. This announcement proved to be the springboard for the movement of Indochinese to Canada.[35]

The defeat of the Liberals in the federal election of May 1979 and their replacement by Joe Clark's Tory government coincided with a huge increase in the number of refugees fleeing Vietnam. In a partial replay of history, many of the same factors that figured in the Hungarian refugee movement resurfaced in the Indochinese immigration saga. These included: mounting international pressure for countries in the West to admit refugees for resettlement; a dramatic upsurge in Canadian media coverage of the refugee question; a corresponding increase in public interest in the issue; and a demand by Canadian churches and voluntary agencies that the government pursue a more aggressive refugee policy.

The stirring plight of the boat people and the lobbying mounted by church congregations and other organizations in the voluntary sector succeeded in wringing a generous commitment of help from the Clark administration. After twisting arms in cabinet, Flora MacDonald, minister of external affairs, and Ron Atkey, minister of employment and immigration, obtained approval for 50,000 refugees to be admitted to Canada by the end of 1980.[36] Announced in July 1979, the decision provided for both privately sponsored and government-sponsored refugees, the government initially agreeing to match each refugee that individuals and church and other voluntary groups supported. Because of this generous response, some 77,000 Indochinese refugees entered Canada between 1975 and 1981.[37]

THE QUEBEC CHALLENGE

In the first decades after the Second World War, public opinion and politicians in Quebec took little interest in the positive role that immigration could play in the economic and cultural development of the province. All this began to change, however, during the Quiet Revolution of the 1960s, when the province entered the immigration field in a decisive and dramatic way. The first initiative was taken by Jean Lesage's Liberal government, which, on February 10, 1965, announced the creation of a Quebec immigration service.[38] Essentially an exercise on paper, it was superseded in 1968 by the Union Nationale government's establishment of an immigration department to promote the integration of immigrants into Quebec's francophone community. This same government also concluded an agreement with Ottawa to place Quebec officials in federal immigration offices abroad to help in the selection of suitable immigrants for Quebec.[39]

When the separatist Parti Québécois came to power under René Lévesque in 1976, it assigned top billing to immigration. Immigration, in fact, was one of the first issues the new government raised with Ottawa. Quebec was eager to establish the rules and to interview and select immigrants to be admitted to the province independently of the procedures then carried out by the federal Department of Manpower and Immigration.

Quebec's requests were bolstered by a provision in the Immigration Act of 1976 (Section 109). This key section not only provides for federal consultation with the provinces regarding measures to promote the integration of immigrants into Canadian society, it also gives the minister authority to enter into agreements with any province to facilitate the drawing up, coordination, and implementation of immigration policies.[40] Although there had been minimal or no demand from provinces other than Quebec for control over immigration, Pierre Trudeau's Liberal government attempted to coax immigration agreements from other provinces as well. As Bud Cullen pointed out in the House of Commons on January 31, 1978, in the face of Conservative charges that special status was being accorded to Quebec, all provinces had the right to conclude immigration agreements with the federal government.

The way was thus paved for the first two such agreements, which were signed on February 20, 1978, one between Ottawa and Quebec and the other between Ottawa and Nova Scotia. By far the most significant was the agreement involving Quebec (the Cullen-Couture agreement), which declared that immigration to the province must contribute to its cultural and social development. Thanks to this accord, Quebec obtained the right to select its own independent-class immigrants — skilled workers and businessmen with their dependents — subject only to federal screening for medical and security/criminal reasons.

Cartoon by Roland Pier that appeared in Le Journal de Montréal.

National Archives of Canada, C136442

Not even the right to select its own immigrants, however, would be enough to satisfy Quebec's need for more immigrants, particularly francophone newcomers. With approximately 25 percent of Canada's population, Quebec would manage in the first nine months of 1990, for example, to attract less than 19 percent of Canada's total immigration for the period. Since it had the lowest birth rate in Canada — 1.5 children for every woman — the province's failure to attract enough new immigrants posed a major challenge to its policy-makers. The problem was further compounded by an inability to hold on to many immigrants who settled in the province and by a dearth of French-speaking immigrants.

MULTICULTURALISM

Multiculturalism was another immigration-related issue that came to the fore in the 1970s. It had been mentioned by the Royal Commission on Bilingualism and Biculturalism (established in 1963 by Prime Minister Lester Pearson to establish the relative use of English and French, Canada's two official languages) in its final volume, which reported that Canada was not bicultural but multicultural. The concept was not thrust into the political limelight, however, until Pierre Trudeau made a warmly received announcement in the House of Commons on Friday, October 8, 1971. On that occasion Trudeau informed the House that his government was adopting a policy of multiculturalism within a bilingual framework. Said Trudeau, "The policy I am announcing today accepts the contention of the other cultural communities that they, too, are essential elements in Canada and deserve government assistance in order to contribute to regional and national life in ways that derive from their heritage and yet are distinctly Canadian."[41]

What the prime minister did not announce, of course, were his government's underlying reasons for officially embracing such a concept. He carefully refrained from mentioning that multiculturalism was politically motivated, intended to persuade non-English and non-French Canadians to accept official bilingualism, the federal policy that had been instituted in 1969 with the passage of the Official Languages Act. Designed to promote the equality of French and English in the operations of all federal departments and agencies, official bilingualism seemed to its sponsors to be a logical response to the tumultuous nationalism that shook Quebec in the 1960s. However, even though its implementation had been urged by the Royal Commission on Bilingualism and Biculturalism, official bilingualism had never received widespread support.

Indeed, from its very inception, official bilingualism had stirred up opposition from a variety of sources. Nowhere, however, had it attracted more hostility than in the West, where westerners of Ukrainian, German, or other non-English or non-French background demanded to know why the federal government attached less importance to their culture than to that of the much smaller French-speaking minorities in Western Canada. When the Royal Commission on Bilingualism and Biculturalism was set up, its terms of reference included the contributions made by other "ethnic groups" (excluding the native peoples) to Canada's cultural enrichment and the measures that should be taken to safeguard these contributions. As a result, in Book IV of its report, the commission outlined a social policy for those Canadians whose origins were not British, French, or native.

The Trudeau government responded to these recommendations and to the increasing assertiveness of the "third force" in Canadian society by adopting a policy of multiculturalism within a bilingual framework. Multiculturalism itself was not new. It was merely an old activity dressed up in a new name. But no matter what guise it assumed, multiculturalism sought to promote equality and mutual respect among Canada's different ethnic or cultural groups. In a sense it was both the logical child of official biculturalism and a polite gesture to non-English and non-French Canadians, who now made up a significant source of potential support for the Liberal Party.

To implement its new policy, the government appointed a minister responsible for multiculturalism in 1972 and in 1973 established a Canadian Multiculturalism Council and a Multiculturalism Directorate within the Department of the Secretary of State. In 1988, an election year, Brian Mulroney's Conservative government, after resisting the idea for years, would set up a separate ministry for multiculturalism. Like official bilingualism, however, multiculturalism would attract opposition, much of which would develop during the turbulent eighties as Canadians became more conscious of the route down which the government had taken them.

— CHAPTER 11 —

The Turbulent 1980s and Beyond

THE REFUGEE CHALLENGE

IN THE 1980s CANADA FACED some of the most challenging immigration issues ever to confront policy-makers and try the souls of policy enforcers. Chief among these was the fast-developing refugee phenomenon, which saw spiralling numbers of individuals claim refugee status within Canada. The refugee question, in fact, dominated the immigration scene during this period, attracting widespread media coverage, igniting public controversy, and radically altering Canada's immigration policy options.

The refugee question was catapulted into new prominence in the 1980s because of a phenomenal upsurge in the numbers of the world's refugees. Two decades earlier, in the early 1960s, the refugee count stood at about 1.2 million. By 1989, however, civil war, ethnic strife, persecution, political upheaval, and natural disaster in the Third World had boosted the world refugee population to a horrendous 14,914,160 and plunged the international refugee system into deep crisis.[1]

The refugee explosion was just one feature of international migration in these years, however. Another major phenomenon was the escalating number of "illegal" or "undocumented" migrants. Improved communications, cheaper transportation, and the growing gulf between rich and poor nations had led to soaring numbers of people seeking to escape overpopulation and a dearth of economic opportunities in their homelands for a better life in developed countries such as the United States, Canada, Australia, and the countries of Western Europe. Since many of these migrants lacked the qualifications or family connections to be admitted to receiving countries by conventional methods, they sought the one means that promised them the best chance of becoming permanent residents — refugee status. As a result, many refugee determination systems became severely tested, and none more so than Canada's. In the mid-1980s, it began to be swamped with claims from "asylum-seekers", i.e., people who arrived on Canada's doorstep claiming refugee status, but who all too frequently did not qualify as refugees under the United Nations Convention of 1951 and its 1967 Protocol. In one month alone, December 1986, more than 3,000 people claimed refugee status within Canada. The first six weeks of 1987 saw over 6,000 claims made. Of the 18,000 claimants in 1986, an estimated two-thirds were not genuine refugees. In fact, commercial operators were believed to have instigated or aided the journeys of a large majority of those claiming refugee status within this country.[2]

DESPERATE VOYAGES

Most of these asylum-seekers came unheralded and unannounced. But some arrived in a more newsworthy fashion, such as the 135 Tamils who were picked up off the southeast coast of Newfoundland in August 1986 after they had been spotted adrift in crammed, powerless lifeboats. At first the strangers claimed they had come directly from Sri Lanka and had been on the high seas for thirty-five days in a ship's hold before taking to the lifeboats. But later, after their pitiful saga unravelled, they confessed that they had travelled to Canadian waters from West Germany, where, except for two in their midst, they had lived for periods of up to two years.

Equally dramatic was the arrival of a group of Sikhs less than a year later. In the July dawn they clambered from lifeboats onto a rocky, desolate stretch of Nova Scotia's southwestern coast near a tiny fishing village and then headed for the road yelling "refugees!" Thus alerted to the presence of 174 Sikhs in their midst, the residents of Charlesville responded by offering the strangers tea, cookies, and peanut-butter-and-jelly sandwiches.[3]

Far less heart-warming was the response of Prime Minister Brian Mulroney's Progressive Conservative Government. A year earlier, Gerry Weiner, the minister of state for immigration, had vowed that boatloads of refugees would never again be turned back as they once were[4] and the

Tamils were granted minister's permits, thereby enabling them to stay in Canada. In the wake of the arrival of the Sikhs, however, the Government recalled Parliament in emergency session to amend the Immigration Act. Bill C-84, the Refugee Deterrents and Detention Bill, was the result.

Hastily drafted by a Government reacting to public outrage, it contained numerous draconian provisions. One, later dropped, even allowed the Government to turn away ships suspected of carrying bogus refugees in Canadian waters.

As might be expected, the bill created a storm of protest from humanitarian organizations, immigration lawyers, Canadian churches, and members of the general public. But, although the acrimonious debate it triggered succeeded admirably in focusing public attention on refugee policy, Bill C-84 diverted attention from important, long-standing immigration questions. "Refugee issues, being hot and always in the media, got all the time and attention, so that other issues suffered" is how one senior official at Employment and Immigration Canada assessed the situation.[5]

There was a great deal of irony in the Government's harsh new attitude towards asylum-seekers. Only a year before, in 1986, the people of Canada had been awarded the United Nations' prestigious Nansen medal in "recognition of their major and sustained contribution to the cause of refugees."[6] This was the first time that the medal, created in 1954, had been awarded to a country. Its award to the people of Canada was tangible recognition of the fact that Canada, during the past decade, had granted a permanent safe haven to more than 150,000 individuals from refugee camps abroad — more per capita than any other country.

CANADA'S REFUGEE DETERMINATION SYSTEM

Individuals seeking conventional entry to Canada as refugees apply outside the country at refugee camps or at Canadian immigration offices around the world, where Canadian government officials process their applications, guided by the provisions of the current Immigration Act and subsequent regulations. Although the points system is not applied to refugees, persons claiming refugee status outside of Canada are screened to make sure that they can adapt to the Canadian labour market and society. Beginning in 1985, however, this orderly system of selection was bypassed by the increasing numbers of asylum-seekers who came to Canada as visitors or students or who arrived illegally like the Sikhs and the Tamils. If these claimants could provide evidence that they were genuine refugees, and that they were not security risks, they were automatically granted refugee status.

The admission of refugees in this manner posed problems, however. One of these was the threat to a carefully thought-out immigration program. The unpredictable arrival of such claimants, and the complex process of determining the validity of their claims, made it extremely difficult for Canadian authorities to implement a coherent immigration program embracing pre-determined numbers of people in the three classes of immigrants. Also, because it was patently obvious that many claimants were not genuine refugees but merely individuals seeking to improve their economic prospects in Canada, this category of newcomers began to excite a lot of controversy.

Probably most Canadians were prepared to accept genuine refugees who sought a safe haven in Canada after fleeing persecution in other parts of the world. Nevertheless, increasing numbers of these same Canadians began to deplore the fact that "economic migrants" could leapfrog over the immigration queue to move ahead of genuine refugees selected overseas and other categories of prospective immigrants. For many of these observers, the influx of economic migrants entering Canada under the guise of political asylum had become an invasion. The government, it seemed, no longer controlled the immigration process.

The refugee determination system that decided the fate of people claiming refugee status within Canada was a cumbersome, multi-step process and the slowness of its operations contributed to a crisis similar to the one that confronted the Immigration Appeal Board during Robert Andras's regime. In place from April 10, 1978 (when the Immigration Act, 1976 came into force) until December 31, 1988, this system, with its numerous loopholes and avenues for appeal, provided just the right blend of incentives to invite delays, and therefore abuse. Its shortcomings were such that they encouraged spiralling numbers of economic migrants and other bogus refugees to flock to Canada, where all too frequently they

were allowed to stay, sometimes courtesy of an amnesty, such as the one in 1986, which probably encouraged the sharp increase that occurred in refugee claimants over the next two years. The numbers could have been slashed if the government had taken prompt action to require citizens of Turkey, Brazil, and Portugal (who had made refugee claims, knowing full well that these were ridiculous but that they were the best route to landed immigrant status) to obtain visas before entering Canada as visitors. But Ottawa, afraid of losing votes in the ethnic community, did not act until abuse of the system had become intolerable.

Requiring citizens of certain countries to obtain visas before entering Canada as visitors constitutes one of the few tools immigration authorities could employ to control refugee flows. Reliable intelligence on organized refugee movements through other countries; cooperation or agreements, such as the Safe Third Country, with other countries, such as the United States (see pages 227–28); quick processing of claims; and early removal of those individuals deemed to be fraudulent refugee claimants are also used to this end. Quick processing of claims, however, necessitates the hiring of more personnel while early removal requires that the home country agree to receive a rejected claimant, two options not always available to immigration authorities.

THE SINGH DECISION

Processing delays and the resultant backlogs work, of course, to the advantage of such claimants, since administrative reviews and amnesties are often the means chosen to resolve backlogs. A major deterrent to the smooth, efficient operation of Canada's refugee determination system was the so-called Singh decision. Viewed as a great victory by refugee advocates, it was handed down by the Supreme Court of Canada on April 4, 1985, after it had deliberated the case of Harbhajan Singh and six other appellants. All seven had been refused refugee status by the minister of employment and immigration and by the Immigration Appeal Board, which, under the old refugee determination system, used to hear re-determination of refugee claims that the minister had concluded were invalid. When the Federal Court of Canada dismissed their applications to have a judicial review of the board's decision, the seven appealed to the Supreme Court.

In their ruling, three of the justices declared that the appellants should be allowed the review they wanted on the basis of the Bill of Rights. The other three judges who participated in the judgment ruled that the appeals should be allowed on the basis of the Charter of Rights and Freedoms. All six justices agreed that fundamental justice requires that a refugee claimant's credibility be determined by a full oral hearing at some stage of the refugee determination process.

The Singh decision had profound implications for the refugee determination system because it meant that refugee claimants in Canada must be guaranteed virtually the same social and legal protections accorded Canadian citizens under the Charter of Rights and Freedoms. Since fundamental justice is one of these rights, it follows that all refugee claimants must be granted a full oral hearing before the Immigration and Refugee Board (at the time of the Singh decision, the Immigration Appeal Board). By way of comparison, the United States and most other refugee-receiving countries do not guarantee such procedural protections to their refugee claimants.

Ideally, of course, claimants should be provided with all these procedural guarantees. But, administratively, the furnishing of such guarantees rules out expeditious hearings, adds considerably to the costs of processing refugee claims, and promotes delays. The end result is a clogged refugee determination system, maintained at great expense by the Canadian taxpayer. The Singh decision did not in itself create a refugee claims backlog but it certainly made the process of weeding out bogus claimants even more complicated and time-consuming. Moreover, it raised the question of whether it was possible to manage an immigration program when aliens were given the same rights as Canadian citizens.

After the Supreme Court handed down the Singh decision, the government decided that it was impossible for it to provide a full oral hearing for each of the 63,000 refugee claimants who were then legally entitled to one.[7] In an attempt to rectify the situation, Ottawa held an administrative review, in effect an amnesty, for all those refugee claimants who had entered Canada before May 21, 1986. Provided they had no security or criminal problems and passed medical examinations, they were allowed to remain in Canada and become permanent residents if they were already successfully employed or likely to become so. The program was effective, but unfortunately the delay that ensued between the time that it ended and the implementation of the new refugee determination system served only to encourage the arrival of the tens of thousands of new refugee claimants.

When the Immigration Act of 1976 was in its lengthy planning stage, experienced immigration officials expressed concern about proposed provisions regarding Canada's acceptance of refugees. These officials feared that if there was extensive reference to procedures governing refugee admission and status determination in the act or regulations, it would encourage misleading claims, which in turn would create unmanageable backlogs. There was also the fear that if Canada accepted too many refugees in any one year, it would do so at the expense of immigrants required for the labour market and the family reunification program. And it was predicted that there would be difficulties not only because of individuals applying for refugee status at Canadian immigration offices overseas but also because of aliens who entered Canada as visitors and then claimed to be refugees.[8]

A NEW REFUGEE DETERMINATION SYSTEM

When many of these fears became harsh reality in the 1980s, Brian Mulroney's Conservative government decided to clamp down on what it conceived to be rampant abuse of the refugee claims system. In May 1987, after many delays, it introduced the controversial Refugee Reform Bill, Bill C-55, designed to produce a refugee determination system that reduced the time required to decide the outcome of an application for refugee status and that cleared up the backlog of claimants already living here and waiting for their claims to be processed. Although the bill recognized Canada's legal and moral obligations to genuine refugees and established a multi-stage screening process, it nevertheless unleashed a torrent of controversy.

The chief source of this uproar was a provision in the proposed law that allowed Canadian immigration officers to refuse entry to refugee claimants who arrived from a safe third country, where they could have filed a refugee claim. Critics charged that some third countries might simply ship these claimants back to danger in their country of origin. They found it reprehensible that the cabinet would draw up a list of "safe" third countries so that immigration officials could quickly pre-screen would-be refugee claimants in an attempt to decide who should be allowed to enter the new hearing process.

As it turned out, opposition critics of the bill were not alone in this view. Barbara McDougall, who was then minister of employment and immigration, also came to entertain such apprehensions regarding at least one country: the United States. Persuaded that Canada's neighbour might send refugee claimants, deported from Canada, back to Central America, where their lives would be in jeopardy, she announced in December 1988 that she was "prepared to proceed with no country on the safe third country list … We think the new system will be able to function without it."[9]

The "safe third country" feature of the act, which the Conservative government never implemented, was not the only complicating factor. Another was the long delay in implementing the new legislation. Although it was introduced in the House of Commons on May 5, 1987, Bill C-55 did not receive royal assent until July 1988 and did not come into force until January 1, 1989. And while the legislative wheels moved slowly along their rocky course, increasing numbers of desperate foreign nationals poured across the United States border and into Canada's international airports. By the time the new legislation was proclaimed, some 125,000 people were in the refugee backlog.

As a result, the new streamlined system, which provided for the establishment of an independent, quasi-judicial body (the Immigration and Refugee Board made up of political appointees) and a two-stage screening process, found itself confronted by a staggering workload from the first day of its operation. Employment and Immigration Canada announced that it wanted claimants in the backlog dealt with in two years, but this would soon prove to be a highly unrealistic goal. Setting up the machinery to deal with claims inherited from the former system would require more time and resources than anticipated. Moreover, the new procedures for processing people who claimed refugee status after December 31, 1988, would soon lead to a parallel backlog of claimants waiting to have their cases resolved.

It was obviously no easy matter to devise a refugee determination system that operated smoothly without significant delays and backlogs and that treated claimants fairly while at the same time allowing Canada to control its immigration program. Indeed, the daunting task faced by the Immigration and Refugee Board would underscore the continuing need to find the right balance between control and fairness. Notwithstanding the criticism directed against the new system, Canada continued to remain true to its tradition of admitting more refugees per capita than any other country in the world. In 1991, for example, this country's Immigration and Refugee Board granted refugee status to 64 percent of the people who sought it. This means that, on a per capita basis, Canada then accepted more than five times as many refugee claims as the United States.

The Refugee Challenge: Deciding who fits the precise definition of Convention Refugee set out in the 1951 Convention relating to the Status of Refugees and subsequent conventions can be a difficult and agonizing experience for those individuals called upon to do so. These are the members of the Immigration and Refugee Board of Canada. In 1990, Geoffrey Howson, who took a leave of absence from the Anglican Diocese of Ottawa to serve in this capacity, recounted some of his thoughts on this question. Writing in the Anglican organ, Crosstalk, he said:

> *It is not easy to determine who is a Convention Refugee and who is not. It is, at times, a heart-rending and gut-wrenching experience to spend my days listening to such horrific stories. I often liken it to being in a hospital emergency ward: I and my colleagues can deal with the immediate crisis, but we can do nothing to attack the root causes of the world's refugee problem....*
>
> *Often I must face the people who do not meet the definition of Convention Refugee. I can understand their desperate need to find a better life for themselves and their families, even read it in their pleading eyes. In their shoes, would I act any differently? No matter now desperate their cases may be, economic refugees are not Convention Refugees, and they must seek other channels for admission to Canada. (Geoffrey Howson, "The Refugee Challenge," Crosstalk, September 1990, 7.)*

Immigration Trends in the 1980s

In the 1980s a trend already under way in the 1970s became even more pronounced. This saw the arrival of increasing numbers of newcomers from Asia and other non-European areas. By 1986, Asian-born immigrants made up the largest group of recent arrivals, accounting for 40 percent of all immigrants in Canada who came to this country between 1978 and 1986.[10] By contrast, people born in Asia represented only 11 percent of those who arrived in Canada before 1978. There were also striking increases in the numbers of other non-European immigrants. People from the Caribbean and from Central and South America who had arrived in the last decade constituted 15 percent of immigrants living in Canada in 1986, whereas they represented only 7 percent of those who arrived before 1978. The proportion of the immigrant population from the Middle East and Africa also continued to rise, from 4 percent of pre-1978 arrivals to 8 percent of those newcomers who arrived in Canada between 1978 and 1986.

At the same time, the proportion of European-born immigrants slid from 70 percent of those who arrived before 1978 to fewer than 30 percent of those who came between 1978 and 1986.[11] The European-born population of Canada is still large, of course, but it is aging. Furthermore, it is not being replenished by enough younger newcomers from Europe to ensure its replacement. As a result, the absolute number of European-born in Canada has been decreasing since 1971.[12] This trend, when coupled with the arrival of growing numbers of Third World immigrants, many of whom are relatively young, has important implications for the changing ethnic character of Canada's population.

The reunification of families continued to be a key factor in immigrant arrivals in the 1980s. In 1971, approximately 27 percent of all immigrants were in the family class while in 1983, this proportion had increased to close to 55 percent.[13] While the family class of immigrants continued to grow in importance, independent-class immigrants continued to decline in numbers, from 72.6 percent of all immigrants who entered Canada in 1971 to less than 30 percent of the total in 1983.[14] Nevertheless, under the Mulroney government there were some shifts in immigration emphasis. One of these saw the Conservatives make a determined attempt to encourage business immigration.

THE BUSINESS CLASS PROGRAM

The energy crisis and rising levels of unemployment in the late seventies together with a recession in the early eighties dampened immigration for about a decade. To reduce immigration, the government slashed Canada's intake of independent immigrants and reduced numbers in the "more distant relatives" category. Politically sensitive areas, such as the close family and refugee categories, were left untouched or reduced only slightly. By 1985, however, the Canadian economy had improved to such an extent that the Conservatives began to plan for a "moderate, controlled increase" in immigration levels, particularly in the economic category, which had been steadily losing ground in recent years.[15] Believing strongly that business is the engine that drives the Canadian economy, the Conservatives expanded a Liberal program, first introduced in 1978, that relaxed immigration requirements for individuals in the business class.

The heart of this program comprised two categories of business immigrants: the self-employed (i.e., skilled workers, such as beauticians, journalists, or carpenters) and entrepreneurs (i.e., experienced business people who would establish, acquire, purchase, or make a substantial investment in an enterprise that employed at least one person —e.g., a garment factory, a beauty salon, a restaurant — and who would participate actively in the management of this venture).

To this program the Conservatives added a third stream in 1986: the investor, a category designed to attract individuals with significant resources who wished to emigrate to Canada but who did not want to become involved in the day-to-day management of a business in which they had invested, or established, in Canada. Investors were to be admitted to this country solely on the basis of money and their proven track record in business. If they had a net personal worth of $500,000 or more, were prepared to sink a minimum of $250,000 in a provincially approved project for at least three years, and had demonstrated success in the business they were in, they could emigrate to Canada as an investor.[16] Two years later the $250,000 minimum for a provincially approved scheme was reduced to $150,000 for the six smaller, less prosperous provinces following complaints to the federal government that they had received no investor projects.

Almost 1,900 entrepreneurs and self-employed immigrants came to Canada in 1981, bringing in excess of $400 million. By 1988, the number of business-class immigrants had climbed to 3,700 and was expected to reach over 4,000 (including investors) in 1990.[16] Of all three categories, the investor class was the fastest growing, although by far the smallest.

At the close of the decade it was unclear what the economic impact of this immigration had been. Nevertheless, in 1991, a respected, but now defunct, advisory body that made recommendations to the federal government on economic matters, questioned the rationale for at least one category of the business program, the entrepreneurial category. Observed the now defunct Economic Council of Canada, "Logic, theory, and evidence all suggest that there would neither be fewer businesses nor a lower rate of business growth in the absence of immigrant entrepreneurs."[17] In other words, Canada could afford to do away with that part of the business program aimed at immigrant entrepreneurs.

Whether or not one accepted this controversial verdict, it is abundantly clear that the business immigration program as a whole, particularly its investor category, attracted a lot of criticism in the press and Parliament. Critics assailed the government for allowing rich immigrants to jump the immigration queue and for not establishing an adequate monitoring system to determine if promised undertakings had been honoured. According to Dan Heap, onetime NDP immigration critic, "We don't need to sell visas. What builds the country is work, not money."[18] And Heap pointed to soaring real estate prices in Vancouver and Toronto that he claimed were caused by the high demand created by rich immigrants from the business class. [19]

Less dramatic were the observations of Sergio Marchi, who was the Liberal immigration critic in 1987 and a tireless defender of the family reunification program. During a lengthy debate on immigration in the House in March 1987, March informed his colleagues:

> Our immigration officers abroad have reported to me personally that as a result of the ambitious entrepreneurship targets imposed by Ottawa and the extensive work required to review and approve each single business proposal, financial and personnel resources are

being shifted away from the family class sector into the business immigration class. The net effect, of course, of the family reunification applications processed is both fewer and slower. This should not occur.[20]

THE POLICY FRAMEWORK

When Sergio Marchi expressed deep concern about the business immigration program, he raised the question of whether Canadians want an immigration policy driven essentially by economics. A timely question then, it would become even more relevant in the 1990s, when Canada was in the grip of inordinately high unemployment and world market forces played an even greater role in her economy.

REALITIES OF THE 1990S

One of these realities was the Canadian birth rate. Canada's annual rate of population growth (natural increase plus net immigration) had declined steadily in recent decades, from 3 percent in the late 1980s to less than 1 percent in the late 1990s. Much of this decline could be attributed to the dramatic plunge in birth rates after the baby-boom period. In 1959, the level of births was 3.9 children per woman while in 1989 it was 1.7 per woman, considerably below the replacement level. Should the birth rate decline to 1.17 children per woman, and net migration remain at 60,000 per annum, Canada's population would begin to decline by 2040.

While the baby boom had been giving way to the baby bust, Canada's population had been aging, in the demographic sense: future populations will contain a higher proportion of the older age groups. By 2040, the number of people over sixty-five in Canada is projected to reach 10 to 11 million.

The decline in the birth rate and the aging of the Canadian population was accompanied by a slowing in the rate of growth of Canada's labour force. After several decades of rapid growth, the rate of growth of the labour force began to slow in the 1980s because of dramatically declining birth rates in the 1960s and 1970s and low immigration levels in the early 1980s. It was becoming highly probable that the labour force's growth rate would continue to fall in the future, particularly if birth rates continued to tumble and if immigration did not increase dramatically.

No Shortage of Prospective Immigrants

Another reality was the growing international population pressures that were being felt on Canada's borders. The influx of "economic migrants" in the 1980s served notice to Canadians that migratory patterns around the world would soon force a rethinking of Canada's immigration policy. At issue was the rapid growth of the world's population and Canada's response to the population pressures created by it. In 1987, the global population had reached 5 billion; by 2020, it was expected to climb to 8 billion. As in the past twenty years, most of the increase in the next decade was expected to take place in the Third World. Population increase was surging ahead so rapidly in these countries that, by the year 2100, they were expected to contain 87 percent of the world's population.[21] Such massive population growth in a part of the globe already subject to extreme environmental and economic pressure was predicted to produce huge numbers of new migrants who would attempt to improve their economic fortunes in developed countries like Canada.

This likelihood was spotlighted by Morton Weinfeld, a sociology professor at McGill University. In a chilling report prepared for the Department of Employment and Immigration, he predicted that population pressure on Canada from Third World countries in the coming century was likely to be intense. "Canada's comparatively empty spaces, political freedoms and high standard of living", he wrote, "will be ever more attractive to large numbers of newcomers, overwhelmingly from the less developed regions. And they will make every effort to get in."[22] Should Canadian immigration policy remain restrictive and selective, he concluded, Canada will have to increase the resources and military personnel required to patrol its waters, air corridors, and the Canada–U.S. border.

National archives of Canada, C136881.

Cartoon by John Lartner. Reprinted with the permission of the
Toronto Star Syndicate.

A foretaste of what might be in store for Canada was provided by developments in Western Europe, where immigrants and political refugees arrived each day from Eastern Europe, the Middle East, and Africa, seeking to escape poverty, civil unrest, and repression. Some observers began to conclude that if gross imbalances in the world's resources and people persisted, Canada might one day find itself emulating the example of Switzerland and Austria. In the summer of 1991 they employed soldiers to help seal their borders against an immigration tide.

THE CONSERVATIVES' FIVE-YEAR IMMIGRATION PLAN

In the fall of 1990, the Mulroney government departed from the practice of previous governments by unveiling a long-range immigration program. After extensive consultation with the provinces and immigrant aid groups, the Conservatives announced a new five-year immigration plan designed to open the immigration gate to tens of thousands more newcomers than had been admitted in previous years, and to introduce fundamental changes in the way immigrants are selected. It was estimated that 250,000 immigrants a year would be admitted to Canada in 1992, an increase of 50,000 over the current level.

Employment and Immigration Minister Barbara McDougall's announcement was notable for several reasons, not least of which was its timing. It was made when the Canadian economy was undergoing painful and wrenching structural change and when Canada was experiencing a recession, a time when, traditionally, Canadians have had little enthusiasm for immigration. What was even more significant, however, was its disclosure that the government intended to change the balance between two types of immigrants, family-class immigrants and independent immigrants.

Prior to the 1988 election the Conservative government had liberalized the regulations for family-class immigrants, thereby precipitating a rush of new applications from people keen to take advantage of the changes. With the new announcement, however, the Tories revealed their intention to impose a Canadian-style definition of family on the immigration process and thereby tighten up on the kinds of relatives who qualify as family members. Under the new arrangement, a prospective immigrant deemed to be dependent on his/her Canadian family would be admitted, while a non-dependent would be required to apply as an independent. The impact of the new regulations would not be felt immediately, though. Because of the earlier loosening of regulations, the numbers of family-class immigrants would continue to grow in 1991 and 1992. Only then would they start to decline, resulting in a better balance between family-style immigrants and independent immigrants by 1995.

The Mulroney government's demonstrated intention to tilt immigration policy away from family-sponsored immigrants, over whom it had little discretionary control, and towards independent immigrants, who must qualify under the points system, unleashed a torrent of criticism. Not surprisingly, there were those who accused the government of ranking economics first and people second, noting that any increase in immigration from 1990 to 1995 would come at the expense of the much vaunted family reunification program. "It's going to have a dramatically restrictive effect on family reunification," charged David Matas, a Winnipeg immigration lawyer, who has written on Canadian immigration policy.[23] Besides, increasing the influx of independent immigrants was "not even a kindness to the independents because when they get over they are going to have the same problem [of being reunited] with their families."[24] Other observers, keenly aware of the tough global competition Canada faced, welcomed the new policy direction. In their view, a sensible immigration policy not only increases the total number of immigrants, it also restores the balance between independent and family-sponsored newcomers. Such a policy, they believed, represents a desirable blend of economic self-interest and humanitarian objectives and helps to marshal public support for more immigration.

Still other observers questioned the government's decision to raise immigration levels at this time. They wondered if Canada did not run the risk of overloading a leaky lifeboat if she admitted more immigrants in the near future. This country, after all, had two serious immigration-related problems of its own: a staggering backlog of unprocessed refugee claims and a fragile economy. To complicate matters further, the already thin budgets of immigration agencies had been stretched by the uncontrolled surge of immigrants in the late eighties. The end result was language and literacy programs that were starved for funds. School boards in cities such as Toronto and Vancouver were also hard pressed to find the resources necessary to provide badly needed language instruction to immigrant children, the majority of whom spoke neither English nor French and many of whom had no academic experience prior to arriving in Canada.

The weak Canadian economy and the situation of immigrants in the Canadian labour force was of special interest to Shirley Seward, one-time director of social policy studies at the Institute for Research on Public Policy. In an appearance before the House of Commons Standing Committee on Labour, Employment and Immigration, she reported that studies had shown that there are two particularly vulnerable groups in the Canadian work force: male immigrants from Europe and North America who came to Canada before the introduction of the points system and recent immigrant women from the Third World. Both, but especially the latter, are well represented in declining industries. Because of their particular characteristics and/or the training opportunities available to them, these groups will have an especially difficult time in adapting to new labour force conditions. In Ms. Seward's words, "Most certainly the 1990s are going to be characterized by very rapid structural change. Under these circumstances, it is critically important for the labour force to be able to adapt. Therefore, it is worrisome that certain groups of immigrant men and women are likely to face quite serious problems of labour adjustment in the future."[25]

Because it is imperative that Canada be able to compete internationally, Ms. Seward concluded that it is more important to increase the educational level, quality, official language ability, and skills of the Canadian labour force than simply to raise the levels of immigration. "If you are going to increase levels," she informed the Standing Committee on Labour, Employment and Immigration in May 1990, "you cannot do so without fundamentally changing the kinds of integration services that are provided to immigrants and non-immigrants."[26]

The Economic Council of Canada, while advocating that Ottawa raise immigration levels significantly, urged a breathing-space. Given the fact that immigration levels in the years 1986–90 rose sharply above the levels of the previous decade, the council cautioned the government to adopt a more gradual approach. If it proceeds with the present plan, said the council, Ottawa runs the risk of "provoking social problems, creating temporary increases in unemployment, and perhaps overstretching the capacity of the institutions that handle the arrival and settlement of immigrants.[27]

BILL C-86

The Conservatives' five-year immigration plan certainly ignited controversy. But this was nothing compared to the controversy that swirled around developments leading to the passage of Bill C-86. Tabled in the

House of Commons on June 16, 1992, it represented the most far-reaching amendments to Canada's immigration laws since 1976–77.

Its introduction was dictated by changing world conditions. The
world in which Canada now delivered its immigration and refugee program had fundamentally changed since the period in which the
Immigration Act of 1976 was drafted. In 1992, people were on the move
— approximately 120 million of them. In 1978, when the Immigration
Act of 1976 came into effect, 4,130 refugees were admitted to Canada,
all of whom were fleeing communism[i]. Few of the 40,000 refugees
admitted into Canada in 1992 could make the same claim. Fifteen years
earlier there was no Charter of Rights and Freedoms to challenge the
rules and assumptions that governed the implementation of immigration and refugee policies. In 1992, there was. And this meant that
Canada had to manage its immigration and refugee program in a far
more litigious atmosphere.[28] To complicate matters further, the years
intervening since 1978 had also seen the globalization of money, crime,
and terrorism, all of which had profound implications for the management of Canada's immigration and refugee program.

In other words, in 1992, Canada's immigration and refugee program operated in a radically altered environment. There was still a political consensus on immigration and refugee issues, but it was an uneasy
consensus. The Canadian public, it was all too apparent, was becoming
increasingly concerned about the implications of immigration for the
rights and responsibilities of citizenship and for the changing face of
such large urban centres as Vancouver, Toronto, and Montreal, which
attracted most of Canada's newcomers. And, in contrast to the earlier
period, many Canadians felt that Canada's refugee and immigration
system was being abused by opportunists.

The clear intent of the 113-page bill was to tighten up the immigration and refugee system by providing more stringent enforcement and
control mechanisms. To this end, the bill provided for, among other
things, the fingerprinting of refugee applicants to discourage welfare
fraud, public hearings of refugee cases, harsher detention procedures,
and deportations without hearings. Even more important, Bill C-86
introduced measures designed to streamline the severely taxed refugee
determination system.

Defending the bill, employment and immigration minister Bernard Valcourt argued that the effectiveness of Canada's immigration and refugee system was being severely tested by mounting international and domestic pressures. Sixteen years ago, when the current immigration act had been developed, times were simpler and there were far fewer abuses of the immigration and refugee program. Using tools fashioned in the seventies, said Mr. Valcourt, militated against Canada's meeting its immigration and refugee objectives in the nineties. For this country to maintain a fair, balanced, and effective immigration program it needed Bill C-86.[29]

Several features of the bill immediately raised a storm of protest, notably the fingerprinting clauses, the provision of public hearings for refugee cases, the detention procedures, and some of the methods proposed for streamlining the refugee determination system. However, representations made by hundreds of individuals and organizations as well as in-depth study conducted by House of Commons and Senate committees succeeded in persuading the government to modify some of the harsher provisions.

In response to criticism that public hearings would place refugee applicants in jeopardy, the government reverted to the old rule that hearings before the refugee board would be in camera. Only in exceptional cases would they be held in public. The government also agreed to change the very harsh detention procedures outlined in the bill and to amend the provisions with respect to fingerprinting. In softening its position on fingerprinting, the government agreed to have an applicant's fingerprints destroyed once he/she had become a Canadian citizen.

The in-Canada refugee determination process outlined in the bill remained essentially the same, however. When passed by the Senate in December 1992, the legislation provided for a single, one-stage hearing process instead of the costly, wasteful two-stage hearing process provided for in Bill C-55, which had introduced a new refugee determination system in 1989. Under Bill C-86, authority previously exercised by board members would be exercised by a senior immigration officer, who would be able to decide if an applicant was eligible to claim refugee status.

Of all the provisions contained in the new legislation, however, it was the "safe third country" provision that unleashed the most controversy. Like its counterpart in Bill C-55, this provision would prevent refugee claimants from entering Canada if they arrived from a "safe" country which was prepared to grant them refugee status. In short, it was designed to curtail a practice commonly known as "asylum shopping", in which potential refugee claimants move around, looking for the country that offers the best benefits. The Conservative government had backed away from this immigration minefield in 1989, but in 1992 it appeared determined to face it head on.

Critics of the measure were no less determined to see it set aside. They attacked the provision for being heartless, noting that it would dramatically reduce the number of refugees allowed into Canada, because about 40 percent of the people who seek asylum in this country each year arrive via the United States. Some opponents of the provision even called the measure racist. The NDP immigration critic, Dan Heap, for example, claimed the policy discriminated against refugee claimants from countries that do not have direct air routes to Canada, i.e., many African, Asian, and Central American countries. Most refugee claimants from Africa and Asia, he pointed out, must travel through Europe or the United States to reach Canada while many Central American refugees reach this country via the United States. By contrast, claimants from the Soviet Union and Eastern Europe usually take direct flights to Canada.[30]

Valcourt was quick to defend the government's policy. Canada, he observed, was merely joining other states that had agreed to share responsibility for refugees. Included in their ranks were European countries which had already negotiated arrangements to distribute responsibility for refugees to prevent "asylum shopping."

Authorities recognized that this provision would take some time to implement, but probably nobody realized that it would take years. Not until midnight, December 28, 2004, would Canada and the United States implement the Safe Third Country agreement. This new legislation would prohibit refugees from transiting through one country before seeking haven in another and would instead require them to seek asylum in whichever country they reached first. The fallout from the provision would become all too evident in 2006, when the number of refugee claimants was down sharply from that of previous years.

Far less controversy greeted the Conservative government's intention to tilt immigration away from family-class immigrants and towards independent immigrants (assisted relatives, skilled workers, entrepreneurs, investors, and self-employed persons). This intention was expressed in a series of planned new immigration regulations that the government announced in January 1993. Scheduled to take effect on January 31, the new regulations reduced the maximum number of bonus points for assisted relatives and increased the number of points for applicants qualified in jobs that required advanced skills. Howard Greenberg, national chairman of the Canadian Bar Association's immigration section, summed up the intention succinctly when he observed, "Clearly, the use of family relationship as a factor in obtaining immigrant status is reduced considerably."[31]

The Conservatives introduced one more major immigration initiative before they were banished from office in the federal election of September 1993. In June of that year, as part of a sweeping reorganization of government, they shifted most immigration functions to a new Public Security ministry. This ill-fated move immediately detonated an explosion of controversy. Furious critics denounced the government for identifying immigration with public security and accused it of reinforcing the public backlash against immigrants. One organization, the Canadian Ethnocultural Council, even labelled the change an "incitement to racism."[32]

The attacks soon ceased, however. For two months after the election, in an attempt to put a new face on immigration, the victorious Liberals tabled legislation creating Citizenship and Immigration Canada (CIC). The new department, which was established on June 23, 1994, combined a range of programs transferred from several other federal departments. As such, it linked immigration services with the registration of citizens and the promotion of the ideals shared by Canadians.

More of the Same

When the Liberals took office in the fall of 1993, they did so at a time when immigration was rapidly becoming a heated issue in Canada. Such a development was to be expected, given the increase of racial tension in Canadian society, the widely perceived belief that the government was inadequately screening and selecting new residents, and the continuing high levels of immigration at a time when Canada was wrestling with excessively high unemployment. Logic dictated that the federal government reduce immigration levels under these circumstances, but in the late 1980s it abandoned the absorptive capacity model approach in favour of setting annual immigration levels independently of short-term economic conditions.

Despite the fact that the Canadian public was becoming increasingly wary of immigration, the government announced, in February 1994, that it intended to maintain immigration at approximately one percent of Canada's population. In other words, it was setting the target for the coming year at 250,000. When making this announcement, Sergio Marchi, now minister of citizenship and immigration, disclosed that his government planned to assign top priority to family-class and "independent skilled immigration."

The government, reported Marchi, would also conduct a Canada-wide series of public meetings and study groups on immigration, after which it would present a new five-year plan to Parliament.[33] Interestingly enough, one consensus that did emerge from this review was that there is not enough reliable information with which to develop really rational immigration policies. Because of this knowledge gap, immigration policy formulators often tend to fall back on myth.[34] When it is also recalled that Canadian immigration policy is not entirely determined by the federal government and that the provinces, municipalities, and non-government organizations (churches, ethnic organizations, professional associations, farmers, businessmen, etc.) also have a role to play in its formulation, one can better appreciate the difficulty of drawing up relevant, coherent policies.

Like the Conservatives before them, the Liberals were determined to curtail misuse of the immigration and refugee system. Accordingly, the government tabled a bill in the House of Commons on June 17, 1994, which contained measures designed to prevent serious criminals from abusing the refugee determination process or from using immigration appeal provisions to delay their removal from Canada.

While cracking down on foreigners who commit crime in Canada, the government extended an olive branch to failed refugee claimants who were still in the country. In an effort to clean up a backlog of refugee cases, Ottawa published new regulations in July 1994 that would permit failed refugees to apply for permanent status if they met certain conditions. Although this initiative had all the earmarks of an amnesty program, Marchi rejected this description, pointing out that unsuccessful claimants, who went underground and then emerged three years later (only refugee claimants who had been in the country for three years could apply for permanent status), would not be able to apply for permanent status.[35]

The flood of new initiatives continued unabated into the autumn of 1994, when the government unveiled an immigration policy with "new directions". In response to pressures from his own department and the general public, the minister of citizenship and immigration announced that the government was lowering immigration levels and shifting the pendulum away from family reunification and toward independent immigrants who have the education, skills, and language to adapt readily to the New Economy. However, what was trumpeted as a policy with "new directions" really represented the continuation of a course charted by the Conservative government.

Even with the Liberals' announced shift toward independent immigrants, by far the largest group of entrants would still be family-class immigrants, and this despite the fact that, under the new regulations announced by Marchi, parents and grandparents would no longer be part of the family class. Indeed, all that was really new in the policy unveiled by the Liberals were provisions designed to realize the tougher attitude toward immigrants and to reduce immigration costs. These would involve the levying of fees and other charges and the requirement that sponsoring relatives post a bond or financial guarantee that the government could cash if sponsored immigrants ended up on welfare.

Little remarked on was a provision in Marchi's guidelines that called for a resumption of the practice of recruiting immigrants. This provision envisaged the setting up of marketing programs in places such as Hong Kong, Taiwan, the Middle East, and Europe. Thanks to the new guidelines, immigration authorities in these locations would re-enter the promotion business with a view to attracting potential immigrants with solid work experience, strong language skills, and a record of success in their native countries.

Prodded by fiscal restraint and world developments, the Liberals announced new changes to the in-Canada refugee determination system in March 1995. These changes would see the panel size for refugee hearings reduced from two members to one. Resulting savings, said Marchi, would be used to help accepted refugees settle in Canada. The target date for full implementation of the new streamlined system was January 1, 1996, by which time the government expected to have an independent advisory group examine the qualifications of all candidates applying for membership to the Immigration and Refugee Board.

THE KOSOVAR REFUGEES

Refugees and refugee assistance captured news headlines in the spring of 1999 when Canada mounted its most recent large-scale refugee aid effort. This was in response to developments in Yugoslavia's Kosovo province, where violent ethnic strife had resulted in huge numbers of ethnic Albanians fleeing to desperately poor, and politically shaky, Albania and Macedonia. When the United Nations High Commissioner for Refugees (UNHCR) issued an urgent appeal to various countries to furnish protection to these refugees, Canada immediately offered to provide a temporary safe haven for 5,000 of them. Once here, they could apply for permanent resident status.

Although this country had often responded to appeals from the United Nations for resettlement assistance, this was the first time it had participated in an emergency humanitarian evacuation program designed to offer temporary protection to persons from a place of mass exodus.[36] Canada responded in two ways to the appeal: by accepting refugees under the UNHCR's emergency evacuation program and then by processing refugees with relatives in this country and refugees with particular needs (the fast-track family reunification program). Between March 1999 and February 2000, 5,051 Kosovar refugees arrived under the emergency humanitarian evacuation program and 2,192 under the family reunification program.[37]

The majority of Kosovar refugees bound for Canada were displaced in Macedonia. Of these, over 90 percent were airlifted to Canada during a three-week period in May 1999, refugee-carrying flights alternately landing at Canadian Forces Base (CFB) Trenton in Ontario and CFB

Corporal François Charest, Department of National Defence.

Kosovar refugees arriving in Canada.

Greenwood in Nova Scotia. Public support for the Kosovars was overwhelming. In fact, from the moment they landed on Canadian soil the newcomers received a warm welcome and assistance from not only the federal and provincial governments but also from a host of charitable and refugee-serving organizations. The federal government, for example, declared that all Kosovars would be eligible for financial assistance and language training for a period of two years.[40] Other assistance took the form of group sponsorships that enabled many of the refugees to move into communities identified by the federal government, in conjunction with the provinces, as having an existing Albanian population and the required support services.

Some of the refugees decided to remain permanently in Canada, but others yearned to return to their homeland. After a peace settlement was reached many did just that, the first group of returning refugees flying out of Halifax on July 7, 1999, on a repatriation flight to Macedonia.

The Kosovar refugee program, like the Hungarian refugee program in 1956–57, attracted widespread support among Canadians. Controversy was the last thing it excited. The same certainly cannot be said, however, for immigration-related developments in the early years of the dawning century.

CHAPTER 12

Immigration Grabs Attention, 1996–2006

T HERE IS NO QUESTION THAT Immigration was an attention-grabbing issue in the late 1990s and the first decade and a half of the twenty-first century. Moreover, in time-honoured tradition, immigration and refugee-related issues continued to whip up controversy in the press and to furnish critics with ammunition with which to attack the government of the day.

There were the usual culprits: the continuing flood of self-selected refugee claimants, most of whom were economic migrants; staggering backlogs in the refugee determination system and in skilled workers' applications; the failure of Ottawa to locate and deport many newcomers in Canada illegally; and immigration levels perceived to be too high.

Developments in these years also made Canadians increasingly conscious of terrorism and the role that security should play in relation to immigration. These twin issues began capturing Canadians' attention after the name Ahmed Ressam surfaced in the daily news in late 1999. Had this young man not appeared nervous when attempting to cross the international border at Port Angeles, Washington, he might have succeeded in carrying out his mission to attack Los Angeles with explosives during the 2000 millennium celebrations. As it was, a suspicious immigration agent arrested the Algerian-born Montreal resident (and Al Queda recruit) and turned him over to the Federal Bureau of Investigation.

The whole issue of security attracted even more attention, of course, after planes sliced into the north and south towers of New York City's World Trade Center and badly damaged the Pentagon building in Washington. In the wake of these horrendous developments of September 11, 2001, security assumed even more importance, leading to increased cooperation between Canada and the United States on "border issues" and the implementation of more stringent controls. Henceforth, it would become increasingly difficult to strike the right balance between facilitating immigration and keeping undesirable individuals out of Canada.

Also competing for attention have been the scandals that plagued the immigration arena. One that caused a significant uproar came to light in 2003, when the RCMP alleged that members of criminal organizations operating in Montreal and Ottawa had been collecting cash bribes from prospective immigrants and channelling payments to two Imigration and Refugee Board (IRB) judges in exchange for favourable decisions.[1] If nothing else, this revelation served as an unwelcome reminder that a key recommendation of the government's own immigration-law advisory committee had not been implemented — namely, that qualified public servants should be named to the Immigration and Refugee Board, not political appointees.

After 278 criminal charges were laid against one of the judges in early 2004, the government moved quickly to reform the selection process for IRB judges. As evidence of Liberal Prime Minister Paul Martin's determination to root out patronage and corruption in government, Ottawa announced that it would implement a new selection system. The Ministerial Advisory Committee would be scrapped altogether, to be replaced by an advisory panel and a selection panel. The independent advisory panel, comprising refugee advocates, lawyers, academics, and human resource experts, would conduct the initial screening of candidates while the selection board would interview prospective board members and make the final selection.

The new selection process, however, was not without its critics. "Has the Minister not heard of conflict of interest?" asked James Bissett, a former diplomat who served as executive director, Employment and Immigration, from 1985 to 1990. "For the most part, these advisors will be refugee activists who have a vested interest in maintaining a wide-open asylum system. It is the lawyers and NGOs who are on the receiving end of the millions of dollars needed to represent and care for those who arrive to apply for asylum," observed the immigration expert.[2]

Then there was "Strippergate," in the fall of 2004, when Immigration Minister Judy Sgro and her department were lambasted for their "exotic dancer program," a program that, before it was reformed, allowed foreign strippers to enter Canada with almost no questions asked. This was damaging enough to the minister's reputation, but what eventually forced her resignation from the Liberal cabinet in early 2005 were the wild and unsubstantiated charges of pizza parlour owner, Harjit Singh. He claimed that Ms. Sgro had promised to grant him asylum in return for free pizza and volunteer assistance in her election campaign. The businessman's charges were later found to be completely baseless and Sgro was subsequently exonerated. Moreover, Harjit Singh, who had been repeatedly appealing his rejected refugee claim (among other things, he was found to have lied about a criminal conviction in India, his homeland) was finally deported to India in February 2005.

Pursuing High Immigration Levels

The Chrétien Liberal government's declared intention to continue the Mulroney government's policy of high immigration levels undoubtedly excited the most controversy. This was especially true after Immigration Minister Elinor Caplan served notice in 1999 that she would like to raise Canada's annual immigration by 70 percent to 300,000 from the expected 175,000 in 1999. A similar reaction greeted the declaration of Immigration Minister Denis Coderre that he wanted to raise the annual intake to one percent of this country's 31.4 million population as soon as possible.[3]

When Elinor Caplan made her announcement, municipal authorities in her own city, Toronto, were already deploring the costs of integrating immigrants in a city that was then receiving more than 42 percent of Canada's immigrants each year. If Toronto, like Vancouver, were to take in even more immigrants, where would housing be found for them? How much additional pressure would be placed on their already overtaxed school systems, social welfare agencies, hospitals, and English-as-a-second-language programs?

Criticism of High Immigration Levels

In view of the stresses associated with large numbers of immigrants, some critics questioned why, for example, Canada should have a per capita immigration level far in excess of that of other large Western nations and twice as high as that of Australia and the United States, the other two major receiving countries with formal immigration programs. Was it because this country desperately needed large numbers of new immigrants due to its low birth rate and aging population? Was it because Canadian business would benefit from a larger domestic market? Or was it because the government wanted to keep the lid on inflation by increasing the supply of labour and thereby suppressing wages?

According to at least one persistent critic of the government's immigration policy, Daniel Stoffman, the federal government has never provided frank answers to these questions. If Ottawa wants to make a demographic case for a high immigration level, then it is on weak ground, declares this well-known journalist. Because of decreasing fertility and increasing longevity, nearly every country, including China, has an aging population. Moreover, where is the evidence that Canada faces a huge shortage of skilled workers? Why Canada, alone among the countries of the world, should address this development by a permanent high immigration level has never been explained, says Hoffman. He concedes that a larger population will create a larger domestic market for Canadian business, but he also noted that Canada, like Sweden, has always depended on foreign exports to earn its living. As for fighting inflation, if the government wants to keep inflation in check by increasing the labour supply, it should admit this openly, insists the author. Hoffman does not oppose immigration. For him the issue is why Canada should promote high immigration levels given the adverse impact that excessive numbers of immigrants can have on the urban infrastructure.[4]

The Fallout from High Immigration Levels

The fallout from high immigration levels is no more graphically illustrated than by the plight of one of Toronto's neighbourhoods. Located on the fringes of the megacity, an hour or so by public transit from the city's core, Malvern boasts the unenviable distinction of being among the worst of Greater Toronto's new ghettos. Formerly a prosperous middle-class neighbourhood, it is now awash in poverty and all the social problems that poverty begets. Malvern's descent into hard times is no great mystery, however: the vast majority of its residents are new immigrants who are finding it much harder to get established in this country than their predecessors in the 1970s and 1980s.[5]

The economic and social stresses imposed by high immigration levels have also been of concern to the well-known columnist and author Jeffrey Simpson. "It's one thing to pluck a number out of the air as the Liberals have done — immigration equivalent to 1 percent of Canada's population, or about 300,000 — but it's quite another to find would-be immigrants overseas, entice them to Canada, then pay for the costs of settling them," observes Simpson. This critic does not dispute the long-term gains from substantial immigration, but he decries Ottawa's penchant for off-loading short-term costs onto provinces, municipalities, school boards, and hospitals. He also predicts that Ottawa's attempts to drive up immigration numbers will result in a smaller portion of skilled and trained immigrants, those newcomers who integrate faster, earn bigger pay cheques, and plough more money back into the economy. If Canadian companies require more labour let them recruit overseas themselves, advises Simpson.[6]

The fallout from high immigration levels also expresses itself in a seldom-acknowledged trend. Since about 90 percent of this country's immigrants settle in its ten largest cities, Canada may be witnessing the creation of two demographic solitudes. This development concerned Larry Bourne, a University of Toronto geographer and urban planner, who observed, "We're turning a half-dozen cities into intensely multicultural and multilingual places and creating these fantastically vibrant but under-serviced cities while the rest of the country remains homogeneous with a declining and aging population." In Bourne's view, this trend is far more important than the east-versus-west division or large city versus small.[7]

Royal Bank of Canada economist Derek Holt took a middle-of-the-road position on immigration and annual immigration targets. Holt ridiculed the idea that demographic charts are a reliable indicator of future trends in everything from stock market prices and housing to government finances and growth. On the other hand, he confidently predicted that Canada could maintain the same mix of ages in 2026 as it had in 2003 if immigration targets were increased substantially, especially for educated workers in their twenties. In advocating higher immigration levels for this category of immigrants, however, Holt urged that more resources be devoted to integrating them into the economy.[8]

The Economic Importance of Immigrants

From academia, Peter S. Li decried the tendency of Canadians to assign overwhelming importance to economic performance when assessing the merits of immigration and the desirability of immigrants. When the subject of immigration comes up for discussion, his fellow countrymen, claims Li, frequently assume that immigrants should only be admitted to this country if they can enrich it economically and that the best way to gauge immigrants' economic value is to establish how their earnings compare to those of native-born Canadians. Such a utilitarian approach to immigration, says the sociology professor, reduces immigrants to two legal categories: the more desirable selected immigrants who qualify as economic immigrants and the less desirable or self-selected immigrants who are admitted as family members or refugees.

However, economic criteria shouldn't be applied to all categories of immigrants. Instead, claims Li, immigrants' performance should be evaluated in accordance with the goals of their admission. If, for example, the objective of admitting families is to permit them to reunite, then measure the success of the family-class program on the ease with which families are reunited in Canada, not on the economic performance of members of this class. Similarly, measure the effectiveness of the refugee admission program on the speed and ease with which Canada offers a safe haven for victims of persecution, not on how well these individuals perform economically in their adopted country.[9]

Li notes that studies of tax returns indicate that skilled immigrants who entered Canada before 1989 earned more, on average, than "Canadian tax filers," while those who arrived after 1989 earned less and this despite their having more education and expertise. This paradox was highlighted in a Statistics Canada study that found that the earnings gap between recent immigrants and Canadian-born men widened dramatically between 1980 and 2000. Although newcomers were arriving more skilled than ever before, they weren't able to capitalize on their skills. In 1980, when differences in age and education were taken into account, recent male immigrants earned 17 percent less, on average, than their Canadian-born counterparts. Twenty years later the gap had more than doubled in size, to 40 percent.[10]

Offsetting these dismal findings are more recent ones, published in 2004. These indicate that after a skilled-worker principal applicant has been in Canada five years he/she earns the same or more than the average Canadian-born worker and that the improvement becomes more evident with successive groups of skilled workers.[11]

Racism and discrimination could partially account for the widening wage gaps. Indeed, some studies reveal a wage gap between visible minority Canadians (both Canadian and foreign-born), while others have found that visible minorities, especially black Canadians, experience nearly double the unemployment rate of others.[12]

UNDERVALUING IMMIGRANTS' FOREIGN EXPERIENCE

Perhaps even more significant, however, is the tendency of Canadian professions and businesses to undervalue foreign work experience and their failure to recognize or appreciate academic credentials earned elsewhere. This has resulted in a shocking waste of talent in Canada, as evidenced by the fact that many foreign-born, highly trained professionals are forced to work in menial jobs in this country for years on end. "The immigration system needs to be tossed on its head and revamped," British Columbia MP, Keith Martin, declared in 2002, after witnessing first-hand the bureaucratic ordeals that foreign doctors had to put up with in order to practise in Prince George, British Columbia, where there was a severe shortage of physicians.[13]

Thirty years ago, Western Europe and the United States were the principal sources of skilled immigrants for Canada. By contrast, Asia and Africa are now the chief sources of skilled immigrants. Asian and African newcomers are finding, however, that their foreign work experience counts for virtually nothing when they are job hunting in Canada. In light of this, Statistics Canada declared bluntly, in the spring of 2004, that lack of recognition of foreign work experience was the principal reason for the plummeting earnings of new Canadians, who now earn about one quarter less today during their first year in Canada than those who arrived thirty years ago.[14]

Canada, it is now widely acknowledged, is doing a poor job of recognizing the skills and work experience of new immigrants, especially those who hail from Africa and Asia. On the one hand, the government's points system favours highly educated professionals, but on the other hand, Canada's overseas immigration officials do not point out the obstacles newcomers face in obtaining employment in their field of expertise. In fact, claims University of Ottawa history professor Mark Stolarik, these immigration officials "deliberately mislead these professionals by not warning them against the closed shops of many Canadian professions, especially medicine."[15]

Lack of recognition of foreign credentials and work experience is certainly widespread. Nevertheless, the situation is perhaps not as bleak as a casual observer might believe, since governments are finally acting to remedy the problem. In the fall of 2004, for example, the Ontario government announced that it would spend $2 million over the next two years to help internationally trained engineers practise in the province. A similar program, it reported, would provide foreign-trained doctors with quicker access to the accreditation they require to practise.[16] Realizing that a strong, vibrant economy depended upon a skilled workforce, British Columbia has established the International Qualifications Unit, designed to help fully utilize the skills of internationally trained immigrants in the B.C. labour market. In February 2004, the unit teamed up with Citizenship and Immigration Canada (CIC) to fund sixteen projects, some of which developed resources to address barriers to employment in the province.[17]

Two years later, in the spring of 2006, the looming shortage of skilled workers and professionals persuaded the Ontario government to announce a pilot project in Ottawa that would earmark $3.8 million for training programs in agriculture, health, teaching, and the trades at Algonquin College, La Cité collégiale, and other institutions. And that autumn, Ottawa Mayor Bob Chiarelli, while campaigning for re-election, floated a plan to assist foreign-trained professionals with finding employment within their chosen fields.[18]

The failure of better-educated immigrants to do as well as their less-educated counterparts did a generation ago has serious implications, not only for the immigrants themselves but also for the Canadian economy. According to the Conference Board of Canada, the frequent failure of Canada to recognize the qualifications of present-day newcomers robs the economy of as much as $3.4 billion annually.

If this were not bad enough, recent arrivals are experiencing significantly higher levels of unemployment than Canadian-born residents. The Canadian Labour and Business Centre spotlighted this trend when it reported that in 1981 the unemployment rate for immigrants in their first year of residence was about ten points above the national average, although five years later it had slid to about the national average. This trend would later reverse itself, however. In fact, by 2001, the unemployment rate for first-year immigrants was twenty-three points higher than the national average.[19]

These trends, which were clearly evident in the early 1990s, provided plenty of fodder for critics of Canada's immigration system. So did the continuing backlog in the refugee determination system and the failure to implement more stringent controls on individuals claiming refugee status. Against this background of mounting criticism and attacks on the system, in the late 1990s the Liberal government appointed an independent three-member advisory panel to examine Canada's immigration policy.

REPORT OF IMMIGRATION ADVISORY COMMITTEE

The panel's report, *Not Just Numbers*, released in January 1998, recommended a massive overhaul of Canada's immigration policy to restore public confidence in what was widely perceived to be a flawed and highly bureaucratic system. In urging the adoption of a simpler but tougher immigration system, the report made 172 recommendations that touched on virtually every area of federal immigration policy.

Among the report's key recommendations were:

- an annual cap on the number of newcomers;
- a greater emphasis on proficiency in English and French among all immigrants, even large investors;
- the close monitoring of refugee claimants in Canada;
- the revamping of the investor program;
- a streamlining of the process for bringing skilled foreign workers into Canada;

- the introduction of a new refugee system that places more emphasis on serving the people most in need — usually women and children — rather than those individuals who succeed in making it to Canada. A new agency, made up mostly of professionally trained public servants, would screen refugee claimants who do make it to this country; and
- the closing of loopholes in the family sponsorship program under which established immigrants agree to provide financial support to relatives for several years after their arrival in Canada. At the time the report was written, the program had an estimated 14 percent default rate.[20]

THE IMMIGRATION AND REFUGEE PROTECTION ACT

When the Liberal government finally embarked on the first large-scale overhaul of Canada's immigration policy since 1976 it did so with a view to streamlining and improving the immigration system, taking into account the changing character of the Canadian labour market, anticipated demographic changes in Canadian society, and the security and safety of the country. The result was Bill C-11, which was introduced on February 21, 2001, by Immigration Minister Elinor Caplan.

After the bill was tabled, the Standing Committee on Citizenship and Immigration conducted a thorough review of its provisions, examining about 160 submissions received from witnesses during cross-Canada hearings. The outcome of these submissions and the committee's deliberations was a series of amendments to Bill C-11. Notable among these was the inclusion of a reference to multiculturalism, considered by the committee to be integrally linked to immigration and therefore a defining characteristic of Canadian society.[21]

The amended bill received third reading on October 31, 2001, and Royal Assent on November 1, 2001. It came into law as the Immigration and Refugee Protection Act on June 28, 2002. From inception to implementation, it had been presided over by three different immigration ministers, each of whom had insisted that the department review and rethink what had already been done before.

The new act outlined several basic economic, social, and cultural goals for Canada's immigration program:

- to pursue the greatest economic, social, and cultural benefits across Canada, while respecting the country's federal, bilingual, and multicultural character;
- to reunite families in Canada;
- to help newcomers integrate into Canadian society while recognizing the mutual obligations of new permanent residents and Canadian society;
- to attract visitors, students, and temporary foreign workers for the purpose of tourism, trade, and cultural, scientific, and educational pursuits;
- to protect the health and safety of Canadians;
- to safeguard the security of Canadian society and promote international justice and security by preventing the admission of criminals or security risks; and
- to cooperate with the provinces in establishing immigration goals, recognizing foreign credentials, and integrating permanent residents.

In addition to these goals, the act also set out four humanitarian goals of refugee protection:

- to fulfill Canada's international legal obligations regarding refugees and to help those who need to resettle;
- to give fair consideration to people arriving in Canada seeking protection, and to offer a safe haven to individuals with a well-founded fear of persecution;
- to maintain the integrity of the refugee determination process while safeguarding human rights and freedoms; and
- to support the well-being and self-sufficiency of refugees by reuniting them with their families.[22]

Part 1V, a key section of the act, provided for the establishment of an independent, quasi-judicial body whose chairperson reports to Parliament through the minister of Citizenship and Immigration. Known as the Immigration and Refugee Board, its mission is "to make well-reasoned decisions on immigration and refugee matters, efficiently, fairly and in accordance with the law."[23] To make these decisions, the act provided for the establishment of four separate tribunals: the Refugee Protection Division (RPD), the Refugee Appeal Division, the Immigration Division, and the Immigration Appeal Division.

When the act came into force then-Immigration Minister Denis Coderre declared that one of its principal objectives was to rectify a major shortcoming of the old act: the regulations governing the skilled-worker program. Under these regulations an applicant's eligibility depended on whether his/her work experience matched a specific occupation on the General Occupations List.[24] Accordingly, under the old act officials tried to pick independent immigrants who could fill perceived skills shortages in the labour market. Today's fast-changing labour market convinced the government that it could no longer be expected to match these applicants with specific occupational vacancies. In the new act, therefore, it adopted a different approach altogether for selecting skilled workers, one that stresses flexible skills rather than an intended occupation.

The new approach requires that a skilled worker be assessed on the basis of his/her *human capital attributes*. "Human capital is much more than just the educational and language skills of an applicant," explained Mark Davidson, director, Economic Policy and Programs for Citizenship and Immigration Canada's Selection Branch. "It is the whole collection of an individual's abilities that allows them to function in a society."[25]

Under the new arrangement, a points system and a list of attributes are employed to evaluate applicants. The criteria include formal education and language proficiency (considered the two most important attributes for success in Canada), work experience, age, arranged employment in Canada, and adaptability. Where education is concerned, up to twenty-five points are awarded for studies up to the Ph.D. level. Up to twenty-four points are awarded for proficiency in Canada's two official languages.

In an attempt to create a more efficient refugee determination system, the Immigration and Refugee Protection Act stipulates that only one member of the Immigration and Refugee Board will hear refugee claimants, not a two-member panel, as was the case under the old act. To counteract this reduction, the act provided for a Refugee Appeal Division to which a refugee claimant can appeal a negative decision. This provision was set aside, however, when the government implemented the act in June 2002.

Compared to the previous act, the Immigration and Refugee Protection Act offers a more generous refugee protection program. Instead of recognizing only the refugee protection criteria of the United Nations Convention Relating to the Status of Refugees, signed at Geneva in 1951, and the Protocol to the Convention, signed at New York in 1967, the new act also recognizes criteria acknowledged by the Convention Against Torture and Other Cruel, Inhuman or Degrading Treatment or Punishment, signed at New York in 1984. As a result, Canada now offers a safe haven "to persons with a well-founded fear of persecution based on race, religion, nationality, political opinion or membership in a particular social group, as well as those at risk of torture or cruel and unusual treatment or punishment."[26]

When Bill C-11 was introduced in February 2001, the threat of terrorism, although a consideration, had yet to assume the importance that it did after the September 11, 2001, attacks that killed over three thousand people on American soil. Nevertheless, the bill did acknowledge the threat of terrorism by decreeing that individuals judged to be security risks and violators of human and international rights could not appeal deportation orders. Other new provisions in the bill declared that there would be no appeal rights for serious criminals, members of organized crime, and for holders of visitors' visas. Furthermore, there would be higher maximum penalties for smuggling ten or more persons into the country and serious penalties for trafficking in persons.[27]

CRITICISM OF THE NEW ACT

The new act, not surprisingly, attracted criticism, most of it directed at the refugee determination system. Some critics questioned whether seventy-two hours was adequate time to run security checks on self-declared refugees before their claims are automatically referred to the Immigration and Refugee Board.

Other critics, notably the Canadian Council for Refugees, the United Nations High Commissioner for Refugees, Canadian churches, and Amnesty International, attacked the Canadian government for not implementing an appeal process that recognized the merits of a refugee's case. "Given that even the best decision-makers may err in passing judgment, and given the potential risk to life which may result from such an error, an appeal to the merits of a negative determination constitutes a necessary element of protection," observed the Inter-American Commission on Human Rights in its February 2000 *Report on the Situation of Human Rights of Asylum Seekers Within the Canadian Refugee Determination System.*

In May 2002, the minister of Citizenship and Immigration, Denis Codere, promised the Canadian Council for Refugees that the appeal process would be implemented within a year. However, the Refugee Appeal Division (RAD) was not launched until December 15, 2012. The RAD considers appeals against RPD decisions to allow or reject claims for refugee protection. Usually there is no hearing, as the RAD bases its decisions on documents provided by the parties involved and the RPD record. Before the RAD was established the Federal Court was allowed to intervene, but only in cases involving procedural mistakes. Notwithstanding this stipulation, there was a 300 percent increase between 1996 and 2006 in the number of refugee and immigration cases heard by the Federal Court; in this period, they comprised 80 percent of the cases before the court.[28]

Since there was then no merit-based appeal process, many rejected refugee claimants used the most promising option available to them, CIC's humanitarian review. In doing so, they argued that they had been in Canada for so long that to would be a hardship for them to leave.

Undoubtedly the most withering criticism was delivered by two former federal civil servants. Leading the charge was James Bissett. A long-time critic of Canadian immigration policy, Bissett regards the new act as deeply flawed, particularly as regards the refugee determination system. In fact, he would scrap the refugee board altogether.

The late Tom Kent, onetime adviser to prime ministers Pierre Trudeau and Lester B. Pearson, was the other critic. From his perch in the school of Policy Studies, Queen's University, Kent excoriated the new legislation for merely fiddling with process and procedure and not introducing a bold new immigration policy suited to the twenty-first century.

In his attack on the new legislation, Kent focused on the refugee question. Canada, he declared, should stop concentrating on refugee claims made by self-selected applicants who have succeeded in getting to this country and instead pursue an activist policy that seeks to help genuine refugees, the people who most need our help and who are languishing in overseas camps. This way we can do more good, insisted the former public servant.

To make this happen, however, Ottawa must invoke the notwithstanding clause of the Constitution to remove Charter rights accorded to refugee claimants by the Supreme Court of Canada in 1985 (the Harbhajan Singh decision). The Charter's legal protections should be extended only to persons who are legally resident in Canada, said Kent, who also noted that Parliament can enact a law providing for this. Once such a law has been adopted, fair but prompt procedures to assess refugee claims and to implement decisions should be established.

Acutely conscious of Canada's low birth rate, Kent proposed that Ottawa focus its efforts on bringing uprooted children, particularly orphans, and then young families to Canada. If such an activist program were carefully developed, he claimed, it could become a significant component of immigration policy. Moreover, it would excite the humanitarian instincts of Canadians.[29]

The Canada Border Services Agency

No sooner was the Immigration and Refugee Protection Act implemented than the Liberal government decided to tackle the lack of coordination among security agencies and weaknesses at airports and border crossings. Its answer was to bring together all the major players involved in facilitating and managing the movement of people and goods at the border and all the related intelligence, interdiction, and enforcement activities into one body, the Canada Border Services Agency (CBSA). Designed to protect Canadians and maintain a safe and peaceful society, it integrates several functions previously divided among three organizations: the customs program from the Canada Customs and Revenue Agency, the import inspection at ports of entry program from the Canadian Food

Inspection Agency, and the intelligence, interdiction, and enforcement program and the immigration program at ports of entry from Citizenship and Immigration Canada. The new agency is an integral part of the Public Safety portfolio, which also includes the Royal Canadian Mounted Police, the National Parole Board, the Canadian Security Intelligence Service, Correctional Service Canada, and the Canada Firearms Centre.[30]

When Prime Minister Paul Martin announced the creation of the CBSA on December 12, 2003, he confirmed the transfer of the intelligence, interdiction, and enforcement functions from Citizenship and Immigration Canada (CIC) to the new agency. At the same time, however, he indicated that the ports of entry program at CIC would not be transferred to CBSA until there had been further discussion with stakeholders. The transfer finally took place in October 2004, the delay having been prompted by Martin's wish that Canada's reputation for welcoming immigrants and refugees not be tarnished by the transfer of these functions to the CBSA.

Non-governmental organizations seized the opportunity presented by the consultation to demand and succeed in obtaining two adjustments to the initial transfer of functions. One involved the Pre-Removal Risk Assessment (PRRA) process, a procedure that allows an individual placed under a removal order to apply for a review of his or her case to ensure that the applicant will not be returned to a country where he or she might face the threat of danger or the risk of persecution. The NGOs insisted that the responsibility for pre-removal assessments be returned to CIC. The other request involved the reinstatement of a requirement that the minister of CIC sign security certificates. These notorious documents allow the Canadian government, by means of a process that engages the Federal Court, to remove non-Canadian citizens deemed to pose a danger to national security or to the safety of any person. The NGOs felt that the December 2003 requirement, that only the minister of Public Safety sign security certificates, lacked the safeguard of a second set of eyes.

These two adjustments and the transfer of the ports of entry functions were effected simultaneously in October 2004 and completed the creation of the new agency. Formal recognition of this was provided by the bill establishing the department, which received Royal assent on November 3, 2005.

When all intelligence, interdiction, and enforcement functions (both policy and operations) and all border management functions were transferred to the CBSA, CIC lost several important responsibilities, to say nothing of approximately 1,900 employees. Still, it retained a number of critical functions. One of these — its mission to optimize the benefits of immigration to Canada — even became more focused. The department also retained responsibility for visa policy and admission policy (with the exception of the three highest-level threats: security, organized crime, and war crime/crimes against humanity), which were transferred to the CBSA. In short, CIC assumed responsibility for attracting people of interest to Canada, be they immigrants or temporary residents, while the CBSA took on the task of targeting and dealing with people who pose a threat or a risk to this country.

Reflecting, in 2006, on the loss of functions by CIC, Craig Goodes, a former CIC officer and CBSA's director in 2015, observed, "It's a little too early to declare that the integration of these Canada Border Services Agency programs has been successful, but to the best of my knowledge nobody has questioned the decision to do this."[31] Goodes conceded that life can become complicated when a client has to deal with two ministries, but he was sanguine that, over time, the delivery of services would improve still further.

— CHAPTER 13 —

Developments 2006–2015:
Pruning the Queue

ABOUT A DOZEN ISSUES DOMINATED the federal election campaign that culminated in the formation of a minority government under Stephen Harper in January 2006. The vital issue of immigration reform, however, was not one of them. Nor did it figure in the centrepiece of the Conservative campaign platform, the "Five Priorities." These were five easy-to-grasp promises that dealt with cleaning up government by enacting and enforcing the Federal Accountability Act; lowering taxes for working Canadians; strengthening the justice system; supporting parents' child-care choices by providing them with direct assistance and by creating additional daycare spaces; and delivering the health care that Canadians need, when they need it.[1]

The first post-election minister of Citizenship and Immigration was the genial Monte Solberg, the MP for Medicine Hat, Alberta, and a former businessman and radio broadcaster. When he took office in February 2006, he was confronted by what can best be described as a failed immigration system. The previous Liberal government had overhauled a flawed and highly bureaucratic system by implementing the Immigration and Refugee Protection Act (IRPA) and by establishing the Canada Border Services Agency. Of the two measures, the IRPA alone could have played a role in helping to scrap the most troubling aspect of the system: the huge number of prospective immigrants who had to wait years for their applications to be processed. However, the act lacked any mechanism that would allow the government to limit the number of applications submitted to it annually.

In the past, the federal government could control the number of newcomers admitted to Canada by altering the selection criteria, which included occupation. When the economy was sluggish, Ottawa could raise the pass mark and adjust downward the number of points awarded to certain occupations. Conversely, when the economy was buoyant the government could lower the pass mark and raise the number of the points assigned to specific occupations. Usually these changes were made by implementing amendments to regulations rather than by changing the act, a cumbersome and time-consuming process. The unamended IRPA also required the government to issue visas to applicants who met the selection criteria (Bill C-11), but because its selection criteria did not include occupation Ottawa could not limit the number of applications submitted to it each year. In other words, the act ignored the fact that there will always be thousands of people who satisfy its selection criteria and who want to settle in Canada, but who could not be either processed or absorbed satisfactorily by the economy. This lack of any mechanism to limit the number of applications submitted annually would prove to be one of the IRPA's major flaws: no sooner had it been implemented than the backlog of applications began to grow. Recognizing the problem, the previous Liberal government took action to correct it. In June 2002, it retroactively introduced more stringent requirements that had to be met by immigrants in the backlog who had already been accepted. Not surprisingly, the courts struck this attempt down. As a result, the backlog continued to grow.[2]

The fact that immigration target figures had been set high for decades only exacerbated the problem. From the end of the Second World War until the mid-1980s, the federal government, no matter what its political stripe, had regulated immigration according to economic conditions. This approach changed in 1985, however, when the newly elected Progressive Conservative government under Prime Minister Brian Mulroney began to plan for "a moderate, controlled increase" of immigration when the economy had yet to fully rebound from the recession triggered by the oil crisis. Five years later, in 1990, Barbara McDougall, the then-minister of Employment and Immigration, endorsed the upward trend when she persuaded her cabinet colleagues to raise the annual immigration intake level to 250,000. Increased immigration, she argued, would help the Progressive Conservative Party to forge stronger ties with Canada's ethnic communities.[3] This thinking was also shared by all the other major political parties, which, like the Progressive Conservative Party, were committed to capturing the immigrant vote. Annual immigration intake levels would therefore remain close to 250,000 throughout the 1990s and into the present century. In fact, in 2010, when Canada had just lost nearly half a million full-time jobs because of a recession, the country received some 280,000 immigrants. (This figure does not include temporary workers, foreign students, and refugees.) On a per capita basis this figure represents more immigrants than are accepted by any other immigrant-receiving country, including the United States.

Not only were large numbers of immigrants being admitted to the country each year, irrespective of the state of the economy, but naturalized immigrants, including educated ones who had entered Canada as economic immigrants, were falling more frequently into poverty and taking longer to attain average Canadian incomes than immigrants in previous decades. This was because six out of ten immigrants were forced, on arrival, to take a shift downward in their job or career. Often this could be attributed to a lack of proficiency in English or French, cultural differences, the absence of a social network, and a lack of so-called "Canadian experience."

In 2011, Yane Brogiollo cited a lack of "Canadian experience" as the reason she could not land a job commensurate with her qualifications in Canada. In her home city of Sao Paulo, Brazil, Brogiollo was an IT professional at Hewlett Packard, where she oversaw fifteen database professionals. She also designed and taught MBA courses at a local university. Despite her years of IT experience, a master of science degree in computer engineering, and seventy job applications, she could not make it past the interview stage with prospective employers. "The first thing they look for is Canadian experience," she told a reporter. "If you don't have that, they don't call you for an interview. And if you don't get an interview, it's hard to show your skills."[4]

No matter what the explanation, many experienced and highly skilled individuals ended up in unsuitable, subsistence jobs, thereby robbing Canada of potential assets. Since these newcomers paid only about half the income tax that Canadians paid, they imposed an estimated fiscal burden on the government of at least $20 billion annually.[5]

It was patently obvious that the number of immigrant arrivals and the demands of the labour market were out of whack. A study by Garnett Pico and Feng Hou found that the number of low-income Canadians among recent immigrants was rising but falling among Canadian-born. Recent immigrants in 1980, for example, had low-income rates 1.4 times that of Canadian-born, but by 2000 the figure had changed to 2.5.[6]

Diane Finley, the MP for Haldimand-Norfolk and Monte Solberg's successor as minister of Citizenship and Immigration, sought to reform the immigration system by introducing important changes to the Immigration and Refugee Protection Act. Her stint as minister of CIC (January 2007–October 2008) is probably best remembered for the alleged threats she received from sex-industry officials vehemently opposed to her support of legislation that allowed immigration officers to refuse temporary visas to prospective strippers suspected of being sex trafficking victims (Bill C-17). This bill died on the Order Paper in September 2008, and was reintroduced twice, eventually being incorporated in Bill C-10, the Safe Streets and Communities Act.

Finley's attempts to overhaul the IRPA and transform Canada's immigration system into a lean recruitment tool merited greater attention. Her instrument for this purpose was Bill C-50, the budget implementation bill introduced in early 2008. Among the countless issues it dealt with was the Immigration and Refugee Protection Act, which Bill C-50 amended and that came into effect on June 28, 2008. Two of the changes would have important implications for the curtailing of application backlogs and the selection of immigrants. Under the amended act, for example, the CIC minister was given the authority to set "the number of applications or requests, by category or otherwise, to be processed in any year" and "provide for the disposition of applications and requests, including those made subsequent to the first application or request." Moreover, if an application or request was not processed, it could be "retained, returned or otherwise disposed of in accordance with the instructions of the Minister."[7] In short, the minister could now instruct departmental officials to prioritize the processing of certain categories of applications or to not process certain applications or categories.

These provisions, however, applied only to applications subject to instructions, i.e., to those applications submitted by economic immigrants and the handful of humanitarian and compassionate applicants outside Canada and received after February 28, 2008. Left untouched were refugee and family-class immigrants, since the new power to issue instructions did not apply to these categories of applicants.

With the government's emphasis on economic immigration (i.e., skilled workers and investors) in mind, the department assigned priority to qualified skilled professionals from certain countries rich in educated people wishing to emigrate. Thanks to another amendment to the act, immigration officials could also deny permanent residence to applicants who met the act's requirements and whose applications had already been approved by them.

The government's attempt to regain control of the immigration program unleashed a volley of speculation about the intent of the regulatory changes. *Toronto Star* columnist Carol Goar wrote, "It is possible that Immigration Minister Diane Finley wants more power to do exactly what she says: clean up her department's enormous backlog of unprocessed applications." But Goar added, "The sweeping nature of the changes proposed in Bill C-50 suggests something bigger than housecleaning is afoot."[8] Long-time immigration lawyer Lorne Waldman weighed in with the observation, "This fundamentally changes our immigration policy." In Waldman's view, Canada would no longer be an immigrant-welcoming country. It would merely be a wealthy Western power that seeks out high-value immigrants, since the minister could set and change the rules at her will.[9] The Canadian Bar Association warned that the use of ministerial instruction would "erode the transparency and accountability that underlie Canada's immigration system."[10]

What critics neglected to note is that the minister did not have unfettered power to do what she wanted: she had to inform Parliament about her instructions regarding the establishment of categories, the order of processing, and the disposition of applications. Although there was much opposition in Parliament to the bill (the NDP and the Bloc Québécois voted against it and many Liberals absented themselves from the vote), the Conservatives succeeded in getting it passed. And despite the fact that the amendments did not apply to the application backlog that had built up prior to February 2008, as of June 2009 the number of federal skilled-worker applicants who had submitted applications after that date had been reduced by 29 percent.[11] The sharp decline in the number of applications can be attributed to the reintroduction of a relatively short occupation list into the selection criteria. As it was then, it is now mandatory to have work experience in one of these occupations.

The amendments to the Immigration and Refugee Protection Act represented a striking achievement during Finley's tenure as minister of CIC. Less striking, but certainly noteworthy, was the establishment of the Foreign Credentials Referral Office. Created in 2007 and designed to improve the assessment and recognition of foreign qualifications, it provides "information, path-finding and referral services to internationally trained individuals in Canada and overseas."[12]

Diane Finley's successor as Immigration minister was Jason Kenney, who would become Canada's longest-serving minister of Citizenship and Immigration to date (October 2008 to July 14, 2013). Before being appointed to the portfolio, the fluently bilingual Kenney wanted nothing to do with immigration. He even refused to become immigration critic when his party was in opposition. However, after Stephen Harper convinced him that the future of Canada's Conservative movement depended on bringing immigrants into its fold, Kenney changed his mind. At Harper's bidding, he became Secretary of State for Multiculturalism on January 4, 2007. He then brought Multiculturalism into Citizenship and Immigration Canada on October 30, 2008, when he was appointed that department's minister.

Jason Kenney was born in Ontario but raised in Saskatchewan, where he graduated from the College of Notre Dame, an independent private school. He then pursued undergraduate studies at the University of San Francisco. After returning to Canada, he served as president and chief executive officer of the Canadian Taxpayers Federation. This became the launching pad for his political career, which began in 1997 with his election to the House of Commons as MP for Calgary Southeast. He was subsequently re-elected five times, most recently with 76 percent of the vote.

As the description so often bestowed on him (he went "for curry in a hurry") suggests, Kenney soon embraced his new job with unbridled enthusiasm. Realizing that personal contact is essential for new immigrants, he went on the road three weekends out of four. On some Sundays in Toronto, Vancouver, or Montreal, he participated in as many as twenty cultural activities, some of which required him to warn new immigrants from China and Tibet, Israel and Iran, and Greece and Turkey not to reproduce the tensions of their homelands in Canada. The work he did courting Canada's ethnic communities was certainly long, complex, and meticulous, requiring, in the words of writer Alec Castonguay, "the patience of a Buddhist monk."[13]

As minister of Citizenship and Immigration, Kenney tirelessly reflected the Harper government's preoccupation with choosing applicants who, it thought, would provide the greatest long-term value to Canada. In speech after speech across the country, the minister singled out our country's low birth rate and predicted that by 2016, 100 percent of Canada's labour growth would have to be provided by immigration. Under these circumstances, he claimed, there should be little room for "electorally driven immigration," whereby governments shamelessly pander to the immigrant communities by expanding family reunification quotas.[14] While stressing the importance of economic immigration, however, Kenney continued to cultivate his strong ties with ethnic communities and to keep family-class immigration numbers near to, or even higher than, previous levels. In 2013, for example, Canada admitted 79,586 permanent family-class members, while in 2011 it admitted 56,450 permanent members in the same category.[15] While continuing to maintain family-class immigration numbers at these levels, the minister nevertheless introduced a requirement that newcomers sponsoring their parents and grandparents commit to covering their financial costs for at least twenty years.

The reason for the marked jump in the admissions of parents and grandparents between 2011 and 2013 can be explained by CIC's desire to reduce the size of the family class applications' backlog. However, the overall robust numbers of family-class members can perhaps also be explained by flack that the minister received from some of his colleagues representing ethnically diverse ridings, who reported that skilled workers and business-class migrants were frustrated by his government's relegating of family sponsorship applications to the bottom of the pile. These people, they explained, wanted to have their parents or grandparents in Canada to help raise the children, who, studies indicated, were more likely to obtain university degrees and high-skill jobs than the children of native-born Canadians.

In stark contrast to this positive view of family-class immigration was the position taken by Herb Grubel, an economist at the Fraser Institute, a conservative thinktank. Alarmed by what he perceived to be the high "fiscal burden" imposed by family-class newcomers, Grubel suggested that the government phase out the sponsorship of parents and grandparents and bring in an employer-driven system to attract economic immigrants.[16]

ATTRACTING ECONOMIC IMMIGRATION

Kenney would not phase out the sponsorship of parents and grandparents, but he would make herculean attempts to increase suitable economic immigration to Canada. For this purpose he used the Canadian Experience Class Program, implemented in 2008, and the Foreign Credentials Recognition Program introduced the following year. The Canadian Experience Class Program is designed to fast track permanent residency applications submitted by international students and temporary foreign workers in skilled occupations. The temporary foreign workers must have lived in Canada for some time, have a good knowledge of English or French, and possess the kind of skilled work experience in demand in this country. International students must have graduated from a Canadian college or university and have skilled work experience in Canada. Since these applicants have spent time in this country on temporary permits or student visas and are therefore familiar with Canadian social mores and work practices, they are considered better able to integrate into the labour market. To ensure that the most suitable candidates were accepted, the minister issued ministerial instructions in June 2010 for mandatory language testing for both skilled workers and Canadian experience-class applicants. Principal applicants in the Canadian Experience Class program numbered 1,775. Two years later, this figure had soared to 4,359, making the program this country's fastest-growing immigration program.[17]

The Foreign Credentials Recognition Program seeks to attract, select, and integrate skilled immigrants into the Canadian economy and society. By means of contribution agreements, it offers financial assistance to provincial and territorial governments and assorted organizations to facilitate the assessment and recognition of credentials obtained in other countries. Partnering organizations often include national associations, regulatory bodies, and credential assessment agencies. In August 2013, for example, the federal government offered Nova Scotia over $1 million to help internationally trained professionals get their credentials recognized. The 125 loans Nova Scotia funded would enable those professionals to overcome the significant financial challenges posed by the cost of licensing, exams, training, and skill upgrades necessary to acquire credential recognition.

The implementation of a provincial nomination program in 1998 has allowed provinces and territories, with the assistance of employers, to nominate individuals who wish to immigrate to Canada and settle in a particular province. Each province and territory, with the exception of Quebec, has its own unique nomination program (Quebec has a different selection system.) The national program has proven very popular over the years, almost guaranteeing a visa if the client has no medical, criminal, or security issues. Nevertheless, Kenney wanted to see a program that would allow employers to participate more directly in the selection of applicants. (They would still be processed by public servants to ensure that they met legislative requirements.) "Employers are going to do a much better job at selection than a passive bureaucracy because they can't afford to recruit people to come to Canada who can't work at their skill level on arrival," Kenney observed.[18] With this in mind, the Conservative government introduced a new "express entry" program in January 2015 that allowed Canadian employers to pick skilled applicants out of the queue for processing, provided there are no Canadians or permanent residents available for the work. Under the new system, skilled immigrants are matched with vacant jobs in at least fifty occupations, but only the "highest" ranking candidates are invited to apply for permanent residence.

In his attempts to develop a faster, more flexible immigration regime, the minister also redesigned the points system to emphasize youth and language ability. To the critics' charge that the Conservatives' approach to immigration was too xenophobic or too market-driven, he argued that Canada was doing people a disservice by allowing them to enter the country without having a decent job lined up.

In order to create the immigration system that Canada lacked, CIC had to deal with its staggering backlog of applications, which it estimated would not be cleared until 2017. It did this in 2012 by bumping hundreds of thousands of people, who had waited for years, from the skilled-worker application list. This was accomplished by means of Bill C-38, which provided for the returning of unprocessed applications and processing fees to clients who had submitted their applications prior to February 2008. In all, some 280,000 applications were culled and $130 million in processing fees returned. Predictably, the government's attempts to eliminate this backlog set off a volley if criticism from appalled observers. Some nine hundred applicants under the skilled-worker program even sued Citizenship and Immigration for violating a pledge to assess and finalize application decisions in a timely manner, i.e., within six to twelve months. In a decision released on June 14, 2012, Federal Court Justice Donald Rennie shot down Kenney's argument that the delay was justified because he had the authority to make immigration policy. The court ruled that those applications deemed eligible for processing must be processed in a "reasonably timely manner." By November of that year, thanks to the cull and earlier measures, only about 100,000 applications remained in the system, down from 640,000 a few years earlier. As a result, Kenney confidently predicted that by the end of 2013 the government would be able to process skilled-immigrant applications within a year, rather than within eight years, which had been the norm.

THE REFUGEE PROBLEM

The means taken to eliminate the immigration application backlog certainly stirred up trouble for Kenney. But an even greater source of controversy was the government's handling of the refugee/asylum issue. As noted earlier in this history, Canada, unlike other countries, allows almost everyone who arrives at its borders claiming persecution to enter. Once in Canada, that individual is granted a hearing before a quasi-judicial board, the Immigration and Refugee Board (IRB), to determine if he/she is a genuine refugee. Since this policy is wide open to exploitation, thousands of individuals have taken advantage of it to circumvent normal immigration procedures. This has resulted in a serious backlog of cases for the IRB, huge costs for government-provided services, and a boon to human smugglers who guarantee their clients a two- to three-year stay in Canada, even if their claim is denied.

This issue was thrown into sharp relief by the arrival of 492 Sri Lankan refugees off the coast of British Columbia in August 2010. After the clandestine Thai freighter *Sun Sea* docked, Public Safety Minister Vic Toews warned that every passenger would be subjected to a criminal investigation. Everyone, including the children, was then swept off to detention. It soon became evident, however, that many of the adults had no connection whatsoever with the Tamil Tigers, a feared terrorist organization. (Nearly eight months after the ship's arrival, only two men were found to be inadmissible to Canada because of their connection to the Tamil Tigers.)[19] Moreover, the IRB found that the vast majority of Sri Lankan asylum seekers "have a well-founded fear of persecution."[20] Despite this, the federal government stubbornly opposed the release of any claimants. When the IRB ordered the release of passengers, the government fought the release orders in Federal Court, even those that involved women and children. The Federal Court went so far as to criticize Ottawa's position as an abuse of power when it continued to detain a passenger who had been ordered released on three different occasions.

In the wake of the boat's arrival came the passage of Bill C-4 (formerly Bill C-49), the Preventing Human Smugglers from Abusing Canada's Immigration System Act. Under this bill, "designated" refugees (based on mode of travel) will be detained for a year, without the possibility of independent review, and denied family reunification for over five years.

As with so many other bills of this nature, Bill C-4 invited a torrent of criticism. One of the harshest criticisms was voiced by the Catholic archbishop of Vancouver, the Most Reverend J. Michael Miller, CSB, who pointed out that the bill punished the smuggled far more than the smugglers. "Refugee claimants arriving in Canada using irregular means do not relinquish the right to respect and dignity that all human beings are entitled to. They need to be dealt with appropriately, but overly harsh conditions do not fulfill the purpose and only compound their suffering," he said.[21]

To reduce the number of what were considered bogus refugee claims that had been ballooning under his watch, Kenney also introduced Bill C-31 (it came into force on December 15, 2012), which overhauled the refugee determination process. Among other provisions, it incorporated "safe country" provisions similar to those employed by European Union countries. "Safe" countries are those deemed unlikely to generate legitimate refugees because, in Canada's view, their governments respect human rights, have an independent judiciary, and are more likely to offer state protection, etc. Applicants from these countries have their claims expedited and, if they are denied refugee status, they cannot appeal to the newly established Refugee Appeal Division. If they don't leave voluntarily they are deported.

As part of his campaign to speed up the deportation process, Kenney ensured that the bill contained provisions to increase the resources required to hire some eight hundred front-line Canada Border Service officers. This produced the desired results. By August 2013 the federal government had succeeded in removing more than 7,500 failed refugee claimants, 60 percent of them to countries designated as "safe."[22] As was to be expected, refugee advocates slammed the torrent of deportations and deplored the fact that in 2013 the number of people claiming refugee status reached what Ottawa called a "historic low."

However, none of Kenney's immigration reforms triggered such a massive backlash as the cuts made to the Interim Federal Health Program, the program designed to furnish basic medical care to refugee claimants while they wait to have their claims processed, and to persons determined to be refugees but not yet eligible for provincial health coverage. If the claims of refugee claimants are validated, they are entitled to receive provincial health coverage. If their claims are rejected, the applicants are required to leave Canada. In 2012, Ottawa slashed medical benefits for claimants, with the result that most of them could receive only essential health care, without supplements such as dental and vision care. Rejected refugee claimants and claimants from so-called "safe" countries could obtain health care only when they posed a threat to public health. To justify the cuts, the government claimed that they were needed to discourage false refugee claims and to provide equity — to restore a balance in the delivery of health-care services, the government falsely contending that refugees were receiving better health care than Canadians.

The opposition to these cuts was unprecedented. As tensions mounted, health professionals crowded onto Parliament Hill to demonstrate and the *Canadian Medical Association Journal* weighed in with a scathing editorial that labelled the cuts "medically irrational" and "economically irresponsible."[23] Cuts to primary and preventive care have led to refugee claimants appearing at hospital emergency departments with costly acute conditions that could have been treated earlier for less cost, observed Deputy Editor Dr. Matthew Stanbrook in the editorial. "This results in a failure to protect either the public or the patient." The cuts came in for further attack in July 2014 when the Federal Court ruled the changes unconstitutional. Justice Anne Mactavish found that the cuts to refugee health care targeted vulnerable people in such a harmful way that they constituted "cruel and unusual treatment." Moreover, the judge found that "lives are being put at risk" and decreed that the government had four months to restore refugee health care.[24] The government immediately appealed the ruling.

Despite the massive opposition, Ottawa did not waver in its commitment to the cuts, although it did change the original legislation to provide full coverage for all those refugees invited by the government. And fortunately for refugee claimants, clinics and hospitals across the country have largely absorbed the cost of refugee health care, while some provinces have introduced their own programs.

The Temporary Foreign Worker Program

First introduced in 1973, the Non-Immigrant Employment Authorization Program, as it was then known, allowed participating workers temporary residency but no access to immigration. The restrictions outlined in the 1973 program established the framework for the current version, the Temporary Foreign Worker Program, which allows Canadian employers to hire foreign workers to fill jobs for which no qualified Canadians or permanent residents are available. Instead of being granted permanent resident status, these workers are issued temporary employment visas. Over the years the program has expanded rapidly, tripling between 2002 and the end of 2012, when a record number of foreign workers (338,189) were admitted to this country.[25] Many of these are lower-skilled workers, whose numbers were boosted by the introduction of a pilot project in 2002 that allowed the admission of minimum-wage workers. Commenting on these developments, Mark Carney, the former governor of the Bank of Canada, stated that the program should concentrate on shortages of skilled workers and not on those in service jobs and other low-wage employment, jobs that critics claim could be filled by Canadians but are now being taken by foreign workers. The solution to this problem, observed Carney, is for employers to pay higher wages and improve productivity.[26]

Thanks to the ease with which Canadian employers could obtain a reliable available work force and, in some cases, reduce labour costs, the program was frequently abused. One of the most flagrant examples of abuse involved the Royal Bank of Canada, which reshuffled IT jobs to outside workers and even required RBC workers to train them. Even greater impetus for changes to the program was provided by a mining company's plan to hire up to two hundred Chinese miners to work on a proposed project in northeastern British Columbia. In response to the public outrage caused by these and other abuses, Kenney proposed a sweeping overhaul of the program in the 2013 budget. The resulting overhaul restricts access to TFWP to ensure that Canadians are first in line for available jobs and provides for tougher enforcement of its rules. These include the requirement that employers pay temporary foreign workers the prevailing wage and limit the number of foreign workers they hire to a percentage of their work force. Employers are also required to increase the length and reach of their job advertising to ensure that no Canadians are available before foreign workers are engaged.

Not surprisingly, business reaction to the new regulations was immediate and scathing. Alberta also voiced its objections, claiming that its economy would be adversely affected. In the face of this opposition, Ottawa stated that it would declare a moratorium on enforcing the rules in the fast food industry. Nevertheless, in one deft move, the government had reformed a program that, left untouched, would have done it much harm in the next federal election.

Before leaving his CIC portfolio, the minister also introduced Bill C-43 (assented to on June 19, 2013) to provide for the faster removal of foreign criminals. This bill would eliminate access to Immigration Appeal Division (IAD) reviews of deportation orders issued against permanent residents of this country on the grounds of criminality. Foreign-born residents of Canada are denied access to the IAD if they have been sentenced to more than six months' imprisonment (it was previously two years), regardless of whether they have been rehabilitated and pose no risk to society, have lived in Canada since childhood, etc.

After his years of feverish activity as minister of Citizenship and Immigration, Kenney could be said to have accomplished much in the way of introducing sorely needed reforms to what had been a highly dysfunctional immigration system. To his successor would fall the task of following up on the reforms and, in some cases, rectifying shortcomings.

Chris Alexander, the Conservative MP for Ajax-Pickering, succeeded Kenney as minister of Citizenship and Immigration on July 15, 2013. After graduating from McGill University with a B.A. in history and politics (1989) he earned an M.A. in politics, philosophy, and economics from Balliol College, Oxford, in 1991. That same year, he joined the Canadian Foreign Service, where his postings included a stint as third secretary and vice-consul of the Canadian embassy in Russia (1993–96), minister counsellor at the Canadian Embassy in Moscow (2002), and Canada's first resident ambassador to Afghanistan (2003–05). After leaving the department, he became deputy special representative of the United Nations Assistance Mission in Afghanistan (2005–mid-2009). The recipient of several leadership awards, Alexander was considered a star candidate when he contested the riding of Ajax-Pickering in the 2006 federal election. After winning his seat in 2011, he was appointed Parliamentary secretary to the minister of National Defence, the last portfolio he filled before joining CIC.

On assuming his new portfolio, fluently bilingual Chris Alexander found himself stoutly defending some of his predecessor's more controversial policies. One of these involved refugee health-care cuts. These, he claimed, would save taxpayers $100 million over five years. (Alexander neglected to mention, however, that this calculation never factored in hidden costs such as those incurred when a patient's condition had not been covered by the health-care program.) But most significantly, he argued that the cuts would reduce the number of bogus refugee claimants headed for Canada simply to access its health care. "It is never compassionate to turn a blind eye to abuse and fraud in our immigration and refugee programs. That kind of mistake penalizes refugees first and foremost," he told *Globe and Mail* reporter Konrad Yakabuski.

When not defending Kenney's reforms, the minister introduced some of his own. One of these was the scrapping of the much-criticized immigrant investor program (the "cash for citizenship" program) that had been introduced in 1986 and then updated in 2010. Used primarily by Chinese investors to gain a foothold in Canada, it required wealthy foreigners to have a net worth of more than $1.6 million and to lend the federal government $800,000 interest free for five years. All told, some 130,000 individuals successfully applied to the program with the view to obtaining residency in Canada and potentially citizenship. After studying the issue, however, the government concluded that many of these investors had only tenuous ties to Canada and that they paid "significantly lower taxes over a lifetime" than other immigrants. Replacing it were two pilot projects: an immigrant investor venture capital fund and a business-skills program.[27]

Under Alexander's watch, the government also lifted a two-year freeze on the parent and grandparent immigration stream. The government had temporarily shelved the program in an attempt to deal with a huge backlog of applications and wait times as long as eight years. With the relaunch, however, came tough new criteria for admission. Still, there were concerns about the program's fairness and the underlying political motivation. Toronto immigration lawyer Sergio Karas, for example, labelled it a "bad" program that should be shelved indefinitely because parents and grandparents are older and less employable. On the other hand, Queen's University immigration law professor Sharry Aiken rejected the argument that parents and grandparents don't contribute to the economy, pointing out that many provide child care, thereby allowing parents to enter the work force.[28]

Chris Alexander also piloted through a bill that sought to make Canadian citizenship "harder to get and easier to lose," as Jason Kenney had earlier promised. Bill C-24, which was passed in 2014, requires prospective citizens to declare their "intent to reside" in Canada, to have a fuller knowledge of the country and its history, to function in either English or French, and to absorb a larger cost of the processing of their applications. Another significant provision in the bill enables the minister or the courts to revoke the Canadian citizenship of dual nationals convicted of terrorism.[29]

To honour a 2013 government pledge to protect immigrant women and girls from violence, the minister tabled Bill S-7 on November 5, 2014. Labelled somewhat bizarrely "Zero Tolerance for Barbaric Cultural Practices Act," it banned anyone in a polygamous, underage, or forced marriage from settling in Canada. It also amended the IRPA, the civil marriage act, and the criminal code to accommodate this ban. In introducing the bill, Alexander declared that the government wanted to send a clear message to anyone wanting to immigrate to Canada that practices such as forced, underage, and polygamous marriages as well as honour killings are "incompatible with Canadian values."

Not surprisingly, Bill S-7 provoked a storm of criticism. When appearing on a CBC radio panel, Deepa Mattoo, staff lawyer and acting executive director of the South Asian Legal Clinic of Ontario, claimed that the government had not consulted experts in the field when drawing up the bill and that its statements in support of its changes were not based on statistical data or research. As a result, the tabled act perpetuated myths about the practices of forced marriages and polygamy and encouraged Canadians to believe that violence against women is a "cultural" issue and occurs only in certain communities.[30]

Writing in the *Toronto Star*, Thomas Walkom conceded that the bill did contain some "reasonable elements," one being the explicit outlawing of forced marriages. He attacked it, however, for pandering to the fear that foreigners, particularly Muslims, threaten the very fabric of Canadian society. Moreover, the bill was unnecessary as most of the practices it sought to curb were already illegal in Canada. The government's motives, he charged, were "crassly political."[31]

The Syrian Refugee Crisis

Far more contentious and attention-grabbing was Chris Alexander and the federal government's tepid response to the so-called Syrian refugee crisis, which erupted in 2015. In the spring and summer of that year an estimated 300,000 asylum seekers from North Africa and the Middle East risked their lives by crossing the Mediterranean to reach Europe and carve out a better life. They were so desperate that they were prepared to pay rapacious smugglers large sums of money to transport them in rickety vessels across the ocean's rough, treacherous waters. Among them were countless Syrians fleeing a brutal civil war in their homeland that had been raging for four years and that had displaced some four million of them, many to squalid refugee camps in neighbouring countries such as Jordan and Turkey.

Prior to 2015, the plight of these asylum seekers had failed to attract a lot of international attention, despite the thousands of fatalities suffered in various attempts to reach Europe and the struggle being waged by various European countries to cope with huge numbers of newcomers. This changed abruptly in the late summer of 2015, however, when the body of a three-year-old Syrian toddler (Alan Kurdi) was discovered washed up on a Turkish beach. When a photograph of the corpse appeared on the front pages of newspapers around the world the hordes of people pressing for entry into the European Union suddenly had a human face. The result was a crystallizing of emotions and outrage around the globe. In Canada, the heartbreaking image resonated even more profoundly when it was revealed that Alan's Canadian aunt, living in British Columbia, attempted in January 2015 to sponsor his father's brother and his family for resettlement in her province. The application was presented personally to Chris Alexander, but was later rejected because it lacked sufficient documentation. The aunt had also hoped to sponsor Alan's father and his family, but these hopes were immediately squelched because Alan's brother and his mother had also drowned while attempting to cross the Mediterranean.

Unfortunately for the Conservative government, this tragedy and the enormity of the migrant crisis gripping Europe occurred in the middle of a federal election campaign (the vote was held on October 19) and when Canadians were eager to assist refugees. In the wake of the Kurdi tragedy, local and provincial governments, community groups, and individuals began frantically raising money to sponsor Syrian refugees. Even Canadian mayors began providing leadership on the refugee issue. Instead of seeing decisive, bold action on the part of Ottawa, however, Canadians found themselves up against Ottawa's business-as-usual approach to refugee admission. In other words, the federal government continued to insist that all parties applying for refugee status be screened individually by the United Nations Refugee Agency, an agency already overtaxed with work. Such screening was unnecessary, claimed critics, since Ottawa carried out its own screening. If there was a political will, they claimed, the government would abandon its customary sclerotic method of handling refugee admission and dramatically increase the numbers. There was simply no excuse for the glacial pace at which refugee applications were being processed.

To support their arguments, these observers pointed out that in the past Canada had quickly and successfully admitted large numbers of refugees, the vast majority of whom had gone on to make valuable contributions to their new homeland. The Hungarians in 1956–57 and the Vietnamese boat people came readily to mind. Several factors contributed to the success of these movements, among them commitment and innovation by immigration staff both in Canada and abroad, and the overwhelming response of Canadian individuals and organizations. But the most important factor was undoubtedly strong political leadership. L. Ian MacDonald, a former chief speech writer to Prime Minister Brian Mulroney and later head of the public affairs division of the Canadian embassy in Washington, noted that in 1991–92, when the former Yugoslavia was imploding, Mulroney, a Progressive Conservative, fast tracked the admission of more than 25,000 refugees from Bosnia. It happened because he informed the minister of immigration and the clerk of the Privy Council that he wanted it done, and it was done.[32]

To the Conservatives' credit they had admitted over two thousand Syrian refugees in the previous couple of years and dispatched humanitarian aid to Syria. However, when approached on the issue, which was now front and centre of the election campaign, Harper maintained that Canada was already doing its fair share by participating in bombing raids against the Islamic State, the brutal, crazed movement occupying a large swath of Syria and part of Iraq. Since he considered this terrorist movement to be the root cause of the Syrian refugee crisis, security concerns were uppermost in the prime minister's mind, not the admission of a much larger influx of refugees to Canada.

By mid-September 2015, refugee advocacy and human rights groups were agitating for the admission of ten thousand Syrian refugees in the following year. It remained to be seen, however, whether public pressure would force the government to expedite refugee applications and admit far greater numbers of refugees, and whether Chris Alexander would succeed in correcting his initial awkward response to the fast-evolving Syrian refugee issue.

— CHAPTER 14 —

Issues in the Twenty-First Century

A HOST OF IMMIGRATION-RELATED issues require study now that Canada has moved into the twenty-first century: questions involving demographic considerations, as well as the possible long-term consequences of immigration. Indeed, as present-day developments and those in the 1980s and 1990s demonstrate, conditions worldwide as well as in Canada itself call for a continuing review of Canadian immigration policy and some hard decisions about the role that immigration should play in this country's development.

If past experience is any guide, we can safely assume that it will not be easy to define goals in this emotionally charged area. Historically, Canada has never had a clearly articulated national consensus about what role immigration should play in its future. Only rarely have Canadian governments felt it necessary to proclaim clearly defined long-range immigration goals, whether economic, social, or demographic, and Canadians themselves have never shared a common view about immigration, except that they do not want to see too many immigrants admitted to this country.[1]

A useful starting point for mapping policy is the Immigration and Refugee Protection Act, 2001, which articulates basic objectives of Canadian immigration policy. These can be characterized as economic, social, and humanitarian. Enunciating immigration goals, however, does not determine how they should be met. Nor does it indicate how much importance should be attached to each type of immigration. This is left to the government, which has to take into account the realities of the twenty-first century when it decides how many and what types of immigrants should be allowed into Canada.

Arguments Favouring Population Growth

From the vast literature that deals with the economic consequences of population growth, decline, and aging, it is possible to identify four main arguments in favour of population growth:

- A larger population enables a country to achieve economies of scale both in production and in the provision of social services. This should result in a lowering of per capita costs of goods and services and raise per capita income.
- A larger population encourages a more rapid pace of technological change.
- An aging population will place a greater burden on what is expected to be a shrinking labour force to finance social benefits, such as pensions and health care, to the expanding population of elderly.
- An aging work force is probably less able and less willing to adapt to changes associated with rapid technological developments.[2]

Some of these arguments are highly controversial. Nevertheless, there does seem to be a reasonable consensus in the academic and policy community that population growth does have a positive impact on the economic growth of a country.[3] As the Economic Council of Canada pointed out in a landmark study, however, the impact of immigration on the economy is marginal. Immigration can, for example, help to create scale efficiencies in the domestic market, but the gains are modest as are those realized through a wider sharing of the tax burden to pay for social security and health costs.[4] In short, the impact of immigration on the economy is not nearly as great as academics and policy-makers had earlier believed. It is also clear that natural increase, not immigration, has driven the growth of Canada's population for much of its history.[5]

There is also general agreement that Canada should have a larger population, but just what the optimum population size for this country should be, nobody seems to know. What is obvious is that Canada can boost its population either by producing more people or by encouraging higher net immigration (by increasing overall immigration and attempting to stem emigration), or both. Of these two options, increasing immigration is the only realistic one, because Canadian governments, with the notable exception of Quebec, have shown little interest in adopting policies to encourage higher birth rates.

An Open-Door Policy on Immigration

Among those observers who want to see Canada boost its population are advocates of an open-door policy on immigration. Not surprisingly, they can be passionate in promoting their point of view, whether it be conditioned by essentially humanitarian motives or the principles of classic laissez-faire liberalism. One outspoken apostle of an open-door policy is the newspaper columnist and conservative Terence Corcoran, who has proposed that Canadian immigration policy be based on just a few simple principles. Such principles, wrote Corcoran in 1990, can be summed up thus: "Canada is a free country open to all who are willing to abide by its laws, regardless of race, creed, wealth, income, nationality, status, or shoe size. From this principle it follows that immigration policy should be directed toward a free border across which the world's people can immigrate and emigrate at will."[6]

For his part, Corcoran was at a loss to explain what gives rise to the unending debate over the immigration selection process. Nor could he understand why there should be a multitude of reasons for raising immigration barriers once an arbitrary number of people have entered the country. But he then concluded that virtually every reason for restricting immigration has an economic foundation.[7] Interestingly, he expressed these views over a decade before the infamous 9/11 attacks gave rise to overarching concerns about security.

Proponents of Reduced Immigration

Among those Canadians eager to see immigration levels reduced are those who abhor the fact that immigration from developing nations now constitutes close to 75 percent of new arrivals each year. Vehemently opposed to more ethnic and cultural diversity, they view Canada's present immigration policy with nothing but misgivings. If this country needs more people, they argue, the government should take steps that will encourage Canadians to have more children. Such measures may be costly, they concede, "But, we must decide whether we want the Canada of the future to be made up of our children or those of others."[8] Immigration, they insist, should not be used as a substitute for natural increase.

Then there are those, like Martin Collacott, who oppose Canada's present immigration levels. Collacott, a former Canadian ambassador and now a senior fellow in immigration studies at the Fraser Institute, has repeatedly denounced Canada's immigration strategy, citing the stagnation of incomes in larger Canadian cities since the 1990s and the fact that recent immigrants earn much less and have higher poverty levels than earlier newcomers. "While a number of factors are involved," claims Collacott, "one that few have been prepared to acknowledge is that we are bringing in far more people than we need or can absorb."[9] Collacott's view is shared by the celebrated environmentalist David Suzuki, who is reported to have said, "Canada is full," and by Gilles Paquet, an economist and professor emeritus at the School of Management and senior research fellow at the Centre on Governance at the University of Ottawa. Professor Paquet has declared that "dealing with such a high volume of immigrants has created problems for their screening."[10] Here, he was alluding to the fact that only about 17 percent of prospective immigrants are fully vetted for their job and language skills.

There are also Canadians who fall into none of these camps but who are deeply concerned about the fact that many recent immigrants, particularly those from Southeast Asia, India, Pakistan, and Africa, hold views about the role of women in the family and the organization of society that are very different from those espoused by the majority of "established" Canadians. Furthermore, many Canadians who are not racist in any way deplore the penchant of some newcomers to import quarrels from their homeland into Canada.

THE DESIRABLE TYPE OF CANADIAN SOCIETY

When immigration issues are studied in this century one economics-related myth that should certainly be discarded is the time-worn contention that immigrants "steal" jobs from Canadians. Research indicates that immigration does not cause unemployment, although the now defunct Economic Council of Canada suggested that very rapid increases in immigration may lead to temporary rises in unemployment.[11]

Having swept this myth aside, Canadians should ask themselves whether they want to see a balance maintained between the different categories of immigration, i.e., economic (selected workers and business-class immigrants), social (family-class immigrants), and humanitarian (refugees). At the opening of the 1990s, less than 20 percent of Canada's immigrants were selected according to the points system. By contrast, in 2011, immigrants in the economic classes (which includes principal applicants chosen by the points system and their family members who are not) accounted for approximately 63 percent of newcomers to Canada. Do Canadians approve of this trend to a more selective immigration policy or would they welcome moves to place more emphasis on those categories not subject to the points system, i.e., family-class members and refugees?

Regrettably, the number of refugees worldwide is increasing. At the end of 2014 the number was 19.5 million, compared with about 16.5 million in 2013. In view of these numbers, Canadians need to consider what role they want refugees to play in Canadian immigration policy. If countless people are fleeing war-torn countries in the Middle East and Africa for Europe, and millions of others languish in squalid camps around the world, should Canadians care? And if they do, do they want their country to accept far larger numbers of these people? Should we embrace the position of the well-known Canadian rabbi and refugee advocate W. Gunther Plaut, who was commissioned by the Trudeau government to draw up models for a reconstituted refugee determination system. He wrote, "To be sure, we like everyone else worry about our own well-being, but our adherence to the U.N. Convention and the incorporation of its principles into Canadian law are flags we have run up on our pole of moral purpose, and there they must continue to wave."[12]

On a related theme, should Canada be prepared to admit more so-called economic migrants or bogus refugees? In other words, should we accept the arguments of the thoughtful and award-winning Canadian author Boyce Richardson that "If we are serious about redressing the imbalances in the distribution of the world's resources and people, we will not be able simply to shovel money and investment into Third World countries. We will be expected to demonstrate our commitment in human terms as well."[13]

Or should we subscribe to the position that Canada's refugee determination system is overly generous and that asylum seekers should be refused admission altogether. In other words, should we abolish a refugee determination system that many, like James Bissett, a retired diplomat and immigration official, feel is outrageously expensive and dysfunctional?

These are just some of the issues that will challenge Canada as the twenty-first century unfolds.

But equally significant is the question of how we manage diversity. For the last four decades we have welcomed a steady stream of newcomers from Asia, the Middle East, and Africa, most of whom have settled in Canada's largest cities, Toronto, Montreal, and Vancouver. These trends, which have transformed Canada into a truly global village, are now too strong to turn back. Nevertheless, we have to address the issue of diversity, the extent we desire and the speed with which we wish to see the defined goal implemented.[14] Moreover, should we be concerned that 80 percent of newcomers settle in just three cities, Toronto, Montreal, and Vancouver? If so, do we encourage new immigrants to spread geographically across the country so that Canada as a whole becomes a society of many peoples and a country well-adapted to globalization?

MULTICULTURALISM UNDER ATTACK

Diversity, of course, is also closely bound up with multiculturalism. Although noble and forward-looking in their goals, the federal government's multiculturalism policies have been viewed with suspicion and hostility by many Canadians. One of the chief criticisms, of course, is that politicians shamelessly use the policies to buy votes at elections, a valid point underscored by the well-known Canadian columnist and author

Richard Gwyn, who has bluntly described the program as "a slush fund to buy ethnic votes."[15] The Trinidadian-born author, Neil Bissoondath, Canada's very vocal and high-profile opponent of the program, has also attacked its link with politics.[16]

The program has also attracted vocal opposition from Quebec, where many observers regard it as injurious to the French Canadians' position as one of Canada's two founding linguistic and cultural communities. In this camp is Guy Rocher, a Quebec sociologist, who has attacked the program because it abandons the concept of a clearly identifiable cultural nucleus. In Rocher's opinion, Canada could have reaped large cultural gains if it had retained the idea of two main cultural communities around which the other ethnic communities could cluster and from which they could derive support.[17]

Most Canadians who object to the perceived policies of official multiculturalism, however, base their opposition on the belief that these policies divide rather than unite Canadians. In the opinion of the Citizens' Forum on Canada's Future, which released its report in early 1991, multicultural programs are divisive because they remind Canadians of their different origins rather than the symbols of Canadian society and the future that they share. Even some members of the ethnic communities themselves have rejected the policies, claiming that they accentuate the differences between various ethnic groups, ignore the tougher issues of racism and bigotry, and prevent "ethnics" from moving into mainstream society. These arguments have been supported by some scholars, who claim the policies serve to buttress the dominance of the Anglo-Saxon community by diverting the attention of the non-English and the non-French into cultural activities and away from political and economic affairs.

Multiculturalism has also been criticized, since the horrific 9/11 attacks, by those Canadians who denounce official multiculturalism for holding that all cultures are worthy of respect. This, they claim, has facilitated the introduction of cultural practices that are inimical to Canada's liberal democratic traditions and discourages newcomers from adopting Canadian values. "Canada is losing out because it drank the Kool-Aid of multiculturalism," observes political scientist Salim Mansur, the author of *Delectable Lie: A Liberal Repudiation of Multiculturalism*. "This has profoundly weakened the country in its ability to get new immigrants to adopt Canadian values. The historical legacy of multiculturalism leads many immigrants to no longer make the effort to become Canadian."[18]

Gilles Paquet likewise challenges the intellectual assumptions that underpin Canada's immigration policy, i.e., multiculturalism, diversity, and tolerance. In his ebook *Moderato Cantabile: Toward Principled Governance for Canada's Immigration Regime*, Paquet argues that these ideological assumptions ill-serve Canadians' sense of solidarity. He also deplores the lack of a clear sense of the responsibilities attached to citizenship. This, he claims, can only "lead to fuzziness in the definition of the limits of tolerance that can legitimately be expected by newcomers."[19]

Criticism of Canada's multicultural policy has ignored the fact that the limited government funding for multicultural activities is no longer, as it once was, devoted almost entirely to promoting cultural pursuits. When visible minorities started to concentrate in large Canadian cities, such as Toronto and Vancouver, and race riots erupted in cities in Britain, the federal government began to change the focus of its spending. Where once it concentrated on the retention of cultures and languages, it now began to stress equality, and ethnic and racial harmony. No longer is it correct to identify official multiculturalism with just the three Ds (dress, diet, and dance). In fact, for years multiculturalism has moved well beyond the so-called song-and-dance approach to focus on fighting discrimination and integrating immigrants into the evolving mainstream of Canadian society.

Shifts in the funding for multicultural initiatives confirm this, as does the Canadian Multiculturalism Act (1988), which commits the Canadian government to supporting the full participation of all Canadians, irrespective of race, national origin, or religion, in all facets of Canadian society. In fact, the Citizenship and Immigration Canada website (the multiculturalism program is now administered by CIC) states, "Through multiculturalism, Canada recognizes the cultural heritage and the potential of all Canadians, encouraging them to integrate into Canadian society and take an active part in its social, cultural, economic and political affairs."[20] The Immigration and Refugee Protection Act, 2001, goes even further, explicitly describing the importance of the "two-way street" approach to integrating immigrants and refugees into Canadian society.

In this piece of legislation the Canadian government acknowledges that the act's goals and, by extension, Canada's immigration program, include: enabling "Canada to pursue the maximum social, cultural, and economic benefits of immigration; to enrich and strengthen the social and cultural fabric of Canada ... to promote the successful integration of permanent residents into Canada, while recognizing that integration involves mutual obligations for new immigrants and Canadian society."[21] In other words, while newcomers are expected to adapt to Canadian society and its accepted practices, Canadian society and its institutions have an obligation to adapt to a diversifying population.

However, despite widespread acknowledgement of the need for mutual adaptation, there is still the nagging question of how far the process of accommodation should go. How, for example, does one respond to those people who view many of Canada's core values, such as democracy, freedom, liberalism, and tolerance, as anathema? It's a question, claims journalist Robert Sibley, that this country must answer.[22]

Discrimination continues to remain a problem in Canada, as hard data provided by the Ethnic Diversity Survey of 2004 proved. It revealed that while only 14 percent of Canadians experienced discrimination or unfair treatment because of their ethno-racial origins, 36 percent of visible minorities had been subjected to discrimination. These findings have only served to encourage the federal government to pursue its multifaceted fight against racism in all forms, employing such tools as the Canadian Charter of Rights and Freedoms, the Canadian Human Rights Act, the Employment Equity Act, the Official Languages Act, the Pay Equity Act, and the Multiculturalism Act.

If properly explained and implemented, multiculturalism policies can help to eliminate racism and to forge a Canadian identity and reality in which Canadians of every ethnic and racial origin can see themselves reflected. Indeed, increased racial tensions in various Canadian cities underline the need for effective multicultural policies. And all indications are that this need will grow. Canada faces and will continue to face a major challenge in finding ways to prevent conflict between different racial and cultural groups as the total number of Third World immigrants and their descendants increases.

THE FUTURE

As was pointed out in the introduction to this book, the decisions that we make now about what sort of people are admitted to Canada will determine the kind of country we will have a hundred years from today. That is why it is so important for Canadians to know something about the history of Canadian immigration and the realities of present-day immigration policy. Only if we are informed about such vital questions can we be truly prepared to participate actively and intelligently in the continuing debate on the direction of Canadian immigration policy, a debate which will have important consequences for Canada's future.

— APPENDIX —

Tables and Figures

TABLE A.1
IMMIGRATION TO CANADA
1852–2014

Year	Number of Immigrants	Year	Number of Immigrants
1852	29,307	1881	47,991
1853	29,464	1882	112,458
1854	37,263	1883	133,624
1855	25,296	1884	103,824
1856	22,544	1885	79,169
1857	33,854	1886	69,152
1858	12,339	1887	84,526
1859	6,300	1888	88,766
1860	6,276	1889	91,600
1861	13,589	1890	75,067
1862	18,294	1891	82,165
1863	21,000	1892	30,996
1864	24,799	1893	29,663
1865	18,958	1894	20,829
1866	11,427	1895	18,790
1867	10,666	1896	16,835
1868	12,765	1897	21,716
1869	18,630	1898	31,900
1870	24,706	1899	44,543
1871	27,773	1900	41,681
1872	36,578	1901	55,747
1873	50,050	1902	89,102
1874	39,373	1903	138,660
1875	27,382	1904	131,252
1876	25,633	1905	141,465
1877	27,082	1906	211,653
1878	29,807	1907	272,409
1879	40,492	1908	143,326
1880	38,505	1909	173,694

Year	Number of Immigrants	Year	Number of Immigrants
1910	286,839	1956	164,857
1911	331,288	1957	282,164
1912	375,756	1958	124,851
1913	400,870	1959	106,928
1914	150,484	1960	104,111
1915	36,665	1961	71,689
1916	55,914	1962	74,586
1917	72,910	1963	93,151
1918	41,845	1964	112,606
1919	107,698	1965	146,758
1920	138,824	1966	194,743
1921	91,728	1967	222,876
1922	64,224	1968	183,974
1923	133,729	1969	161,531
1924	124,163	1970	147,713
1925	84,907	1971	121,900
1926	135,982	1972	122,006
1927	158,886	1973	184,200
1928	166,783	1974	218,465
1929	164,993	1975	187,881
1930	104,806	1976	149,429
1931	27,530	1977	114,914
1932	20,591	1978	86,313
1933	14,382	1979	112,096
1934	12,476	1980	143,117
1935	11,277	1981	128,618
1936	11,643	1982	121,147
1937	15,101	1983	89,157
1938	17,244	1984	88,239
1939	16,994	1985	84,302
1940	11,324	1986	99,219
1941	9,329	1987	152,098
1942	7,576	1988	161,929
1943	8,504	1989	192,001
1944	12,801	1990	214,230
1945	22,722	1991	230,781
1946	71,719	1992	252,842
1947	64,127	1993	255,819
1948	125,414	1994	223,759
1949	95,217	1995	212,845
1950	73,912	1996	226,039
1951	194,391	1997	216,014
1952	164,498	1998	174,159
1953	168,868	1999	189,922
1954	154,227	2000	227,346
1955	109,946	2001	250,484

Year	Number of Immigrants	Year	Number of Immigrants
2002	229,091	2009	252,170
2003	221,340	2010	280,687
2004	235,823	2011	248,747
2005	262,228	2012	257,903
2006	251,640	2013	259,023
2007	236,753	2014	260,404
2008	247,244		

Source: Citizenship and Immigration Canada

TABLE A.2
OCCUPATIONAL DISTRIBUTION OF IMMIGRANTS AND NON-IMMIGRANTS, BY SEX, 1986

	Men		Women	
	Immigrants	Non-immigrants	Immigrants	Non-immigrants
		%		
Professional	16.1	12.4	18.9	21.3
Managerial	13.5	12.4	7.5	7.8
Clerical	5.9	7.0	28.2	34.7
Sales	7.4	9.1	8.5	9.6
Service	11.6	9.9	17.5	15.8
Primary	3.9	8.8	2.2	2.6
Processing	10.0	7.8	3.1	2.2
Product fabricating	12.4	9.4	10.1	2.9
Construction	10.0	10.1	0.3	0.3
Other	9.3	13.1	3.7	2.8
Total	100.0	100.0	100.0	100.0

Source: Statistics Canada, 1986 Census of Canada

TABLE A.3

IMMIGRATION BY TOP TEN SOURCE COUNTRIES, 1999-2001

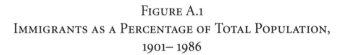

IMMIGRATION BY TOP TEN SOURCE COUNTRIES
(Principal Applicants and Dependants)

COUNTRY	1999			2000			2001		
	#	%	Rank	#	%	Rank	#	%	Rank
China, People's Republic of	29,112	15.33	1	36,715	16.15	1	40,296	16.10	1
India	17,429	9.18	2	26,086	11.48	2	27,812	11.11	2
Pakistan	9,295	4.89	3	14,182	6.24	3	15,339	6.13	3
Philippines	9,170	4.83	4	10,086	4.44	4	12,903	5.15	4
Korea, Republic of	7,216	3.80	5	7,626	3.35	5	9,604	3.84	5
United States	5,528	2.91	7	5,814	2.56	7	5,894	2.35	6
Iran	5,907	3.11	6	5,608	2.47	8	5,736	2.29	7
Romania	3,461	1.82	14	4,425	1.95	11	5,585	2.23	8
Sri Lanka	4,723	2.49	9	5,841	2.57	6	5,514	2.20	9
United Kingdom	4,478	2.36	10	4,647	2.04	10	5,345	2.14	10
Taiwan	5,464	2.88	8	3,511	1.54	14	3,111	1.24	19
Yugoslavia	1,490	0.78	29	4,723	2.08	9	2,786	1.11	22
Total for Top Ten Only	98,322	51.78		121,328	53.38		134,028	53.54	

FIGURE A.1

IMMIGRANTS AS A PERCENTAGE OF TOTAL POPULATION,
1901– 1986

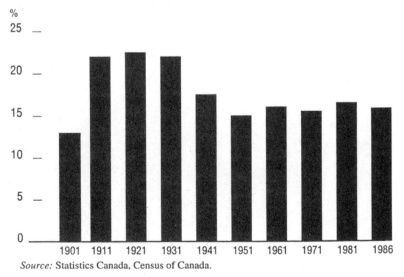

Source: Statistics Canada, Census of Canada.

FIGURE A.2

IMMIGRANT POPULATION, BY PLACE OF BIRTH AND PERIOD OF IMMIGRATION, 1986

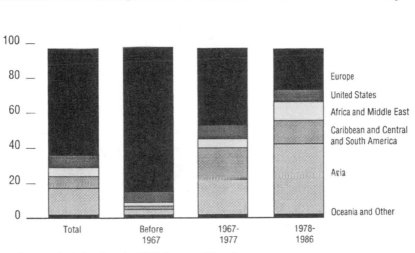

Source: Statistics Canada, 1986 Census of Canada.

FIGURE A.3

IMMIGRANTS AS A PERCENTAGE OF PROVINCIAL POPULATIONS, 1986

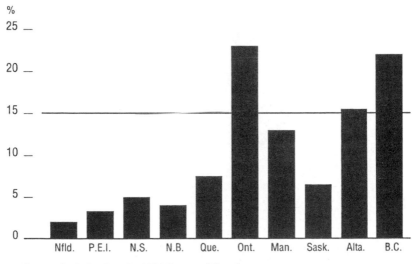

Source: Statistics Canada, 1986 Census of Canada.

FIGURE A.4
LEADING COUNTRIES OF BIRTH IMMIGRANTS TO CANADA

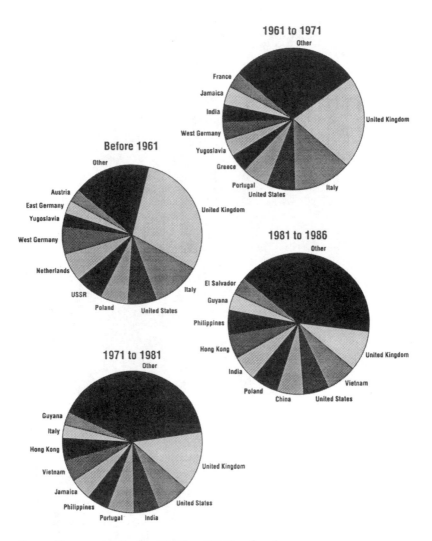

Source: Demographic Review, Health and Welfare Canada.

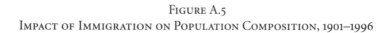

FIGURE A.5

IMPACT OF IMMIGRATION ON POPULATION COMPOSITION, 1901–1996

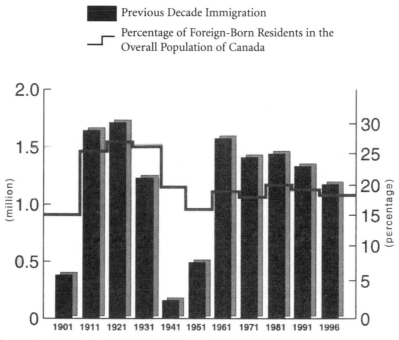

Source: Demographic Review, Health and Welfare Canada.

— NOTES —

CHAPTER 1: THE BEGINNINGS

1. André Vaccine in collaboration with Victor Cabot and Andre Defrosters, *Dreams of Empire: Canada before 1700* (Ottawa: National Archives of Canada, 1982), 121.
2. Ibid., 120.
3. Marcel Trudel, *The Beginnings of New France, 1524–1663* (Toronto: McClelland & Stewart, 1972), 234.
4. Ibid., 184.
5. Serge Courville and Jacques Mathieu, "A French Stamp on the Land," *Horizon Canada* 2, no. 17: 405.
6. Quotation supplied by Cornelius Jaenen.
7. R.C. Harris, ed., *Historical Atlas of Canada*, vol. 1: *From the Beginning to 1800* (Toronto: University of Toronto Press, 1987), plate 45 by Hubert Charbonneau and Normand Robert.
8. W.J. Eccles, *Canada under Louis XIV 1663–1701* (Toronto: McClelland & Stewart, 1964), 47–48.
9. Vachon et al., *Dreams of Empire*, 127.
10. Information supplied by Cornelius Jaenen.
11. Harris, ed., *Historical Atlas of Canada*, vol. 1, plate 45.
12. Vachon et al., *Dreams of Empire*, 144.
13. Figures supplied by Cornelius Jaenen.
14. Ibid., 155.
15. Dale Miquelon, *New France 1701–1744: A Supplement to Europe* (Toronto: McClelland & Stewart, 1987), 120.
16. Information supplied by Cornelius Jaenen.
17. Figure supplied by Cornelius Jaenen.
18. Ibid.
19. Harris, ed. *Historical Atlas of Canada*, vol 1, plate 24 by Kenneth Donovan.
20. Graeme Wynn, "On the Margins of Empire," Craig Brown, ed., *The Illustrated History of Canada*, (Toronto: Key Porter Books, 2002), 211.
21. W.S. MacNutt, *The Atlantic Provinces: The Emergence of Colonial Society 1712–1857* (Toronto: McClelland and Stewart, 1965), 36–37.
22. Ibid., 37.
23. Norah Story, *The Oxford Companion to Canadian History and Literature* (Toronto: Oxford University Press, 1967), 341.

24. Robert McLaughlin, "New England Planters Prior to Migration: The Case of Chatham, Massachusetts," Margaret Conrad and Barry Moody, eds., *Planter Links: Community and Culture in Colonial Nova Scotia* (Fredericton: Acadiensis Press, 2001), 12, 19.

25. John Mannion and Selma Barkham, "The 16th Century Fishery," *Historical Atlas of Canada*, vol. 1, Plate 22.

26. Mannion and Barker, "The 17th Century Fishery," *Historical Atlas of Canada*, vol. 1, plate 23.

27. Shannon Ryan, "The Fishing Station," *Horizon Canada*, vol. 1, no. 8, 174.

28. Cecil J. Houston and William J. Smyth, *Irish Emigration and Canadian Settlement: Patterns, Links and Letters* (Toronto: University of Toronto Press, 1990), 16.

CHAPTER 2: CANADA'S FIRST LARGE INFLUX OF REFUGEES

1. Donald Laing, "MacCanada," *Horizon Canada* 6, no. 72: 1720.

2. K.J. Duncan, "Patterns of Settlement in the East," W. Stanford Reid, ed., *The Scottish Tradition in Canada* (Toronto: McClelland & Stewart in association with the Secretary of State of Canada and Supply and Services Canada, 1967), 50–52.

3. Cameron Nish, "The 1760s," J.M.S. Careless, ed., *Colonists and Canadiens 1760–1867* (Toronto: Macmillan of Canada, 1971), 9.

4. Ramsay Cook with John T. Saywell and John C. Ricker, *Canada: A Modern Study* (Toronto: Clarke Irwin, 1967), 5.

5. Bruce Wilson, *Colonial Identities: Canada from 1760 to 1815* (Ottawa: National Archives of Canada, 1988), 68.

6. Wallace Brown, *The King's Friends: The Composition and Motives of the American Loyalist Claimants* (Providence: Brown University, 1965), 262.

7. Ibid., 48.

8. William H. Nelson, *The American Tory* (Oxford: Clarendon Press, 1961), 147–48.

9. Christopher Moore, "Old Loyalties," *Horizon Canada* 2, no. 20: 458.

10. Mary Beacock Fryer, *King's Men: The Soldier Founders of Ontario* (Toronto: Dundurn Press, 1980), 308.

11. Christopher Moore, *The Loyalists: Revolution, Exile, Settlement* (Toronto: Macmillan of Canada, 1984), 141.

12. Margaret Ells, "Settling the Loyalists in Nova Scotia," *Canadian Historical Association Report for 1934*, 108.

13. Robin Winks, *The Blacks in Canada* (Montreal: McGill-Queen's University Press; New Haven: Yale University Press, 1971), 33.

14. Moore, *The Loyalists*, 143.

15. Graeme Wynn, "Paradise North," *Horizon Canada* 3, no. 33: 774.

16. Gerald Craig, *Upper Canada: The Formative Years 1784–1841* (Toronto: McClelland & Stewart, 1968), 25.

17. Ibid., 48.

18. Ibid., 43.

CHAPTER 3: BRITISH IMMIGRATION TRANSFORMS THE COLONIES

1. Helen I. Cowan, *British Emigration to British North America: The First Hundred Years* (Toronto: University of Toronto Press, 1961), 20.

2. Gerald M. Craig, *Upper Canada: The Formative Years 1784–1841* (Toronto: McClelland & Stewart, 1968), 124.

3. Helen Cowan, *British Immigration before Confederation* (Ottawa: Canadian Historical Association, 1978), 8.

4. Cecil J. Houston and William J. Smyth, "Irish Emigrants to Canada: Whence They Came," Robert O'Driscoll and Lorna Reynolds, eds., *The Untold Story: The Irish in Canada* (Toronto: Celtic Arts of Canada, 1988), vol. 1, 30.

5. Ibid., 87.

6. Craig, *Upper Canada*, 88.

7. K.J. Duncan, "Patterns of Settlement in the East," W. Stanford Reid, ed., *The Scottish Tradition in Canada* (Toronto: McClelland & Stewart, 1976), 56.

8. Valerie Knowles, *Capital Lives: Profiles of 32 Leading Ottawa Personalities* (Ottawa: Book Coach Press, 2005), 52–53.

9. Craig, *Upper Canada*, 129.

10. Cowan, *British Immigration before Confederation*, 10.

11. W.S. MacNutt, *The Atlantic Provinces: The Emergence of Colonial Society 1712–1857* (Toronto: McClelland & Stewart, 1965), 117.

12. Cowan, *British Emigration to British North America*, 133.

13. Craig, *Upper Canada*, 138.

14. *Canada Year Book 1957–58* (Ottawa: Queen's Printer, 1958), 166.

15. John Cameron, "Legislation Relating to Immigration in Canada Prior to Confederation" (M.A. dissertation, University of Toronto, 1935), 4.

16. Stanley Johnson, *A History of Emigration from the United Kingdom to North America, 1763–1912* (London: George Routledge & Sons, 1913), Appendix 1, Table 1, 344.

17. Adam Shortt, "Immigration and Land Settlement," *Canada and Its Provinces* (Toronto: Publishers' Association of Canada, 1913), vol. 4, 577.

18. Johnson, *A History of Emigration*, 21.

19. Cecil Woodham-Smith, *The Great Hunger: Ireland 1845–1849* (New York and Evanston: Harper & Row, 1962), 210.

20. Shortt, "Immigration and Land Settlement," 577.

21. J.M.S. Careless, *Canada: A Story of Challenge* (Cambridge: Cambridge University Press, 1953), 148.

22. Ibid.

23. Gerald M. Craig, "The 1830s," J.M.S. Careless, ed., *Colonists and Canadiens 1760–1867* (Toronto: Macmillan of Canada, 1971), 179.

24. Jean-Pierre Wallot, "The 1800s," Careless, ed., *Colonists and Canadiens*, 116.

25. Gerald M. Craig, ed., *Lord Durham's Report* (Toronto: McClelland & Stewart, 1963), Carleton Library, no. 1, 172.

25. Ibid., 115.

26. Woodham-Smith, *The Great Hunger*, 211.

27. Frances Morehouse, "Canadian Migration in the Forties," *The Canadian Historical Review*, 1928, 310.

28. Ibid., 311.

29. Daniel Francis, "Boat People," *Horizon Canada* 4, no. 42: 985.

30. S.J. Jacques Monet, "The 1840s," Careless, ed., *Colonists and Canadiens*, 221.

31. Julian Gwyn, "The Irish in the Napanee River Valley: Camden East Township, 1851–1881," O'Driscoll and Reynolds, eds., *The Untold Story*, 355.

32. Bruce S. Elliott, "Regionalized Immigration and Settlement Patterns of the Irish in Upper Canada," *The Untold Story*, 309.

33. Padraic O. Laighin, "Grosse-Ile: The Holocaust Revisited," *The Untold Story*, 95.

34. Paul W. Gates, "Official Encouragement to Immigration by the Province of Canada," *The Canadian Historical Review* 15, no. 1 (March 1934): 25.

35. Ibid., 30.

CHAPTER 4: IMMIGRATION IN THE MACDONALD ERA

1. H. Gordon Skilling, *Canadian Representation Abroad: From Agency to Embassy* (Toronto: Ryerson Press, 1945), 15.

2. Canada, House of Commons, *Debates*, June 19, 1869, col. 887.

3. Maurice Pope, ed., *Public Servant: The Memoirs of Sir Joseph Pope* (Toronto: Oxford University Press, 1960), 38.

4. Skilling, *Canadian Representation Abroad*, 3.

5. Report of a Committee of the Privy Council approved by the Governor General, December 12, 1874, Vertical Files, Library, Department of Employment and Immigration Canada.

6. Christopher Moore, "Confronting the Dragons," *The Beaver,* February/March 2006, vol. 86:1, 52.

7. Foon Sien, "The Chinese in Canada" (essay submitted to the Royal Commission on Bilingualism and Biculturalism, 1967), 8.

8. Patricia E. Roy, "A Choice Between Evils: The Chinese and the Construction of the Canadian Pacific Railway in British Columbia," *The CPR West: The Iron Road and the Making of A Nation* (Vancouver and Toronto: Douglas & McIntyre, 1984), 30–31.

9. Pope, ed., *Public Servant*, 192.

10. Carl Berger, *The Writing of Canadian History: Aspects of English-Canadian Historical Writing Since 1900*, 2nd ed. (Toronto: University of Toronto Press, 1986), 309.

11. K.H. Norrie, "The Rate of Settlement of the Canadian Prairies, 1870–1911," in *Perspectives on Canadian Economic History*, ed. Douglas McCalla (Toronto: Copp Clark Pitman, 1987), 168.

12. Norman Macdonald, *Canada: Immigration and Colonization, 1841–1903* (Toronto: Macmillan of Canada, 1966), 236.

13. Ibid., 240.

14. Canada, House of Commons, *Journals*, 1878, Appendix 2, 16.

15. Irving Abella, *A Coat of Many Colours: Two Centuries of Jewish Life in Canada* (Toronto: Lester & Orpen Dennys, 1990). 78.

16. John A. Eagle, *The Canadian Pacific Railway and the Development of Western Canada, 1896–1914* (Montreal: McGill-Queen's University Press, 1989), 174–76.

CHAPTER 5: THE SIFTON YEARS

1. Mabel Timlin, "Canada's Immigration Policy, 1896–1910," *Canadian Journal of Economics and Political Science* 26 (1960): 518.

2. Canada, House of Commons, *Debates,* July 15, 1903, col. 6699.

3. Robert Craig Brown and Ramsay Cook, *Canada 1896–1921: A Nation Transformed* (Toronto: McClelland & Stewart, 1974), 54–55.

4. Canada, House of Commons, *Debates*, July 27, 1899, cols. 8654–55.

5. David J. Hall, Clifford Sifton, vol. 1: *The Young Napoleon, 1861–1900* (Vancouver: University of British Columbia Press, 1985), 258.

6. Harold Troper, "Official Canadian Government Encouragement of American Immigration, 1896–1911" (Ph.D. thesis, University of Toronto, 1971), 195.

7. R. Douglas Francis, Richard Jones, and Donald B. Smith, *Destinies: Canadian History Since Confederation* (Toronto: Holt, Rinehart and Winston of Canada, 1988), 121.

8. Canada, House of Commons, *Journals*, 1903, vol. 38, Part 11, Appendix 2, 73–74.

9. Robert Hamilton and Dorothy Shields, *The Dictionary of Canadian Quotations and Phrases*, rev. ed. (Toronto: McClelland & Stewart, 1979), 458.

10. Marjorie Harper, *Emigration from North-East Scotland* (Aberdeen: University of Aberdeen Press, 1989), vol. 2, 102.

11. Francis, Jones, and Smith, *Destinies*, 118.

12. R.G. Moyles, "War at Heart," *Horizon Canada* 3, no. 27: 637.

13. Donald Avery, *"Dangerous Foreigners": European Immigrant Workers and Labour Radicalism in Canada, 1896–1932* (Toronto: McClelland & Stewart, 1979), 20.

14. Kenneth Bagnell, *The Little Immigrants* (Toronto: Macmillan of Canada, 1980), back cover.

15. Canada, House of Commons, *Debates*, July 10, 1903, col. 6359.

16. Joy Parr, article on George Everitt Green, *Dictionary of Canadian Biography* online, April 10, 2006.

17. Canada, House of Commons, *Debates,* July 10, 1903, col. 6359.

18. Margaret Ormsby, *British Columbia: A History* (Toronto: Macmillan of Canada, 1971), 314.

19. John Norris, *Strangers Entertained: A History of the Ethnic Groups of British Columbia* (Vancouver: Evergreen Press Limited for the British Columbia Centennial 71 Committee, 1971), 231.

20. Ibid., 127.

21. Jean R. Burnet with Harold Palmer, *"Coming Canadians": An Introduction to a History of Canada's Peoples* (Toronto: McClelland & Stewart in association with the Multiculturalism Program, Secretary of State Department and the Canadian Government Publishing Centre, 1989), 29.

22. H.R. Ferns and B. Ostry, *The Age of Mackenzie King: The Rise of the Leader* (London: William Heinemann, 1955), 77.

CHAPTER 6: FORGING A NEW IMMIGRATION POLICY

1. Ruth Cameron, "The Wheat from the Chaff" (M.A. thesis, Concordia University, 1976), 13.

2. Canada, House of Commons, *Debates*, vol. 3, July 14, 1903, cols. 6562–63.

3. David J. Hall, "Room to Spare," *Horizon Canada* 7, no. 7: 1805.

4. Canada, House of Commons, *Debates*, June 13, 1906, col. 5196.

5. Barbara Roberts, *Whence They Came: Deportations from Canada, 1900–1935* (Ottawa: University of Ottawa Press, 1988), 12.

6. Report of the Superintendent of Immigration, Sessional Paper No. 25, *Report of the Department of the Interior, 1908*, 61.
7. Canada, House of Commons, *Debates*, vol. 111, June 13, 1906, col. 5233.
8. Ibid., col. 5231.
9. Cameron, "The Wheat from the Chaff," 4.
10. In a brief prepared for the Department of Citizenship and Immigration by L. Couture, departmental solicitor in 1952, the Immigration Act, 1910 is described as Canada's first immigration act. Conventional sources, however, all appear to assign this distinction to the Immigration Act, 1869.
11. William Scott, "Immigration and Population," Adam Shortt and Arthur Doughty, eds., *Canada and Its Provinces* (Toronto: Publishers' Association of Canada, 1913), vol. 7, 573.
12. *Statutes of Canada 1909–1910*, vol. 2, chap. 27, section 38, 14.
13. Scott, "Immigration and Population," 575.
14. *Statutes of Canada 1909–1910*, vol. 2, chap. 27, section 41, 15.
15. Roberts, *Whence They Came*, 14.
16. Scott, "Immigration and Population," 574.
17. J. Castell Hopkins, *The Canadian Annual Review of Public Affairs 1910*, 384.
18. Scott, "Immigration and Population," 586.
19. Evidence of William Scott, superintendent of immigration, before the Select Standing Committee on Agriculture and Colonization, Canada, House of Commons, *Journals*, vol. 43, 1907–1908, Appendix 2, 328.
20. Canada, House of Commons, *Debates*, June 13, 1906, col. 5229.
21. Richard Clippingdale, *Laurier: His Life and World* (Toronto: McGraw-Hill Ryerson, 1979), 141.
22. Ibid.
23. Donald Avery, *"Dangerous Foreigners": European Immigrant Workers and Labour Radicalism in Canada, 1896–1932* (Toronto: McClelland & Stewart, 1979), 21.
24. *Report of the Department of Immigration and Colonization for the Fiscal Year Ended March 31, 1924*, Sessional Paper No. 13, 7.
25. Evidence of William Scott, superintendent of immigration, before the Select Standing Committee on Agriculture and Colonization, Canada, House of Commons, *Journals*, vol. 43, 1907–1919, Appendix 2, 324–25.
26. Cameron, "The Wheat from the Chaff," 18–20.
27. Ibid.
28. Scott, "Immigration and Population," 555.
29. Robert Craig Brown and Ramsay Cook, *Canada 1896–1921: A Nation Transformed* (Toronto: McClelland & Stewart, 1974), 72.
30. Scott, "Immigration and Population," 555.
31. J. Castell Hopkins, *The Canadian Annual Review of Public Affairs* 1910, 387–88.
32. Harold Troper, "Official Canadian Government Encouragement of American Immigration, 1896–1911" (Ph.D. dissertation, University of Toronto, 1971), 230.
33. Scott, "Immigration and Population," 531.
34. Troper, "Official Canadian Government Encouragement of American Immigration, 1896–1911," 254.

35. Ibid., 253.

36. Trevor Slessing, "How They Kept Canada Almost Lily White," *Saturday Night*, September 1970, 30–32.

37. W. Peter Ward, *White Canada Forever* (Montreal: McGill-Queen's University Press, 1978), 66.

38. *Canadian Immigration Historical Society Bulletin*, Supplement "A," no. 4 (March 1988): 1–2.

39. Ibid., 2.

40. M.C. Urquhart and K.A.H. Buckley, eds., *Historical Statistics of Canada* (Toronto: Macmillan of Canada, 1965), Table A 284–299, 25.

41. Cameron, "The Wheat from the Chaff," 5.

42. Brown and Cook, *Canada 1896–1921*, 73.

43. J.S. Woodsworth, *Strangers Within Our Gates*, Michael Bliss, ed., The Social History of Canada series (Toronto: University of Toronto Press, 1972), 234.

44. Joseph Schull, *Laurier: The First Canadian* (Toronto: Macmillan of Canada, 1967), 461.

45. Brown and Cook, *Canada 1896–1921*, 74.

CHAPTER 7: IMMIGRATION DOLDRUMS

1. Immigration to Canada by calendar year, 1852–1896, Canada Employment and Immigration Commission.

2. Donald Avery, *"Dangerous Foreigners": European Immigrant Workers and Labour Radicalism in Canada, 1896–1932* (Toronto: McClelland & Stewart, 1979), 66.

3. Robert Craig Brown and Ramsay Cook, *Canada 1896–1921: A Nation Transformed* (Toronto: McClelland & Stewart, 1974), 224.

4. Roger Graham, "Through the First World War," J.M.S. Careless and R. Craig Brown, eds., *The Canadians, Part I* (Toronto: Macmillan of Canada, 1968), 189.

5. Canada, House of Commons, *Debates*, June 8, 1917, 2140.

6. Ibid., March 22, 1918, 103–4.

7. Avery, *"Dangerous Foreigners,"* 77.

8. Ibid., 86.

9. *Statutes of Canada 1919*, 9–10 Geo. V, vol. 1, chap. 25, 97.

10. Foon Sien, "The Chinese in Canada" (essay submitted to the Royal Commission on Bilingualism and Biculturalism, 1967), 38.

11. Canada, House of Commons, *Debates*, March 20, 1923, 1341.

12. Ibid., May 17, 1923, 2844.

13. *The Canadian Annual Review 1925–1926* (Toronto: Canadian Review Company, 1926), 163.

14. Ibid.

15. Avery, *"Dangerous Foreigners,"* 97.

16. Ibid., 96.

17. James B. Hedges, *Building the Canadian West* (New York: Macmillan, 1939), 351.

18. Nicholas Faith, *The World the Railways Built* (London: Bodley Head, 1990), 126.

19. Valerie Knowles, *Capital Lives: Profiles of 32 Well-Known Ottawans* (Book Coach Press, 2005), 140.

20. Edward Ziegler, *Refugee Movements and Policy in Canada*, May 1988, National Archives of Canada (hereafter NAC), RG 76, 89-90/035, 14.

21. Ibid., 15.

22. Avery, *"Dangerous Foreigners,"* 98.

23. Ibid.

24. John Herd Thompson and Allen Seager, *Canada 1922–1938: Decades of Discord* (Toronto: McClelland & Stewart, 1985), 131.

25. Valerie Knowles, *First Person: A Biography of Cairine Wilson, Canada's First Woman Senator* (Toronto: Dundurn Press, 1988), 196.

26. Avery, *"Dangerous Foreigners,"* 114.

27. Barbara Roberts, *Whence They Came: Deportations from Canada, 1900–1935* (Ottawa: University of Ottawa Press, 1988), 8.

28. R. Douglas Francis, Richard Jones, and Donald B. Smith, *Destinies* (Toronto: Holt, Rinehart and Winston of Canada, 1988), 255.

29. Maurice Mitchell, *"A Man of Big Heart": The Memoirs of Maurice Mitchell* (Ottawa: Canadian Immigration Historical Society, 1988), 19.

30. Ibid., 21.

31. Canada, Senate Standing Committee on Immigration and Labour, brief presented by the Canadian National Committee on Refugees, 1946, 234.

32. Ziegler, *Refugee Movements and Policy in Canada*, 17.

33. Irving Abella and Harold Troper, *None Is Too Many: Canada and the Jews of Europe, 1933–1948* (Toronto: Lester & Orpen Dennys, 1982), 151.

34. Peter and Leni Gillman, *"Collar the Lot"!* (London: Quartet Books, 1980), 276.

35. NAC, RG 76, vol. 453, files 693, 670, part 2.

36. Martin Laflamme, "The $21,000 Question," *Ottawa Citizen*, January 30, 2005, C9.

CHAPTER 8: IMMIGRATION'S POST-WAR BOOM (1947–1957)

1. Gerald Dirks, *Canada's Refugee Policy: Indifference or Opportunism?* (Montreal: McGill-Queen's University Press, 1977), 144.

2. Brief submitted by the Canadian Congress of Labour to the Senate Standing Committee on Immigration and Labour, July 25, 1946, Eugene Forsey Papers, NAC, MG 28, I 103, vol. 347.

3. Canada, Senate, *Report of the Standing Committee on Immigration and Labour* (Ottawa, 1946), 240.

4. Canada, House of Commons, *Debates*, August 27, 1946, 5492.

5. Canada, Senate, *Report of the Standing Committee on Immigration and Labour*, 1946, 239.

6. Ibid., 235.

7. Ibid., 628.

8. Ibid., 635.

9. Dirks, *Canada's Refugee Policy*, 139.

10. Laura Neilson Bonikowsky, "War Brides: They Crossed the Sea for Love," *Ottawa Citizen*, February 10, 2003.

11. Canada, House of Commons, *Debates*, May 1, 1947, 2644.

12. Ibid., 2645.

13. John W. Holmes, *The Shaping of Peace: Canada and the Search for World Order, 1943–1957*, vol. 1 (Toronto: University of Toronto Press, 1979), 101.

14. Franca Iacovetta, "The Political Career of Senator Cairine Wilson, 1921–62," *Atlantis* 2, no. 1 (1985): 101.

15. Gerald Dirks, "Canada and Immigration: International and Domestic Considerations in the Decade Preceding the 1956 Hungarian Exodus" (unpublished paper delivered to a Canadian Immigration Historical Society symposium, April 28, 1990), 6–7.

16. Alti Rodel, extracts from the report "Nazi War Criminals in Canada: The Historical and Policy Setting From the 1940's to the Present" (report commissioned by the Deschenes Commission), 168.

17. *Globe and Mail*, editorial, May 28, 1947.

18. Canada, House of Commons, *Debates*, June 2, 1947, vol. 4, 3704.

19. Ibid., April 24, 1953, 4351–52.

20. Ibid., June 10, 1952, 3078.

21. Hawkins, *Canada and Immigration*, 102.

22. John Manion (deputy minister, Employment and Immigration Canada, 1977–79), "Hungarian Refugee Movement — Implementing the Policy" (unpublished paper delivered to a Canadian Immigration Historical Society symposium, April 28, 1990), 2.

23. Ibid., 3–4.

24. NAC, RG 76, vol. 865, file 553-54-607.

25. Interview with Michael Shenstone, March 15, 1991.

26. NAC, RG 76, vol. 865, file 555-54-607.

27. David Corbett, *Canada's Immigration Policy: A Critique* (Toronto: University of Toronto Press, 1957), 22.

28. Dirks, *Canada's Refugee Policy*, 194.

29. Department of Citizenship and Immigration, *Annual Report, Fiscal Year Ended March 31, 1958*, 25.

30. Canada, Senate, *Debates*, 1946, 629.

31. Mabel F. Timlin, *Does Canada Need More People?* (Toronto: Oxford University Press, 1951), 122.

32. Reg Whitaker, *Double Standard: The Secret Story of Canadian Immigration* (Toronto; Lester & Orpen Dennys, 1987) 55–58.

CHAPTER 9: MAJOR NEW INITIATIVES

1. Quoted in a speech given by L.D. Crestohl, Canada, House of Commons, *Debates*, February 27, 1962, 1327.

2. *U.S. News and World Report*, April 18, 1958.

3. NAC, RG 25, vol. 2, box 33, file 232-AF-40, memorandum on Italian immigration, February 23, 1960.

4. Canada, House of Commons, *Debates*, April 22, 1959, 2933.

5. Ibid., 2934.

6. Canada, House of Commons, *Debates*, March 5, 1959, 1629.

7. Ibid., 1630.

8. John T. Saywell, ed., *Canadian Annual Review for 1962* (Toronto: University of Toronto Press, 1963), 203.

9.   Peyton Lyon, ed., *Canada in World Affairs, 1961–63* (Toronto: Oxford University Press, 1968), 359.

10. Freda Hawkins, *Canada and Australia: The Dilemmas of Modern Migration* (Canada House Lecture Series, no. 30, 1985), 6.

11. Lyon, ed., *Canada in World Affairs, 1961–63*, 359.

12. Canada, House of Commons, *Debates*, January 19, 1962, 11.

13. Ibid., February 27, 1962, 1327.

14. Lyon, ed., *Canada in World Affairs, 1961–63*, 360.

15. John Saywell, ed., *Canadian Annual Review for 1963* (Toronto: University of Toronto Press, 1964), 220.

16. Jean R. Burnet with Howard Palmer, *"Coming Canadians"* (Toronto: McClelland & Stewart in association with the Department of the Secretary of State and the Canadian Government Publishing Centre, 1988), 45.

17. Canada, House of Commons, *Debates*, September 25, 1967, 2441.

18. Saywell, ed., *Canadian Annual Review for 1962*, 204.

19. Canada, House of Commons, *Debates*, May 9, 1966, 4872.

20. Ibid.

21. Ibid., May 29, 1966, 5435.

22. Ibid., May 30, 1966, 5731.

23. Tom Kent, *A Public Purpose: An Experience of Liberal Opposition and Canadian Government* (Montreal: McGill-Queen's University Press, 1988), 408.

24. Ibid., 410.

25. Canada, House of Commons, *Debates*, October 26, 1967, 3536.

26. Kent, *A Public Purpose*, 409.

27. Freda Hawkins, *Canada and Immigration*, 2nd ed. (Montreal: McGill–Queen's University Press, 1988), 102.

CHAPTER 10: A NEW ERA IN IMMIGRATION

1.   Charles M. Beach, Alan G. Green, and Jeffrey G. Reitz, eds., *Canadian Immigration Policy for the 21st Century* (Kingston: John Deutsch Institute for the Study of Economic Policy, 2003), 1.

2.   Freda Hawkins, *Critical Years in Immigration: Canada and Australia Compared* (Montreal: McGill-Queen's University Press, 1989), 283.

3.   Peter C. Dobell, *Canada in World Affairs*, vol. 17: *1971–1973* (Toronto: Canadian Institute of International Affairs, 1985), 319.

4.   Paul Stevens and John Saywell, "Parliament and Politics," John T. Saywell, ed., *Canadian Annual Review of Politics and Public Affairs, 1972* (Toronto: University of Toronto Press, 1974), 82.

5.   Canada, House of Commons, *Debates*, June 20, 1972, 4952.

6.   Ibid., 4950.

7.   Hawkins, *Critical Years in Immigration*, 48.

8.   Ibid., 48.

9.   Interview with Richard Tait, March 22, 1991.

10. Canada, Department of Manpower and Immigration, White Paper on immigration (Ottawa: Queen's Printer, 1966), 7.

11. Canada, Minister of Manpower and Immigration, *Immigration Policy Perspectives*, vol. 1: *Canadian Immigration and Population Study* (Ottawa: Information Canada, 1974), 5.
12. Ibid., 6.
13. Canada, House of Commons, *Debates*, February 3, 1975, 2819.
14. Ibid.
15. Interview with Richard Tait, March 22, 1991.
16. *Report to Parliament by the Special Joint Committee on Immigration Policy* (Ottawa: Queen's Printer, 1975), 2.
17. Ibid., Table 3, 71.
18. Ibid.
19. Ibid., 5.
20. Hawkins, *Critical Years in Immigration*, 72.
21. Reg Whitaker, *Double Standard: The Secret Story of Canadian Immigration* (Toronto: Lester & Orpen Dennys, 1987), 269.
22. Interview with Cal Best (executive director, Immigration Branch, Employment and Immigration Canada, 1979–85), July 20, 1990.
23. R. Douglas Francis, Richard Jones, and Donald B. Smith, *Destinies: Canadian History Since Confederation* (Toronto: Holt, Rinehart and Winston of Canada, 1988), 407.
24. "Profiles of Canadian Immigration," narrative and discussion guide (Ottawa: Supply and Services Canada, 1987), 7.
25. Gerald Dirks, *Canada's Refugee Policy: Indifference or Opportunism?* (Montreal: McGill-Queen's University Press, 1977), 230.
26. Ibid.; letter from James George to the author, February 12, 1992; and summary of a study done on the Tibetan refugee program by the Research Projects Group, Department of Manpower and Immigration.
27. Dobell, *Canada in World Affairs*, vol. 17: 1971–1973, 324.
28. Ibid., 326.
29. Renee Goldsmith Kasinsky, *Refugees from Militarism: Draft-Age Americans in Canada* (Totowa, NJ: Littlefield, Adams and Company, 1976), 6.
30. Mark Fruitkin, unpublished memoir.
31. Howard Adelman, "An Immigration Dream: Hungarian Refugees Come to Canada. An Analysis" (unpublished paper delivered to a Canadian Immigration Historical Society symposium, April 28, 1990), 16.
32. Whitaker, *Double Standard*, 257.
33. Howard Adelman, *Canada and the Indochinese Refugees* (Regina: L.A. Weigl Educational Associates, 1982), 1.
34. Gerald Dirks, "Immigration Policy," *The Canadian Encyclopedia*, 2nd ed. (Edmonton: Hurtig Publishers, 1988), 1048.
35. Interview with Cal Best, July 20, 1990.
36. Ibid.
37. Adelman, *Canada and the Indochinese Refugees*, 45.
38. Freda Hawkins, *Canada and Immigration: Public Policy and Public Concern* (Montreal: McGill-Queen's University Press, 1988), 214.
39. Ibid.

40. Tom Traves and John T. Saywell, "Parliament and Politics," R.B. Byers and John T. Saywell, eds., *Canadian Annual Review of Politics and Public Affairs*, 1978 (Toronto: University of Toronto Press, 1980), 79.
41. Canada, House of Commons, *Debates*, October 8, 1971, 8545–46.

CHAPTER 11: THE TURBULENT 1980S AND BEYOND
1. "Refugees and Others of Concern to UNHCR — 1998 Statistical Overview," Table 1.4, UNHCR website.
2. Freda Hawkins, *Critical Years in Immigration: Canada and Australia Compared* (Montreal: McGill-Queen's University Press, 1989), 192.
3. Canada, House of Commons, *Debates*, September 2, 1987, 8716; and *Globe and Mail*, July 13, 1987, A3.
4. "Desperate Voyage," *Maclean's*, August 25, 1986, 12.
5. Joe Bissett (executive director, Immigration Branch, Employment and Immigration Canada, 1985–90) quoted in "The Reorganization of Immigration," *The Canadian Immigration Historical Society Bulletin*, no. 7: Supplement "C," 1.
6. Canada, House of Commons, *Debates*, December 10, 1986, 1976.
7. Gary Segal, *Immigrating to Canada: Who Is Allowed? What Is Required? How to Do It!*, 9th ed. (North Vancouver: Self-Counsel Press, 1990), 122.
8. Gerald Dirks, "A Policy within a Policy: The Identification and Admission of Refugees to Canada," *Canadian Journal of Political Science 17*, no. 2 (June 1984): 285.
9. Matas with Simon, *Closing the Doors*, 300.
10. Jane Badets, "Canada's Immigrant Population," *Canadian Social Trends*, Autumn 1989, 3.
11. Ibid.
12. Alan B. Simmons, "'New Wave' Immigrants: Origins and Characteristics," Shiva S. Halli, Frank Throvato, and Leo Driedget, eds., *Ethnic Demography* (Ottawa: Carleton University Press, 1990), 154.
13. Shirley B. Seward and Marc Tremblay, "Immigrants in the Canadian Labour Force: Their Role in Structural Change" (discussion paper prepared for Institute for Research on Public Policy, 1989), 7.
14. Ibid.
15. Ibid.
16. Segal, *Immigrating to Canada*, 27.
17. Economic Council of Canada, *New Faces in the Crowd: Economic and Social Impacts of Immigration* (Ottawa: Minister of Supplies and Services Canada, 1991), 10.
18. Theresa Tedesco, Shaffin Sharif, and Dan Burke, "The Moneyed Class," *Maclean's*, July 10, 1989, 19.
19. Ibid.
20. Canada, House of Commons, *Debates*, March 24, 1987, 4486.
21. Boyce Richardson, *Time to Change: Canada's Place in a World in Crisis* (Toronto: Summerhill Press, 1990), 167.
22. *Globe and Mail*, March 6, 1989.
23. Rudy Platiel and Gene Allen, "Family Reunification Harder, Lawyer Says," *Globe and Mail*, October 26, 1990.

24. Ibid.
25. House of Commons, Standing Committee on Labour, Employment and Immigration, *Minutes of Proceedings and Evidence*, no. 34, May 15, 1990, 34.9.
26. Ibid., 34.14.
27. Economic Council of Canada, *New Faces in the Crowd*, 35–36.
28. Unpublished report provided by Citizenship and Immigration Canada.
29. Peter Harder, bout de papier, vol. 12, no. 3, 30–3.
30. House of Commons, *Debates*, November 24, 1992, 13911.
31. Jacquie Miller, "Redefining Refugees," *Ottawa Citizen*, December 14, 1992.
32. Estanislao Oziewicz, "Vocational Skills to Count More for Immigration," *Globe and Mail*, January 1, 1993.
33. Jacquie Miller, "Immigrant Refugee Groups Protest Inclusion in Public Security Ministry," *Ottawa Citizen*, July 27, 1993.
34. News release published by Citizenship and Immigration Canada, February 2, 1994.
35. Information supplied by Lucien Dubois.
36. Lila Sarick, "Deportation Crackdown Unveiled," *Globe and Mail*, July 8, 1994.
37. Theresa Wallace, *The Role of Transportation in Canadian Immigration, 1900–2000* (Ottawa: Public Works and Government Services Canada, 2001), 62, and www.web. net/~iccr/edu/ISSUE.htm, accessed April 20, 2004.
38. House of Commons, *Debates*, February 8, 2000, 3216.

CHAPTER 12: IMMIGRATION GRABS ATTENTION, 1996–2006

1. Andrew McIntosh, "RCMP Says Refugee Judges Bribed," *National Post*, June 6, 2003, http://proquest.umi.com/pqdweb?index=3&sid=10&srch, accessed March 31, 2005.
2. James Bissett, "Scrap the Refugee Board," *National Post*, March 30, 2004.
3. Jeffrey Simpson, "The Politics of Immigration," *Globe and Mail*, November 23, 1999, A15.
4. Daniel Hoffman, "The Mystery of Canada's High Immigration Levels," *Canadian Issues, Themes Canadiens*, April 2003, 23–24.
5. Margaret Wente, "Inner Cities on the Outer Edges," *Globe and Mail*, April 13, 2004.
6. Simpson, *Globe and Mail*, November 23, 1999, A15.
7. Marina Jiménez and Kim Lunman, "Canada's Biggest Cities See Influx of New Immigrants," *Globe and Mail*, August 19, 2004, A1.
8. James Daw, "Tough Decisions Now Best For Boomers," *Ottawa Forever Young*, November, 2003, 17.
9. Peter S. Li, "Understanding Economic Performance of Immigrants," *Canadian Issues*, April, 2003, 24–25.
10. Ingrid Peritz, "Wage Gap Grows For Newcomers to Canada," *Globe and Mail*, October 8, 2003.
11. "The Economic Performance of Immigrants," *The Monitor*, Spring 2004, Citizenship and Immigration Canada, www.cic.gc.ca/english/monitor/issue05/06-feature.html, November 2005.
12. John Biles, Erin Tolley, and Humera Ibrahim, "Does Canada Have a Multicultural Future?" *Canadian Diversity/Diversité Canadienne*, vol. 4:1, winter 2005 hiver.
13. Mary Janigan, "Immigrants How Many Is Too Many? Who Should Get In? Can We Tell Them Where To Live and What To Do?" *Maclean's*, December 16, 2002, 21.

14. Erin Andersen, "Foreign Work Not Respected, Statscan Says," *Globe and Mail*, May 18, 2004.

15. Mark Stolarik, Letter to the Editor, *Ottawa Citizen*, April 21, 2005.

16. Pauline Tam, "Immigrant MDs Get Long-Awaited Provincial Help," *Ottawa Citizen*, October 27, 2004.

17. See www.ecdev.gov.bc.ca/ProgramsAndServices/IQU/index.htm, accessed January 15, 2006.

18. Jake Rupert, "Chiarelli Floats Plan to Help Foreign-Trained Professionals," *Ottawa Citizen*, September 28, 2006, C1 and C7.

19. Jeffrey Simpson, "Facts We've Swept Under Our Welcome Mat," *Globe and Mail*, August 27, 2003.

20. Andrew Duffy, "Report Urges Tougher, Simpler Immigration System," *Ottawa Citizen*, January 7, 1998, A1–A2.

21. See www.cic.gc.ca/english/irpa/C11-amend.html, accessed May 6, 2004.

22. CIC website, www.cic.gc.ca/english/pub/you-asked/section-03.html, accessed March 10, 2005.

23. Immigration and Refugee Board home page, March 29, 2005.

24. Susan Hagopian, "Canada's Skilled Worker Program: Speaking to the Experts," *Metropolis*, March 2003, 4.

25. Ibid.

26. CIC Canada Facts and Figures, 2002, Immigration Overview: www.cic.gc.ca/english/pub/facts2002/refugee/refugee-_1.html, accessed May 5, 2004.

27. Frank N. Marrocco, Q.C. and Henry M. Goslett, *The 2003 Annotated Immigration Act of Canada* (Toronto: Carswell, 2003), 2.

28. "Citizenship and Immigration Overview 7: Canada and Refugee Protection at Home and Abroad," Part 2, Citizenship and Immigration Canada, 2005.

29. Tom Kent, "Immigration Now: How to Regain Control and Use it Well," http://policy.queensu.ca/spspi/docs/tk1001.shtml, accessed March 15, 2005.

30. Robin MacKay, "Bill C-26: Canada Border Services Agency Act," Legislative Summaries, Library of Parliament, Parliamentary Information and Research Service, accessed September 26, 2005.

31. Interview with Craig Goodes, September 25, 2006.

CHAPTER 13: DEVELOPMENTS 2006–2015: PRUNING THE QUEUE

1. Paul Wells, *The Longer I'm Prime Minister: Stephen Harper and Canada, 2006 –* (Toronto: Random House Canada, 2013), 22.

2. James Bissett, "The Current State of Canadian Immigration Policy," paper delivered to the Fraser Institute, 3, www.fraserinstitute.org, accessed July 29, 2014.

3. Ibid., 2.

4. Tavia Grant and Rita Trichur, "Shortchanging Immigrants Costs Canada," *Globe and Mail*, December 17, 2011, B8.

5. Patrick Grady, "Conservative Immigration Policy Reform Has Not yet Produced Any Significant Improvement in the Aggregate Labour Market Performance of Recent Immigrants," October 1, 2013, Immigration Papers Global Economics Limited, http://econpapers.repec.org/paper/prampaper/55586.htm, accessed July 8, 2014.

6. Jeffrey Simpson, "Robust Immigration Isn't Working as it Once Did," *Globe and Mail*, February 23, 2007, www.theglobeandmail.com/news/politics/robust-immigration-isnt-working-as-it-once-did/article1325655, accessed November 22, 2014.

7. Parliament of Canada, Parliamentary business, Part 6, Immigration and Refugee Protection Act, Amendments to the act, 87.3 (3), http://openparliament.ca/bills/39-2/C-50/?page=12, accessed September 1, 2014.

8. Carol Goar, "Bill Would Transform Immigration," *Toronto Star*, May 26, 2008, www.thestar.com/opinion/columnists/2008/03/26/bill_would_transform_immigration,html, accessed November 22, 2014.

9. Ibid.

10. Canadian Bar Association paper, "Current Status," June 2014, www.cba.org/CBA/advocacy/pdf/immigration-refugee.pdf, accessed September 5, 2014.

11. Government of Canada, Annual Report to Parliament on Immigration, 2009, Permanent Residents, http://www.cic.gc.ca/english/pdf/pub/immigratio2009_e.pdf, accessed November 18, 2014.

12. Mark Davidson, "Building a Fast and Flexible System," Canada-China Human Capital Dialogue, November 28, 2012, www.asiapacific.ca/research-report/canada-china-human-capital-dialogue-second-conference, accessed September 8, 2014.

13. Alec Castonquay, "The Inside Story of Jason Kenney's Campaign to Win Over Ethnic Votes," *Maclean's*, February 2, 2013.

14. Charlie Gillis, "Who Doesn't Get Into Canada," *Maclean's*, June 17, 2010.

15. Citizenship and Immigration Canada Preliminary Tables — Permanent and Temporary Residents, 2013, Permanent Residents By Category, 2009–2013.

16. Peter O'Neil, "Think-Tank Calls For Immigration Reform," *Ottawa Citizen*, August 29, 2013.

17. Citizenship and Immigration Canada Preliminary Tables — Permanent and temporary residents, 2013. Permanent residents by category, 2009-2013. Retrieved from the Internet, October 2, 2014.

18. Anna Mehler Paperny, "Kenney in a hurry to recruit world's top talent," *Globe and Mail,* April 5, 2012, A 10.

19. Peter Showler, "Detained Tamils case exposes Canada's brutal refugee policy," *Ottawa Citizen*, April 18, 1911.

20. Carol Goar, "Canada shows the world a forbidding new face," *Toronto Star*, August 20, 2010, A21.

21. "Concerns about Bill C-49." Retrieved from the Internet October 21, 2014.

22. Tobi Cohen, "Refugee advocates slam flood of deportations," *Ottawa Citizen*, August 23, 2013. Retrieved from the Internet November 22, 2014.

23. Tobi Cohen, "Refugee health cuts 'irresponsible,'" *Ottawa Citizen*, January 29, 2014, A5.

24. "A cruel policy struck down," editorial, *Globe and Mail*, July 7, 2014. Retrieved from the Internet November 22, 2014.

25. Tavia Grant, "Foreign workers program seen as growing too fast," *Globe and Mail*, April 9, 2013. Retrieved from the Internet November 22, 2014.

26. "Major Shortcomings Overshadow Progress Made In Canada's 2013 Immigration And Refugee Policy Performance." Press release issued by Centre for Immigration Policy Reform, 2.

27. Iain Marlow, "Investor road to Canada hits a dead end," *Globe and Mail*, February 12, 2014, A10.

28. Tobi Cohen, "Immigration of grandparents, parents reopens," *Ottawa Citizen*, January 3, 2013, A 4.

29. Konrad Yakabuski, op. cit.

30. CBC Radio, The Current, November 20, 2014. Retrieved from the Internet November 23, 2014.

31. Thomas Walkom, *Toronto Star*, November 7, 2014. Retrieved from the Internet, November 23, 2014.

32. L. Ian MacDonald, "Harper is bungling the refugee issue — and it will cost him," iPolitics.ca/2015/09/08/harpers-blowing-the-refugee-issue-and-it-will-cost-him/, accessed September 10, 2015.

CHAPTER 14: ISSUES IN THE TWENTY-FIRST CENTURY

1. Irving Abella in panel discussion on Canada's immigration objectives, "Levels, Composition, and Directions," Charles M. Beach and Alan G. Green eds., *Policy Forum on the Role of Immigration in Canada's Future* (Kingston, ON: John Deutsch Institute for the Study of Economic Policies, 1989), 81.

2. Shirley Seward, *The Relationship Between Immigration and the Canadian Economy* (Ottawa: Institute for Research in Public Policy, 1987), 5.

3. Ibid.

4. Economic Council of Canada, *New Faces in the Crowd*, 8, 11.

5. Ibid., 2.

6. Terence Corcoran, "Xeconophobia [sic] Versus Free Immigration," *Globe and Mail*, October 27, 1990.

7. Ibid.

8. Paul Fromm, "Government Policy Ignores Views of Majority," *Ottawa Citizen*, August 14, 1990.

9. Martin Collacott, "Turn Off the Taps," *Ottawa Citizen*, April 30, 2004, A-17.

10. Gilles Paquet, *Moderato Cantabile: Toward Principled Governance for Canada's Immigration Regime* (Ottawa: Invenire Books, 2012). (For a discussion of Suzuki's statement, see *Globe and Mail* editorial, July 13, 2013, www.theglobeandmail.com/globe-debate/editorials/david-suzuki-and-jason-kenney-amplify-each-other/article13205288, accessed Mach 2, 2015.

11. Economic Council of Canada, *New Faces in the Crowd*, 34.

12. W. Gunther Plaut, Refugee Determination in Canada: Proposals for a New System, Report to the Hon. Flora MacDonald (Ottawa: Minister of Supplies and Services, 1985), 179.

13. Boyce Richardson, *Time to Change*, 159.

14. Alan Green, *Canadian Immigration Policy for the 21st Century* (Montreal: McGill-Queen's University Press, 2003), 43.

15. R. Douglas Francis, Richard Jones, and Donald B. Smith, *Destinies: Canadian History Since Confederation* (Toronto: Holt, Rinehart and Winston of Canada, 1988), 412.

16. For a detailed criticism of Canada's multicultural policies see Neil Bissoondah, *Selling Illusions: The Cult of Multiculturalism in Canada* (Toronto: Penguin Books, 1994).

17. Peter Woolfson, "An Anthropological Perspective: The Ingredients of a Multicultural Society," William Metcalfe ed., *Understanding Canada: A Multidisciplinary Introduction to Canadian Studies* (New York and London: New York University Press, 1982), 305.

18. Robert Sibley, "Canada After 9/11 Part 2: The Trouble With Multiculturalism," www.canada.com/life/Canada+after+Part+trouble+with+multiculturalism/5358736/story.html, accessed February 24, 2015.

19. Paquet, *Moderato Cantabile: Toward Principled Governance for Canada's Immigration Regime.*

20. See Citizenship and Immigration Canada website.

21. See http://laws-lois.justice.gc.ca/eng/AnnualStatutes/2001_27/page-1.html#s-3, accessed September 9, 2015.

22. Robert Sibley, "Rethinking Multiculturalism," *Ottawa Citizen,* June 10, 2005, A1.

— SELECT BIBLIOGRAPHY —

BOOKS

Abella, Irving. *A Coat of Many Colours: Two Centuries of Jewish Life in Canada.* Toronto: Lester & Orpen Dennys, 1990.

Abella, Irving, and Harold Troper. *None Is Too Many: Canada and the Jews of Europe, 1933–1948.* Toronto: Lester & Orpen Dennys, 1982.

Adelman, Howard. *Canada and the Indochinese Refugees.* Regina: L.A. Weigl Educational Associates, 1982.

Avery, Donald. *"Dangerous Foreigners": European Immigrant Workers and Labour Radicalism in Canada, 1896–1932.* Toronto: McClelland & Stewart, 1979.

Beach, Charles M., Alan G. Green, and Jeffrey G. Reitz, eds. *Canadian Immigration Policy for the 21st Century.* Kingston: John Deutsch Institute for the Study of Economic Policy, Queen's University, 2003.

Beach, Charles M., and Alan G. Green, eds. *Policy Forum on the Role of Immigration in Canada's Future.* Kingston: John Deutsch Institute for the Study of Economic Policy, Queen's University, 1989.

Berger, Carl. *The Writing of Canadian History: Aspects of English-Canadian Historical Writing Since 1900,* 2nd ed. Toronto: University of Toronto Press, 1986.

Brown, Craig, ed. *The Illustrated History of Canada.* Toronto: Key Porter Books, 2002.

Brown, Robert C., and Ramsay Cook. *Canada 1896–1921: A Nation Transformed.* Toronto: McClelland & Stewart, 1974.

Brown, Wallace. *The King's Friends: The Composition and Motives of the American Loyalist Claimants.* Providence: Brown University Press, 1965.

Burnet, Jean, with Harold Palmer. *"Coming Canadians": An Introduction to a History of Canada's Peoples.* Toronto: McClelland & Stewart, 1988.

Clippingdale, Richard. *Laurier: His Life and World.* Toronto: McGraw-Hill Ryerson, 1979.

Conrad, Margaret, and Barry Moody, eds. *Planter Links: Community Culture in Colonial Nova Scotia.* Fredericton, NB: Acadiensis Press, 2001.

Cook, Ramsay, with John Saywell and John Ricker. *Canada: A Modern Study.* Toronto: Clarke Irwin, 1967.

Corbett, David C. *Canada's Immigration Policy: A Critique.* Toronto: University of Toronto Press, 1957.

Cowan, Helen I. *British Emigration to British North America: The First Hundred Years.* Toronto: University of Toronto Press, 1961.

———. *British Immigration Before Confederation*. Volume 22 of the Canadian Historical Association Booklets. Ottawa: The Canadian Historical Association, 1978.

Craig, Gerald M., ed. *Lord Durham's Report*. Carleton Library, no. 1. Toronto: McClelland & Stewart, 1963.

———. *Upper Canada: The Formative Years 1784–1841*. Toronto: McClelland & Stewart, 1968.

Dirks, Gerald. *Canada's Refugee Policy: Indifference or Opportunism?* Montreal: McGill-Queen's University Press, 1977.

Dobell, Peter C. *Canada in World Affairs*. Vol. 17: 1971–73. Toronto: Canadian Institute of International Affairs, 1985.

Eagle, John A. *The Canadian Pacific Railway and the Development of Western Canada 1896–1914*. Montreal: McGill-Queen's University Press, 1989.

Eccles, William I. *Canada Under Louis XIV, 1663–1701*. Toronto: McClelland & Stewart, 1964.

Faith, Nicholas. *The World the Railways Made*. London: Bodley Head, 1990.

Ferns, Henry, and Bernard Ostry. *The Age of Mackenzie King: The Rise of the Leader*. London: William Heinemann, 1955.

Francis, R. Douglas, Richard Jones, and Donald B. Smith. *Destinies: Canadian History Since Confederation*. Toronto: Holt, Rinehart, and Winston of Canada, 1988.

Fryer, Mary Beacock. *King's Men: The Soldier Founders of Ontario*. Toronto: Dundurn Press, 1980.

Hall, David J. *Clifford Sifton: Volume 1, The Young Napoleon, 1861–1900*. Vancouver: University of British Columbia Press, 1985.

Hamilton, Robert, and Dorothy Shields. *The Dictionary of Canadian Quotations and Phrases*. Rev. ed. Toronto: McClelland & Stewart, 1979.

Harper, Marjory. *Emigration from North-East Scotland: Beyond the Broad Atlantic*. Vol. 2. Aberdeen: University of Aberdeen Press, 1989.

Harris, R. Cole, and Geoffrey J. Matthews. *Historical Atlas of Canada Vol. 1: From the Beginning to 1800*. Toronto: University of Toronto Press, 1987.

Hawkins, Freda. *Canada and Australia: The Dilemmas of Modern Migration*. Canada House Lecture Series, no. 30, 1985.

———. *Canada and Immigration: Public Policy and Public Concern*. Montreal: McGill-Queen's University Press, 1972 and 1978.

———. *Critical Years in Immigration: Canada and Australia Compared*. Montreal: McGill-Queen's University Press, 1989.

Hedges, James B. *Building the Canadian West: The Land and Colonization Policies of the Canadian Pacific Railway*. New York: Macmillan Company, 1939.

Holmes, John W. *The Shaping of Peace: Canada and the Search for World Order, 1943–1957*, Vol. I. Toronto: University of Toronto Press, 1979.

Hopkins, J. Castell. *The Canadian Annual Review of Public Affairs: 1910*. Toronto: Annual Review Publishing Company, 1911.

Houston, Cecil J., and William J. Smyth. *Irish Emigration and Canadian Settlement: Patterns, Links and Letters*. Toronto: University of Toronto Press, 1990.

Johnson, Stanley. *A History of Emigration from the United Kingdom to North America, 1763–1912*. London: George Routledge & Sons, 1913.

Kasinsky, Renée G. *Refugees from Militarism: Draft-Age Americans in Canada.* Totowa, NJ: Littlefield, Adams and Company, 1976.

Kent, Tom. *A Public Purpose: An Experience of Liberal Opposition and Canadian Government.* Montreal: McGill-Queen's University Press, 1988.

Knowles, Valerie. *First Person: A Biography of Cairine Wilson, Canada's First Woman Senator.* Toronto: Dundurn Press, 1988.

Lyon, Peyton. *Canada in World Affairs, 1961–63.* Toronto: Oxford University Press, 1968.

Macdonald, Norman. *Canada: Immigration and Colonization, 1843–1903.* Toronto: Macmillan of Canada, 1966.

MacNutt, W.S. *The Atlantic Provinces: The Emergence of Colonial Society 1712–1857.* Toronto: McClelland & Stewart, 1965.

Malarek, Victor. *Heaven's Gate: Canada's Immigration Fiasco.* Toronto: Macmillan of Canada, 1987.

Matas, David, and Ilena Simon. *Closing the Doors: The Failure of Refugee Protection.* Toronto: Summerhill Press, 1989.

Metcalfe, William, ed. *Understanding Canada: A Multidisciplinary Introduction to Canadian Studies.* New York: New York University Press, 1982.

Miquelon, Dale. *New France, 1701–1744: A Supplement to Europe.* Toronto: McClelland & Stewart, 1987.

Mitchell, Maurice. *"A Man of Big Heart": The Memoirs of Maurice Mitchell.* Ottawa: Canadian Immigration Historical Society, 1988.

Moore, Christopher. *The Loyalists: Revolution, Exile, Settlement.* Toronto: Macmillan of Canada, 1984.

Nelson, William H. *The American Tory.* Oxford: Clarendon Press, 1961.

Ormsby, Margaret. *British Columbia: A History.* Toronto: Macmillan of Canada, 1971.

Ouellet, Fernand. *Lower Canada, 1791–1840: Social Change and Nationalism.* Toronto: McClelland & Stewart, 1980.

Paquet, Gilles. *Moderato Cantabile: Toward Principled Governance for Canada's Immigration Regime.* Ottawa: Invenire Books, 2012.

Pope, Maurice, ed. *Public Servant: The Memoirs of Sir Joseph Pope.* Toronto: Oxford University Press, 1960.

Richardson, Boyce. *Time to Change: Canada's Place in a World in Crisis.* Toronto: Summerhill Press, 1990.

Roberts, Barbara. *Whence They Came: Deportations from Canada, 1900–1935.* Ottawa: University of Ottawa Press, 1988.

Roberts, John A., ed. *The Canadian Family Tree: Canada's Peoples.* Don Mills, ON: Corpus Information Services, 1979.

Schull, Joseph. *Laurier: The First Canadian.* Toronto: Macmillan of Canada, 1967.

Segal, Gary. *Immigrating to Canada: Who Is Allowed? What Is Required? How to Do It!* 9th ed. North Vancouver: Self-Council Press, 1990.

Seward, Shirley. *The Relationship Between Immigration and the Canadian Economy.* Ottawa: Institute for Research in Public Policy, 1987.

Skilling, H. Gordon. *Canadian Representation Abroad: From Agency to Embassy.* Toronto: Ryerson Press, 1945.

Story, Norah. *The Oxford Companion to Canadian History and Literature*. Toronto: Oxford University Press, 1967.

Timlin, Mabel E. *Does Canada Need More People?* Toronto: Oxford University Press, 1951.

Trudel, Marcel. *The Beginnings of New France, 1524–1663*. Toronto: McClelland & Stewart, 1972.

Urquhart, M.C., and K.A. Buckley. *Historical Statistics of Canada*. Toronto: Macmillan Company of Canada, 1965.

Vachon, Andre, et al. *Dreams of Empire: Canada Before 1700*. Ottawa: Public Archives of Canada, 1982.

Ward, W. Peter. *White Canada Forever: Popular Attitudes and Public Policy toward Orientals in British Columbia*. Montreal: McGill-Queen's University Press, 1978.

Wells, Paul. *The Longer I'm Prime Minister: Stephen Harper and Canada, 2006–*. Toronto: Random House Canada, 2013.

Whitaker, Reg. *Double Standard: The Secret Story of Canadian Immigration*. Toronto: Lester & Orpen Dennys, 1989.

Wilson, Bruce. *Colonial Identities: Canada from 1760 to 1815*. Ottawa: National Archives of Canada, 1988.

Winks, Robin. *The Blacks in Canada: A History*. Montreal: McGill-Queen's University Press, 1977.

Woodham-Smith, Cecil. *The Great Hunger: Ireland 1845–1849*. New York: Harper & Row, 1962.

Woodsworth, J .S. *Strangers within Our Gates*. Michael Bliss, ed. The Social History of Canada series. Toronto: University of Toronto Press, 1972.

ARTICLES

Allen, Gene, and Rudy Platiel. "Family Reunification Harder, Lawyer Says." *Globe and Mail*, October 27, 1990, AF.

Badets, J. "Canada's Immigrant Population." *Canadian Social Trends*, Autumn 1988, 2.

Biles, John, Erin Tolley, and Humera Ibrahim. "Does Canada Have a Multicultural Future?" *Canadian Diversity/Diversité Canadienne*, vol. 4:1, winter 2005 hiver, 23–28.

Bissett, James. "Scrap the Refugee Board." *National Post*, March 30, 2004, A14.

Canadian Immigration Historical Society. *CIHS Bulletin SHIC*, Supplement "A," Issue no. 4, March 1988.

Collacott, Martin. "Turn Off the Taps." *Ottawa Citizen*, April 30, 2004, A17.

Corcoran, Terence. "Xeconophobia [*sic*] Versus Free Immigration." *Globe and Mail*, October 27, 1990, B4.

Courville, Serge, and Jacques Mathieu. "A French Stamp on the Land." *Horizon Canada* 2, no. 17: 404–08.

Craig, Gerald M. "The 1830s." J.M.S. Careless, ed. *Colonists and Canadiens 1760–1867*. Toronto: Macmillan of Canada, 1971, 173–99.

Day, Patricia. "A Choice between Evils: The Chinese and the Construction of the Canadian Pacific Railway in British Columbia." Hugh A. Dempsey, ed. *The CPR West: The Iron Road and the Making of a Nation*. Vancouver and Toronto: Douglas & McIntyre, 1984, 13–34.

Dirks, Gerald. "A Policy within a Policy: The Identification and Admission of Refugees to Canada." *Canadian Journal of Political Science* 17, no. 2 (June 1984): 279–307.

———. "Immigration Policy." *The Canadian Encyclopedia*, Vol. 2. Edmonton: Hurtig Publishers, 1988, 1047–48.

Duncan, K.J. "Patterns of Settlement in the East." W. Stanford Reid, ed. *The Scottish Tradition in Canada*. Toronto: McClelland & Stewart, 1976, 49–75.

Elliott, Bruce S. "Regionalized Immigration and Settlement Patterns of the Irish in Upper Canada." Robert O'Driscoll and Lorna Reynolds, eds. *The Untold Story: The Irish in Canada*. Toronto: Celtic Arts of Canada, 1988.

Ells, Margaret. "Settling the Loyalists in Nova Scotia." *Canadian Historical Association Report for 1934*, 105–09.

Forster, Donald. "The Economy." John T. Saywell, ed. *Canadian Annual Review for 1962*. Toronto: University of Toronto Press, 1963.

———. "The National Economy." John T. Saywell, ed. *Canadian Annual Review for 1963*. Toronto: University of Toronto Press, 1964.

Francis, Daniel. "Boat People." *Horizon Canada* 4, no. 42: 985–91.

Fromm, Paul. "Government Policy Ignores Views of Majority." *Ottawa Citizen*, August 14, 1990, A11.

Gates, Paul W. "Official Encouragement of Immigration by the Province of Canada." *Canadian Historical Review* 15 (March 1934): 24–38.

Goar, Carol. "Bill Would Transform Immigration." *Toronto Star*, May 26, 2008.

———. "Canada Shows the World a Forbidding New Face." *Toronto Star*, August 20, 2010, A21.

Grant, Tavia and Rita Trichur. "Shortchanging Immigrants Costs Canada." *Globe and Mail*, December 17, 2011, B8.

Gwyn, Julian. "The Irish in the Napanee River Valley: Camden East Township, 1851–1881." Robert O'Driscoll and Lorna Reynolds, eds. *The Untold Story: The Irish in Canada*. Toronto: Celtic Arts of Canada, 1988.

Hall, David. "Room to Spare." *Horizon Canada* 7, no. 76: 1801–07.

Hamilton, Sylvia D. "On the Way to Africa." *Horizon Canada* 5, no. 54: 1292–96.

Hoffman, Daniel. "The Mystery of Canada's High Immigration Levels." *Canadian Issues, Themes Canadiens*, April 2003, 23–24.

Houston, Cecil J., and William J. Symth. "Irish Emigrants to Canada: Whence They Came." Robert O'Driscoll and Lorna Reynolds, eds. *The Untold Story: The Irish in Canada*. Toronto: Celtic Arts of Canada, 1988.

Laighin, Padraie. "Grosse-Ile: The Holocaust Revisited." Robert O'Driscoll and Lorna Reynolds, eds. *The Untold Story: The Irish in Canada*. Toronto: Celtic Arts of Canada, 1988.

Laing, Donald. "MacCanada." *Horizon Canada* 6, no. 72: 1718–23.

Li, Peter S. "Understanding Economic Performance of Immigrants." *Canadian Issues, Themes Canadiens*, April 2003, 24–25.

Lower, Arthur. "The Myth of Mass Immigration." *Maclean's*, May 15, 1949, 69–71.

McLaughlin, Robert. "New England Planters Prior to Migration: The Case of Chatham, Massachusetts." Margaret Conrad and Barry Moody, eds. *Planter Links: Community and Culture in Colonial Nova Scotia*. Fredericton: Acadiensis Press, 2001, 12–19.

Monet, Jacques. "The 1840s." J.M.S. Careless, ed. *Colonists and Canadiens 1760–1867*. Toronto: Macmillan of Canada, 1971, 200–25.

Moore, Christopher. "Confronting the Dragon." *The Beaver*, February/March 2006, 52–53.

———. "Old Loyalties." *Horizon Canada* 2, no. 20: 457–63.

Morehouse, Frances. "Canadian Migration in the Forties." *Canadian Historical Review* 9, no. 1 (March 1928): 302–29.

Moyles, R.G. "War at Heart." *Horizon Canada* 3, no. 27: 632–37.

Nish, Cameron. "The 1760s." J.M.S. Careless, ed. *Colonists and Canadiens 1760-1867*. Toronto: Macmillan of Canada, 1971, 1–19.

Norrie, K.H. "The Rate of Settlement of the Canadian Prairies, 1870–1911." Douglas McCalla, ed. *Perspectives on Canadian Economic History*. Toronto: Copp Clark Pitman, 1987, 168–81.

Peritz, Ingrid. "Wage Gap Grows for Newcomers to Canada." *Globe and Mail*, October 9, 2003, A10.

"Re Singh and Minister of Employment and Immigration." *Dominion Law Reports* (fourth series), Vol. 17. Canada Law Book Inc., 1985.

Ryan, Shannon. "The 17th Century Fishery." *Horizon Canada*, vol. 1, no. 8, 169–75.

Scott, William. "Immigration and Population." Adam Shortt and Arthur Doughty, eds. *Canada and Its Provinces*, Vol. 7. Toronto: Publishers' Association of Canada, 1913, 517–90.

Sessing, Trevor. "How They Kept Canada Almost Lily White." *Saturday Night*, September 1970, 30–32.

Sibley, Robert. "Rethinking Multiculturalism." *Ottawa Citizen*, June 10, 2005, A4.

Simmons, Alan B. "'New Wave' Immigrants: Origins and Characteristics." Shiva S. Halli, Frank Trovato, and Leo Driedger, eds. *Ethnic Demography*. Ottawa: Carleton University Press, 1990, 151–59.

Simpson, Jeffrey. "The Politics of Immigration." *Globe and Mail*, November 23, 1999, A15.

Tedesco, Theresa, et al. "The Moneyed Class." *Maclean's*, July 10, 1989, 19.

Timlin, Mabel F. "Canada's Immigration Policy, 1896–1910." *Canadian Journal of Economics and Political Science* 26 (1960): 517–32.

Traves, Tom, and John T. Saywell. "Parliament and Politics." R.B. Byers and John T. Saywell, eds. *Canadian Annual Review of Politics and Public Affairs*, 1978. Toronto: University of Toronto Press, 1980.

Wallot, Jean-Pierre. "The 1800s." J.M.S. Careless, ed. *Colonists and Canadiens 1760– 1867*. Toronto: Macmillan of Canada, 1971, 95–121.

Wente, Margaret. "Inner Cities on the Outer Edges." *Globe and Mail*, April 13, 2004, A19.

Woolfson, Peter. "An Anthropological Perspective: The Ingredients of a Multicultural Society." William Metcalfe, ed. *Understanding Canada. A Multidisciplinary Introduction to Canadian Studies*. New York: New York University Press, 1972, 297–399.

Wynn, Graeme. "Paradise North." *Horizon Canada* 3, no. 33: 769–75.

Zieman, Margaret K. "The Story Behind the Real Uncle Tom." *Maclean's*, June 1, 1954, 20–21, 42–44.

THESES

Cameron, John. "Legislation Relating to Immigration in Canada Prior to Confederation." M.A. dissertation, University of Toronto, 1935.

Cameron, Ruth. "The Wheat from the Chaff." M.A. dissertation, Concordia University, 1976.

Troper, Harold. "Official Canadian Government Encouragement of American Immigration, 1896–1911." Ph.D. dissertation, University of Toronto, 1–71.

REPORTS, BRIEFS, STUDIES, PAPERS

Adelman, Howard. "An Immigration Dream: Hungarian Refugees Come to Canada — An Analysis." Unpublished paper delivered to a Canadian Immigration Historical Society symposium, 28 April 1990.

Bissett, James. "The Current State of Canadian Immigration Policy." Paper delivered to the Fraser Institute, 3, www.fraserinstitute.org, accessed July 29, 2014

———. Unpublished notes on Bill C11, prepared for Senate hearing [2001].

Canadian Bar Association paper. "Current Status," June 2014. www.cba.org/CBA/advocacy/pdf/immigration-refugee.pdf, accessed September 5, 2014.

Davidson, Mark. "Building a Fast and Flexible System." Canada-China Human Capital Dialogue, November 28, 2012. www.asiapacific.ca/research-report/canada-china-human-capital-dialogue-second conference, accessed September 8, 2014.

Seward, Shirley, and Mark Tremblay "Immigrants in the Canadian Labour Force: Their Role in Structural Change." Discussion paper prepared for Institute for Research on Public Policy, 1989.

Sien, Foon. "The Chinese in Canada." Essay submitted to the Royal Commission on Bilingualism and Biculturalism, 1967. Ottawa: Queen's Printer, 1967.

Zeigler, Edward. "Refugee Movements and Policy in Canada." Unpublished study prepared for the Department of National Health and Welfare's Demographic Review, 1988.

GOVERNMENT PUBLICATIONS AND DOCUMENTS

Canada. Department of Citizenship and Immigration. *Annual Report, Fiscal Year ended March 31, 1958.*

Canada. Department of Citizenship and Immigration files. RG 76, vol. 865. NAC.

Canada. Department of Employment and Immigration. *Annual Report of the Department of Employment and Immigration for the fiscal year 1986–87.*

Canada. Department of External Affairs files. RG 25, vol. 2., LAC.

Canada. Department of Immigration and Colonization. *Report of the Department of Immigration and Colonization for the Fiscal Year Ended March 31, 1924.*

Canada. Department of the Interior. *Report of the Superintendent of Immigration,* Sessional Paper No. 25, *Report of the Department of the Interior, 1908.*

Canada. Department of Manpower and Immigration. *Immigration Policy Perspectives, Vol. 1: Canadian Immigration and Population Study.* Ottawa: Information Canada, 1974.

Canada. Department of Manpower and Immigration. *White Paper on Immigration.* Ottawa: Queen's Printer, 1966.

Canada. Statistics Canada. *Canada Year Book 1957–58.* Ottawa: Queen's Printer, 1958.

Canada. *Statutes of Canada 1909–1910,* vol. 1.

Canada. *Statutes of Canada 1919*, vol. 1.
Canada. *Statutes of Canada 1976–1977*, vol. 2.

CANADA, PARLIAMENT

Canadian Congress of Labour. Brief Submitted to the Senate Standing Committee on Immigration and Labour, July 25, 1946. Eugene Forsey Papers, LAC.

Couture, L. Brief Prepared for the Department of Citizenship and Immigration, 1952.

Economic Council of Canada. *New Faces in the Crowd: Economic and Social Impacts of Immigration.* Ottawa: Minister of Supplies and Services Canada, 1991.

House of Commons. *Debates*, June 19, 1869, July 27, 1899, July 10, 1903, July 15, 1903, June 13, 1906, June 8, 1917, March 22, 1918, March 20, 1923, May 17, 1923, August 27, 1946, May 1, 1947, June 2, 1947, April 24, 1953, June 10, 1952, April 22, 1959, March 5, 1959, January 19, 1962, February 27, 1962, May 9, 1966, May 29, 1966, May 30, 1966, October 26, 1967, October 8, 1971, June 20, 1972, February 3, 1975, December 10, 1986, March 24, 1987, and September 2, 1987.

House of Commons. *Journals*, 1878, Appendix 2.

———. *Journals*, vol. 38, 1903.

———. *Journals*, vol. 43, 1907–1908.

Manion, John. "Hungarian Refugee Movement — Implementing the Policy." Unpublished paper delivered to a Canadian Immigration Historical Society symposium, April 28, 1990.

Plaut, W. Gunther. *Refugee Determination in Canada: Proposals for a New System. A Report to the Hon. Flora MacDonald, Minister of Employment and Immigration.* Ottawa: Minister of Supplies and Services Canada, 1985.

Privy Council committee. *Report approved by the Governor General, December 12, 1874.* Vertical files, library, Employment and Immigration Canada.

Rodel, Alti. *Nazi War Criminals in Canada: The Historical and Policy Setting from the 1940s to the Present.* Report prepared for the Commission of Inquiry on War Criminals, September 1986.

Senate. *Report of the Standing Committee on Immigration and Labour, 1946.* Ottawa: King's Printer, 1946.

———. *Report to Parliament by the Special Joint Committee of the Senate and House of Commons on Immigration Policy.* Ottawa: Queen's Printer, 1975.

Standing Committee on Labour, Employment and Immigration, Minutes of Proceedings, no. 34, May 1990. Ottawa: Queen's Printer, 1990.

INTERVIEWS

Cal Best
James Bissett
Bernard Brodie
Craig Goodes
Barbara Jackman
Daniel Jean
Mary Joseph
Jack Manion

Michael Molloy
Donald Page
Michael Shenstone
Richard Tait
Mary Tatham
Gerald Van Kessel
Richard Weatherston

— INDEX —

Acadia, 13, 20, 24–25, 28
Adjustment of Status Program, 202, 203, 214
Aiken, Sharry, 279
Alexander, Chris, 278, 279, 280, 281, 282
Alexander, Sir William, 16
Alien Labour Act, 86, 103, 168
Allan, Sir Hugh, 74, 79
Allen, James, 37–38
Anderson, R.K., 136–37
Andras, Robert, 198, 199, 200, 202–03, 204, 206, 207, 208, 214
    amends Immigration Appeal Board Act, 202, 214
    and immigration act, 208
    view of immigration policy, 204, 206
Annapolis Royal, 14, 16, 25, 42
anti-Semitism, 145, 146, 154, 165
Assisted Passage Loan Scheme, 171
asylum-seekers, 222, 224
Atkey, Ron, 217

Bagot, Sir Charles, 64
Barnardo, Thomas John, 96, 97–98
Barr, Rev. Isaac, 99, 100
Barr Colony, 99–100
Bata, Thomas, 148
Bathurst, Lord, 51, 52
Bell, Richard, 190–91, 193, 196
    view of immigration, 190
Berry, S.R., 114
Bill C-4, 274

Bill C-10, 267
Bill C-11, 259, 265
Bill C-17, 267
Bill C-24, 279
Bill C-31, 274–75
Bill C-38, 273
Bill C-43, 277
Bill C-49. *See* Bill C-4
Bill C-50, 268
Bill C-84. *See* Refugee Deterrents and Detention System
Bill C-86, 238, 239–40
Bill of Rights, 187–88, 226
Bill S-7, 279–80
Birt, Louisa, 96
birth rate, 233, 266
Bissett, James, 248, 261, 269
Bissoondath, Neil, 270
Blair, Frederick Charles, 145–46
    view of refugees, 146, 147
Borden, Sir Robert, 131
Bourassa, Henri, 125
Bourne, Larry, 251
Brandeau, Esther, 26
Brant, Joseph, 40
British American Land Company, 56
British Columbia, settlement of, 101–02
British North America Act. *See* Constitution Act, 1867
British Queen (ship), 49
Brogiollo, Yane, 266
Buchanan, Alexander Carlisle, the elder, 57

Budka, Bishop Nykyta, 128
business class program, 231–33

Cabot, John, 11
Cadillac, Lamothe, 27
Canada Border Services Agency,
    262–63, 264
Canada Company, 56–57
Canada Manpower and Immigration
    Council Act, 197
Canada West Land and Agency
    Company, 74
Canadian Bar Association, 268
Canadian Christian Council for
    Resettlement of Refugees
    (CCCRR), 170
Canadian Congress of Labour, 156–57
Canadian Council of Churches, 215
Canadian Experience Class program, 271
Canadian Medical Association Journal,
    275–76
Canadian National Committee on
    Refugees (CNCR), 147–48, 159, 160
Canadian Pacific Railway (CPR), 72, 80,
    81–82, 86, 87, 139
    Department of Colonization and
        Development, 139
    and western settlement, 81–82, 139
Cape Breton, 11, 28, 39
Caplan, Elinor, 249, 257
Card, Charles Ora, 90
Carignan-Salières regiment, 22
Carleton, Sir Guy, 35–36, 42
Carney, Mark, 276–77
Cartier, Jacques, 12
Champlain, Samuel de, 13–14
Chapleau, Joseph-Adolphe, 71–72
Charlesbourg-Royal, 12
Chinese Immigration Act, 1923, 136, 163
cholera epidemic of 1832, 60–61
Citizens' Committee of One Thousand, 133
City of Benares (ship), 153
"Clearances," 50
Coderre, Denis, 249, 259, 261
Colbert, Jean-Baptiste, 19, 20

Coldwell, M.J., 167–68
Collacott, Martin, 286
Communauté des Habitants, La, 19
Compagnie de la Nouvelle France. See
    Company of New France
Compagnie des Indes occidentales, 19–20
Company of New France, 15–16, 18, 19
Company of One Hundred Associates.
    See Company of New France
Conception Bay, Newfoundland, 31
Conservatives' five-year immigration
    plan, 236–38
Constitution Act, 1867, 69–70
Constitutional Act of 1791, 45
continuous journey regulation, 121, 144
Contract Labour Regulation, 144
Corbett, David, 187, 188
Corcoran, Terence, 266–67
Cornwallis, Colonel Edward, 29
Craig, Sir James, 62
Crerar, Thomas, 145–46, 149, 152
Crestol, Leon, 189
Croll, David, 158–59
Cullen, Bud, 216, 218
Cullen-Couture Agreement, 218

Davidson, George, 188
Davidson, Mark, 259
Dawson route, 79
deportation process, 108, 143
deportations, 108, 111–12, 143
deportations of Japanese Canadians.
    See discrimination, Japanese
    Canadians as victims during
    Second World War
d'Esterhazy, Count Paul, 78
Diefenbaker, John, 179–80, 182, 187
Dionne, Ludger, 168
discrimination
    blacks as victims of racism, 42,
        117–19
    elimination in immigration policy,
        187, 188, 197
    First World War and anti-foreign
        sentiment, 127–29

hostility towards immigrants from eastern, central, and southern Europe, 104
immigration policy regarding Asians, 120, 121
immigration policy regarding blacks, 117–19
immigration policy regarding Chinese, 71, 72
Japanese Canadians as victims during Second World War, 153–54
nativist attitudes towards immigrants, 104
See also anti-Semitism
Dixon, William, 70
Dominion Lands Act, 1872, 73–74, 78, 80, 87
Douglas, W.A.B., 152–53
Doukhobors. *See* Immigration, Doukhobors
Du Gua de Monts, Pierre, 14
Dunkards. *See* Immigration, Dunkards
Dunlop, William "Tiger," 57
Duplessis, Maurice, 149
Durham, John George Lampton, Earl of, 62–63
Durham Report, 62–63

Economic Council of Canada, 232, 238, 266, 268
"economic migrants." *See* asylum-seekers
emigration
Arthur Lower on, 91
from Canada, 81, 186
from Canada East, 45
from Newfoundland, 32
from Nova Scotia, 29
from Upper Canada, 42, 43
Empire Settlement Act, 1922, 137–38
engagés, 22
Evian Conference, 144, 145
Express Entry Program, 272

Fairclough, Ellen, 180–81, 182, 184, 185, 187, 188

introduces non-racist immigration policy, 187
and sponsored immigration, 181–82
and World Refugee Year, 183, 185
filles du roi, 22–23
Finley, Diane, 267, 268
Flavelle, Sir Joseph, 140
Fleming, Stewart, 184–85
Foreign Credentials Referral Office, 269
France, 11–32
colonial policy of, 13, 15–16, 19–20, 24–25
severance of Canada from, 27, 33
Freiman, A.J., 139
Freiman, Lillian, 139
French West Indies Company. *See* Compagnie des Indes occidentales

Galt, Alexander, 77, 78
Galt, John, 57
George, James, 212
German, W.M., 109
Gilbert, Sir Humphrey, 31
Glen, J.A., 162
Goar, Carol, 268
Gotlieb, Allan, 203
Green, George Everitt, 98
Green Paper of 1975, 203, 204, 205–06, 207
Greenberg, Howard, 242
Grubel, Herb, 270
guest children from Great Britain. *See* Immigration, guest children
Gwyn, Richard, 270

Haldimand, Frederick, 38–39
Halifax, Lord, 29
Halifax, Nova Scotia, founding of, 28–29
Harbhajan Singh decision. *See* Singh decision
Harper, Stephen, 264
Harris, Walter, 169, 180
Hawke, A.B., 67
head tax, 71, 72–73

Heap, Dan, 232, 241
Hector (ship), 48
Henson, Josiah, 59
Herbert, H.G., 122
Holmes, John, 165
Holt, Derek, 251
home children. See immigration, home
    children
Hospitalières, 17
Hou, Feng, 266
Howe, C.D., 167
Howson, Geoffrey, 229
Huguenots, 12, 24
Hutterites. See immigration, Hutterites

Île Royal. See Cape Breton
Île St. Jean. See Prince Edward Island
immigrant investor program, 278–79
immigration
    African, 211, 230, 254
    agriculturists during Sifton regime,
        103, 104
    during Oliver years, 107, 116
    American, 48, 88–89, 90, 102, 104
    Arthur Lower on, 157
    Asian, 211, 230, 254
    Balts, 166
    blacks, 91, 118, 169
    border inspection service, 121–22
    British, 48, 49, 94, 95, 96, 99–100,
        101, 102, 104, 111, 114, 115,
        137, 138, 175, 176
    business class, 232
    Canadian war brides, 162
    Caribbean, 190, 211, 230
    Central American, 230
    Chinese, 29–30, 136, 186
    departments, 130, 169, 192, 194, 242
    Doukhobor, 93–94, 104, 135
    Dunkards, 46
    Dutch, 22, 177
    "enemy aliens, " 127, 128, 129, 132
    enemy aliens, Second World War,
        150–51
    family class, 171, 236, 268

famine (1840s), 65–66
female, 22–23, 69
Finnish, 103
First World War, 127
French, chapter 1, 56
German, 22, 35, 56, 141
    during Great Depression, 142
    guest children from Great Britain,
        151, 152–53
    home children, 95–98
Hungarian, 78
Hutterite, 135
Icelandic, 76–77
illegal, 166, 186, 221
impact on economy, 190, 191, 232
impact on population, 191
independent class, 171, 236, 268
Indian, 121
investor category, 231–32
Irish, 31–32, 49, 53–54, 55, 60, 64,
    65, 66
issues in the 21st century, 283–92
Italian, 103, 181, 182, 183
Japanese, 101, 119, 120, 121
Jewish, 77–78, 139–40
Mennonite, 46, 75, 135
Mormon, 90
nativist attitudes towards, 104,
    106–07
Norwegian, 77, 101, 102
Planters, 29–30
Polish, 56, 161
Portugese, 11, 22
post-Second World War boom,
    155, 164
pro-immigration lobby (1946–52),
    156, 158, 159–60
"push factors"
    Great Britain, 50
    Ireland, 5–51
Quakers, 45, 46
riots over. See Vancouver riot of 1907
Salvation Army's role in, 95
Scandinavian, 77, 89
Scottish, 33, 48–49, 52–53, 55, 60, 64

Sikh, 101
South American, 190, 230
sponsored, 181, 182, 183, 191, 107,
   256
trends in the 1980s, 230
Ugandan Asians, 212–13
Ukranian, 102–03, 104, 156
Immigration Act
   of 1869, 71
   of 1906, 107–09
   of 1910, 110–12
   revisions of, 133–34, 135
   of 1952, 170, 171, 179, 203, 204
   of 1976, 198, 208, 217, 224, 227, 239
   of 2001. *See* Immigration and
      Refugee Protection Act, 2001
Immigration and Refugee Board of
   Canada, 226, 228, 229, 248, 258
Immigration Appeal Board, 192, 197,
   200–01
immigration promotion
   Canada, 69, 70, 72, 88, 92, 93, 94
   Province of Canada, 67
Immigration and Refugee Protection
   Act, 2001, 257–62, 265, 271
immigration regulations
   1962, 187–88
   1967, 197
   1978 , 210
immigration service, establishment of,
   57, 70
Institute for Research on Public Policy, 237
Interim Federal Health Program, 275–76
Island of St. John. *See* Prince Edward
   Island
Ivens, William, 133, 134

Japanese Canadians. *See* discrimination,
   Japanese Canadians as victims
   during the Second World War
Jesuits, 15, 17
Joliffe, A.L., 159

Karas, Sergio, 279
Keenleyside, Hugh, 165–66

Kenney, Jason, 269–70, 271, 272, 273,
   274, 275, 277, 278, 279
Kent, Tom, 194, 195, 196, 261–62
King, Mackenzie, 162, 163, 179
   immigration policy statement,
      1947, 162–64
   and Japanese immigration, 120
Kirke, Sir David, 31
Kirke, Lewis, 16
Kirke, Thomas, 16
Komagata Maru (ship), 121
Kurdi, Alan, 281

La Tour, Charles de, 25
Lang, Otto, 199
Lapointe, Ernest, 145
Laurier, Sir Wilfrid, 83
Le Jeune, Father Paul, 17
League of Nations Society in Canada,
   148
Lemieux, Sir Rodolphe, 120, 121
Lennox, Haughton, 100–01
Lévesque, René, 217
Li, Peter S., 252, 253
Lloyd, Rev. George, 99, 100
Louisbourg, 28, 29
Lowe, John, 75
Lower, Arthur, 91, 157–58
Loyalists, 36–47, 48
   impact of, 44–45
   numbers, 36, 37, 38, 39, 42, 43, 44
   origins, 36, 38
   settlement of, 37, 39, 40–44, 45–46
   soldiers, 38, 39
   "late" loyalists, 47

MacDonald, Flora, 216
Macdonald, Sir John A., 68, 69, 77, 79,
   80, 81, 188
   on Chinese immigration, 72
   on immigration, 69
   on Jewish immigration, 77–78
   and western settlement, 79, 80
MacEachen, Allan, 199, 211
Mackasey, Bryce, 199, 201, 202, 213

Mackenzie, Prime Minister Alexander, 79–80
Mackenzie, Daniel, 130–31
Macpherson, Annie, 96
Mactavish, Justice Anne, 276
Maisonneuve, Paul Chomedy de, 18
Mance, Jeanne, 18
Manion, John, 171
Mansur, Salim, 289–90
Marchand, Jean, 193–94
Marchi, Sergio, 232–33
Martin, Keith, 253–54
Martin, Prime Minister Paul, 263
Matas, David, 237
Mattoo, Deepa, 280
Mauritania (ship), 162
Mavor, James, 93
McDougall, Barbara, 228, 236
Meighen, Arthur, 133
Mennonites. *See* immigration, Mennonite
Menou d' Aulnay, Charles de, 25
mercantilism, 15
Merchant Adventurers, 31
Meulles, Jacques de, 24
military settlements, 52–53
Millard, Charles H., 189
Miller, The Most Rev.J. Michael, 274
Mitchell, Maurice, 146, 147
Monk, Frederick, 109, 113
Montreal, founding of, 18
Mulroney, Brian, 265
multiculturalism, 219–20
    federal government policy, 257, 271, 272
    opposition to, 270
Murray, General James, 35

Nansen medal, 223
Netherlands Farm Families Movement, 177
New Brunswick, settlement of, 43
New Brunswick and Nova Scotia Land Company, 56
Newfoundland, settlement of, 31–32

Non-Immigrant Employment Authorization Program. *See* Temporary Foreign Worker Program
North Atlantic Trading Company, 92–93, 112, 113
Not Just Numbers, 255
Nova Scotia, settlement of, 13, 28–30, 34–35, 40, 41, 42. *See also* Acadia

Oleskow, Dr. Josef, 102
Oliver, Frank, 94, 105, 115, 121
    immigration policy of, 106–07, 110, 112–13, 118, 119
Onderdonk, Andrew, 72

Papineau, Louis Joseph, 62
Paquet, Gilles, 286, 290
Parr, John, 41
Patterson, Walter, 44
Pearson, Prime Minister Lester B., 191, 194, 219
Perth, Ontario, 52–53
Pickerskill, J.W., 171, 174, 175, 182, 188–89
Pico, Garnett, 266
Pinhey, Hamilton Kirkes, 53
Placentia, Newfoundland, 31
Planters. *See* immigration, Planters
Plaut, Rabbi W. Gunther, 269
points system, 190, 194, 195, 196, 210, 223, 237, 238, 259, 268
Pope Sir Joseph, 73
Port Royal. *See* Annapolis Royal
Pre-Removal Risk Assessment (PRRA), 262
Preston, W.T.R., 93
Prince Edward Island, 44, 55, 60
Proclamation of 1763, 34, 35
Provincial Nomination Program, 272
Pursuer (ship), 152

Quakers. *See* immigration, Quakers
Quebec, attitude towards refugees, 145, 173–74

immigration agreement (1978), 218
opposition to federal multiculturalism policy; settlement of, 14, 16, 17, 18, 22–23
Quebec Act, 36
railway agreement of 1925, 141, 142

Rat River settlement, 75
Razilly, Isaac de, 25
Récollets, 14, 15
Red River colony, 55–56
refugee determination system, 223–24, 225, 226, 227–29, 239, 240, 241, 256, 258, 259, 260, 261
Geoffrey Howson on refugee determination system, 229
Refugee Deterrents and Detention Bill (Bill C-84), 223
Refugee Reform Bill (Bill C-55), 227–29
Refugee Status Advisory Committee, 210
Refugees, 158, 185, 209, 210, 211, 216. *See also* Canadian National Committee on Refugees
boat people, 215–17
Chilean, 214–15
civilian internees (Second World War), 148, 150, 151
Czech, 148–49
and displaced persons, 157, 163, 164, 165, 166, 167, 168
economic. *See* asylum-seekers
European (post-Second World War), 155, 157–58, 160
during Great Depression, 143–44, 146, 147, 148, 149
Hungarian, 173–76, 183
from Iberian Peninsula (1944), 148
Kosovar, 245–46
labour "bulk labour" schemes, 161, 167, 168
Loyalist. *See* Loyalists
Palestinian, 171–73
Polish, 149

Sikh, 222
Singh decision. *See* Singh Decision
Tamils, 222
Tibetan, 212
Ugandan, 212–13
World Refugee Year, 183, 185
Rennie, Justice Donald, 273
Ressam, Ahmed, 247
Richardson, Boyce, 269
Richelieu, Cardinal, 15, 17
Robertson, Gideon, 133
Roberval, Jean-Francois de La Rocque, Sieur de, 12
Robinson, Peter, 53, 54
Roche, William James, 129–30
Rocher, Guy, 270
Royal Bank of Canada, 277
Royal Commission on Bilingualism and Biculturalism. *See* multiculturalism
Rye, Maria Susan, 96, 97

"Safe country" provisions, Safe Third County agreement, 240–41
St. Laurent, Louis, 179, 188
St. Louis (ship), 144
Salvation Army. *See* immigration, Salvation Army's role in
Sandwell, B.K., 158, 159
Scott, William, 104, 112, 113, 116, 117, 118
Sedgewick, Joseph, 191–92
Sedgewick Report, 191
Select Committee of the British House of Commons, 1826, Report of, 59–60
Selkirk, Thomas Douglas, Fifth Earl of, 55, 56
Senate Standing Committee on Immigration and Labour, 159
Seward, Shirley, 237–38
Sewell, Jonathan, the elder, 37
Sewell, Jonathan, the younger, 61–62
Sgro, Judy 249
Shelburne, Nova Scotia, 41, 44
Sibley, Robert, 271

Sifton, Clifford, 84, 105, 138, 141
    immigration policy, 85, 86, 87,
        91–92, 93, 94, 106
    immigration promotion, 88, 94
Simcoe, John Graves, 45, 45–47
Simpson, Jeffrey, 251
Singh, Harbajan, 225
Singh, Harjit, 249
Singh decision, 226
slaves, 26, 42
Smart, James A., 90–91
Smith, Goldwin, 117
Societé de Notre-Dame de Montréal
    pour la conversion des Sauvages de
    la Nouvelle France, 18
Solberg, Monte, 264
Somerville, James, 97
Special Joint Committee on Immigration
    Policy, 1975, 207–08
Stanbrook, Dr. Matthew, 276
Starr, Michael, 193
Stewart, Alistair, 170
Stoffman, Daniel, 250
Stolarik, Mark, 254
Stowe, Harriet Beecher, 96–97
Strum, Gladys, 168
Sun Sea (ship), 274

Tait, Richard, 9, 204
Talbot, Colonel Thomas, 46, 47
Talon, Jean, 20–22, 24
Temporary Foreign Worker Program,
    276–77
"Three Thousand Families Scheme," 137
Timlin, Dr. Mabel, 177–78
Toews, Vic, 274
Tolstoy, Leo, 93
Trudeau, Pierre, 199, 212, 219
Turner, Frederick Jackson, 89

Ursulines, 17

Valcourt, Bernard, 240, 241
Vancouver Riot of 1907, 119
Van Horne, Sir William, 109–10

Verrazano, Giovanni da, 11–12
Vikings, 11
Ville Marie. See Montreal
Wagner, William, 67
Wakefield, Edward Gibbon, 58, 59
Waldman, Lorne, 268
Walkom, Thomas, 280
War Measures Act, 128
Wartime Elections Act, 1917, 129
Weiner, Gerry, 222
Weinfeld, Morton, 234
West Coast Merchants. See Merchant
    Adventurers
White Paper of 1966, 191, 204–05
Wilks, James, 103
Wilson, Senator Cairine, 148
Winnipeg General Strike, 132–35
Winslow, Edward, 40, 43
Woodsworth, J.S., 117, 124–25, 133,
    134, 136
World Refugee Year. See refugees, World
    Refugee Year

Yakabuski, Konrad, 278

Zero Tolerance for Barbaric Cultural
    Practices Act. See Bill S-7